See The colors
Know The light

For those who walk out of the cave,
And are unafraid, and do not return
Stare in wonder
Afresh with youthful exuberance
And proceed, ever forward
Tumble on in torn blue jeans
Crystalline eye
Interlocking gnashing teeth
Tear into the heart,
Let it drip upon your life
Warm, sinuous, infused

THIS RULER

BY MARK DUFF

AGS Publishing, Inc., Carbondale, Colorado
Copyright ©2019 by Mark Duff
All rights reserved. Published in 2019
Printed in the United States of America
25 24 23 22 21 20 19   1 2 3 4 5

ISBN 78-0-9991218-2-5

Library of Congress Catalog Number available upon request.

Cover design: Mark Duff
Cover illustration: Hannah Condon
Book design & layout: Marjorie DeLuca

To order books write:
Mark Duff
PO Box 1824
Carbondale, CO 81623
mark@authormarkduff.com

...or visit
amazon.com
barnesandnoble.com

Printed by Ingram-Spark

EPIGRAPH

Education needs:
1. a little honesty
2. functioning infrastructure
3. some stability

Perhaps the day will come when educators conscript the
publishing companies to produce products for kids,
not for ambitions and profit margins.

CONTENTS

INTRODUCTION

We all know that being a teenager is a harrowing experience wrought with many changes. If you zoom in and look at a high school, obviously it is a hectic place with a dynamic environment, and no one story could possibly catch all the happenings and nuances. This is not a typical high school story of getting laid, the big blowout party, adventurous hijinks, fun ditch day, finding true love, stupid adults etcetera. Those stories have been told.

And yes, I know teenagers are not always nice pleasant critters to be around. They can be selfish, self-centered, hyper-plugged-in, prone to tantrums, unruly, quite dangerous, absolutely tribal, thoughtless, wild, sexually charged, feral, depressed and quite frankly a pain in the ass. Well—duh!

But also, there really is a particular beauty to their youth, a tumbling exuberance, energy, and unprecedented growth and maturation. There exists within The Fray: the other, technology, deceit, façade, good, evil, sex; all in a look and a thought. And from this, one has to ask some very important questions: What is the journey? What is transcendence? Are tax dollars getting to the kids? How to see beauty? Who do we want to be? How can you reconcile inequality? Can a good deed balance out something bad? Are ambition and pride good? Can we become good? Do you know yourself? First do no harm?

This story is a weird, metaphoric statement against the publishing companies, standardized testing, educational consultants, and others adults that harm children. The money, our tax dollars, is not getting to the kids. It is going to endless multiple ever-changing schemes to make money for a few adults.

The children are being harmed. Every piece of artwork, every history lesson, every chunk of natural history is a metaphor for this argument. Just remember conquistadors, monoliths, parasites and invasive species. Regardless, each kid proceeds with their own particular journey.

I

MONEY-CHANGER
AND HIS WIFE

Solemque suum, sua sidera norunt
"And they know their own sun and their own stars…"

—Virgil, The Aeneid, Book VI

Here, open this," James says as he hands Sandy a condom.
"How big will it get? Sandy says."

"Oh, you'll see."

She fumbles with extracting the condom. "Ah, it's all gooey. Okay, grab me here around the waist." Sandy turns around and James grabs her around the waist. She opens the back window of the car. She holds the edge of the condom out the window as the car races down the highway at sixty mph. The condom inflates like a windsock at an airport.

The other four kids in the car explode into laughter, as the condom balloons to three feet long, flapping in the wind. James has his arms around Sandy's waist and his head on her abdomen, as half her body is out the window. Blond hair is whipping around her smiling face. In the reflection of her mirrored sunglasses is Hector hanging out the front passenger's window videoing the whole thing. The condom flies out of her hand as she rolls back into the laps of James, Helen and Sialia crammed into the back seat. Ryan is driving and looking around, and over corrects; the car jerks and changes lane. All falls silent for a second, then everyone bursts out into boisterous laughter again.

James yells out, "Hurry, I can't be late. Park in Africa, don't look for a closer spot. We'll run from there." Africa is the kids name for the far dirt parking lot at school.

The gang parks the car; laughing and giggling, they enter school and proceed down the hallway with a stream of other students.

One kid yells out, "Dude, nice," as he looks up from his phone at the video posting.

"Yo, Mali. Totally outrage man. Yeah."

"Mr. Malachite," the principal formally addresses him.

James turns to face his fate. "So, you're playing soccer today. Good luck."

"Ah, thanks Dr. Stufa."

"Now, let's get a move on."

The group disperses down to the junction of the hallways as teachers bark out, "Ladies let's get to class now."

Helen and Sandy, arm in arm giggling, split down separate hallways. Sialia rolls on to art class. James glides down the hallway empty handed, snatching a pencil off the ground as he jumps into his classroom. A lone kid is left in the now nearly empty hall as he kicks his locker that is stuck half open. Teachers are closing doors in every direction. Exasperated, he kicks the door one more time, turns and runs for his class.

Sialia Torres sits in a lounge chair in the corner of the art room at Elysium Hills High School. Outside the afternoon light is illuminating the school on the bench-like hill, as traffic flows by on the highway down the hill. In the corner of the art room is a large soft chair with padded armrests. The air duct vent, in the ceiling, is immediately above the chair. Hot or cold, the air duct hums with a slight clanking rattle. The chair is partially hemmed in by a low bookshelf. Paint brushes by the handful sit on paper plates stained by water and pigments. Large oversized art books are stacked, leaning to one side. Sialia sits cross-legged in the chair with a giant book in her lap. It is here the world unfolds, blazing color, violence, some story she does not know. A chosen place. She reaches out and touches the color on the page with her fingertip. She sighs and leans back and stares out the window to the north. And so, we look at a journey that goes nowhere in place, but so very far within.

The elegant, smooth hand of Sialia turns the pages of the art book. The large-format book lies heavy upon her lap. Flipping and skimming these pages deep in the book reveals subtitles such as: *16th-Century Art, Northern Europe*; within these sections there are old maps, woodcuts, visionary imagery during Reformation, divergent views, shrines and gilded panels from far off lands from a time long ago.

The line and form of her thin wrist show her tendons pushing against the purple embroidered bracelet tied in a knot, a bright contrast to her golden-brown skin and pink painted nails. There on the left-hand page, Sialia's right hand falls heavy with her forearm across the entire book. At the top left is Quinten Matsys's *Money-Changer and His Wife,* 1514. Oil on panel. She stops flipping pages, lets gravity take her hand and arm so that they lie still across the pages.

Strange and odd are the clothes of the man and woman in the painting. But that is not what captivates Sialia. No, it is the gaze of the woman, so transfixed looking at the money in the balance scale and in her husband's hand next to her. Gold and silver coins lie on the green table top. Golden standards of weights and a small pile of pearls on velvet also lie there.

Sialia's head is cocked to the side, and the lines of muscle are taut in her neck showing down to her exposed collar bone. She breathes softly but does not blink. The thick jet-black braid of her hair hangs across her right shoulder as she leans to her right and looks intently down to her left.

The woman in the painting has both hands on the Bible. The painting depicts her flipping the page, but distracted, she holds the page still. It could fall either way, barely held by the tips of her fingers. The money is there; you can hear the coins clink and ring as they fall through the man's deft, thin hands. The pious biblical words are silent on the pages. Also, on the table is a small round mirror-like orb reflecting a window to the outside world. Within the mirror is an entire other painting, so small as to seem an insignificant image within the painting. Dark and mystical—the dream of haunting thick green black oil flows underneath, caught in the edges of the reflection. Money, the balance, the Good Book, transfixed with eyes on one thing, mind elsewhere. Silent; but for the metallic sound of coins dropping.

At that moment, the entire school spins a hundred and eighty degrees upon the green slick oil underneath and zooms in to a back conference room.

There, Principal Dr. Jonathan Stufa, an educational consultant, the superintendent, and two school board members sit around a long scratched-up wood table. The table is almost too big for the room, so that once seated, each individual is pinned between the wall and the table. Projected on the whiteboard on the wall is the school's Mission Statement. It is projected as an overlay to a shadow of weakly erased words that were hastily wiped away. The room, even with the shades drawn and closed, is too bright, and the projection is weak and almost confusing. A strange reflected sheen bounces off the whiteboard making it difficult to look at the words projected.

Stufa's hands are holding the paper copy of the Mission Statement. But his eyes are on the consultant, Joel Haustoria, as Stufa speaks. The reason they are here is for a presentation by Haustoria about the new curriculum adoption. The Spring Forward curriculum put out by Bradmoor Publishing is aligned to the new state standards and standardized tests. Stufa has just purchased a new car for his wife and is staying in a large well-furnished home on the golf course. In the hollow wall behind the screen a mouse deftly scurries along the top of a copper pipe. Pipes and wires thread their way behind the walls, under the concrete and in the space above the drop ceiling.

The pipes and wires, behind and underneath the school, lead to the science room of Zack Tyndall. There on his desk is a cluttered array of piled papers, science magazines, shiny rocks, old bones and a feather or two. There is a fist-sized piece of green-black obsidian reflecting the light. Within the shiny rock is a dream-like image of shadowy dark thick hands moving erratically. Black oil flows underneath. Blood drips red over the edge of a white stone table, red and bright, squirting in long rhythmic spurts from a slit throat. Large towering stone pyramids with iconic monster heads jut out from the sidewalls. These images dance within the rock like a tiny painting within a painting, then they disappear with the blink of an eye.

The coins and pearls slide through the fingers. The pearls slide and roll onto a black velvet cloth. Papers slide and roll off printing presses. Uniform sized boxes slide down rollers into boxcars that are then attached to semi-trucks that roll down highways like a mouse running on a pipe. Traffic sits frozen at a red light, commuters look down and read texts, a mother looks in the rear-view mirror at the infant in the seat facing backwards. It all flows by.

The balance of the scales. To load one side and then add to the other. Sway, sway down, swing up, rock back-and-forth. Does it balance? Can one good deed balance out the bad action? The mind with its own rationalization is pulled by actions and real consequences. Mystic forces run underneath, weigh heavily on the mind in the tearing agony of sleeplessness uncompromised in the brightness of the day.

Youthful beauty gazes at an image of a painting. Clear, bright and strong, straight limbs, impressionable and naïve; lost in a world of dreamy thoughts. So free from the scales that weigh us all. So capable—capable of seeing, rational, wise, a royal gift of insight, a blessing for one who can truly see. Set upon the path.

2

LE BONHEUR DE VIVRE

Mr. Tyndall stands in front of his science class and watches the kids file in for River Watch class. It's all seniors, and it's essentially the great breakdown here at the end of the school year. So, he has one last big three-week project to keep them busy. He thinks, *It's like trying to herd cats, keep it together.* The students shuffle in, with Miguel Angel and Josue sitting down at the far right and talking in a low guttural dialect of Spanish. Sialia stands in the back of the classroom talking on the phone in Spanish. Hector, James and Ryan come in and sit pretty much in the middle front of the room. In the far-left corner Helen and Sandy plop down in back seats and talk in hushed tones looking around and then back down at their phones. At the far back table, sitting alone, is JR doodling in a notebook with his headphones on, oblivious to it all. Another twenty-some-odd kids come in, mix and assemble themselves with some level of push and pull in the ever-complex medium of high school.

Tyndall has been teaching now for ten years, all at Elysium Hills. He thinks, *Well, I'm thirty-six now; I guess this is my career. Can't wait for summer, ugh, just don't lose it here at the end.* He repeats to himself over and over again: *Do not strike the children. In a couple of weeks, you'll feel good again, and will be fishing up at the cabin.* He finishes outlining the last project this group of seniors will do in high school. "Okay we have about three weeks to finish this up. What y'all are going to do is draw and describe insects we collected down at the river. Up here are some examples from the Big Bug Books done by other students in previous years. Mostly, you guys, it's in your hands to finish this up by Friday in three weeks, on the last day for seniors."

After Tyndall demonstrates what to do, the students grab their specimens and materials and sit down at the big lab tables in the sunny science room at the end of the hall on that warm day in May. Tyndall pushes his brown hair out of his face as he leans over to fill the coffee cone with coffee. Then he pulls the kettle off the hot plate, pours the hot water through it. The aroma of fresh coffee fills the room. Ever watching, the frogs float in the green water of the aquarium on the countertop. Tyndall got the frogs during his first year of teaching. They have been watching for many years now.

Sialia says, "Can you believe it? We're at the end, less than three weeks left."

James is standing at the back table extracting an insect from a jar. His long curly light-brown hair is almost blond at the tips from so much time outside in the bright Colorado sun. He says, "Yeah, I'm not quite sure how we got here."

"I don't think we were supposed to make it—you know, some of us," Hector says. He has an almost permanent smile on his round face, a contrast with his tough stocky, muscular build.

James, sitting down, says, "Yeah, fuck it, here we are." His hazel eyes get bigger as he emphatically cusses.

"Hey, watch it. You guys talk as if I weren't here," Tyndall says.

Josue says, "We all, didn't like each other at the start."

Helen glides gracefully across the room and adds, "Now, it all don't matter anymore. You know what I'm say'n?"

Miguel Angel adds in with a singsong high-pitched voice, "So simple a thing, that we're sitting here."

"Yeah you know; we get our graduation gowns tomorrow, then graduation practice at the end of next week," Sandy says.

JR sits in the far corner, his thin flat hair, dyed dull-green, sticks out in a funny way under his headphones. He pipes up all enthusiastic, "I think I'll climb up the hill and paint one last picture of campus and the fields—real early in the morning."

Ryan responds, "God, that's so cool."

Tyndall sits with his feet up on the desk, sipping his afternoon coffee, while looking over at and contemplating the piled-over inbox of tests and labs that he has to grade before the end of the year. He says, "I like it here at the end—so different. Another cohort."

Ryan, tall, thin and lanky, quickly sets up the chess board on the stone table. He says, "So Tynd, you want to play chess?"

"Yeah sure, you think you got what it takes?" Tyndall says, jiving Ryan, knowing that he is the old dog to beat. The chess game proceeds with Tyndall occasionally turning around and giving directions to kids. He lifts up his white bishop, moves it, and says, "Check."

On the other side of the chess board, Ryan assertively moves his black pawn and blocks the move. It is on. So here they all sit together in the sunny science room; a particular place that most of these kids have spent so much time in over the last four years. Though not necessarily in a together fashion. It is a didactic poem unraveled, out of time. Here in the light, the color unfolding, smelted and forged; believable yet unlikely. All told, out of sequence, on golden panels in a Baptistery of fate and luck. The biggest pebble yet to be carried. Plunge in. And there is something underneath it all; from the savage hand of nature to the fine paintings. All color, bold, naked and so beautiful a vision; a painting within a painting; within it—*The Dance.* Other imagery is more angular and foreboding—factories within factories. But in the end, the bronze statue of Perseus stands with his adamantine sword in one hand and the head of Medusa in the other. It is an impossible task that is hidden within a mystic tale from an extinct culture. Win and lift the severed head. Do it with honor, joy, peace and the truth unleashed with knowledge; as well as just a little bit of clever. To lean so hard against it. Remember we were all there once. Pick the people and the place up; turn it in the light. See the colors.

3

COMMUTE IN

The inexplicable moment between being awake and asleep is when the dream is most vivid. At the forge, the heated iron is hit by a hammer. Orange-red sparks fly from the hot metal and bounce on the floor. They float and zip on a layer of air at the interface of the floor. Propelled by the heat they generate and the gases that rise. Each spark is a tiny suspended piece of steel, like a raft on a swift stream.

The machinist stands at the machine press. His hands are stained along the ripped seam of his torn leather gloves. His legs are spread wide as he leans into the press. His right foot pivots as he pushes the steel plate through the jaws of the machine. It is a downward push to his left. There are two worn depressions, crater-like in the wood floor. One well-worn crater for each foot, the right one slightly off center and deeper. Each foot-shaped imprint is a testament of years of men standing at this machine and pushing, and pivoting, as each 10" x 10" steel plate is forced into the press. The finished cog assembly falls into a pushcart with a harsh clanking sound.

A flash of orange-red streaks along the floor as Zach Tyndall is jolted awake by the alarm at 5:45 am. Shower, make coffee, feed the dog; he opens the back door to let the pup out. The house is quiet, he pours boiled water through the open cone into a travel mug. NPR is on the radio; intro music is playing as the commentary begins with an overview about the state budget.

After the news report about the budget, there is an excerpt about a street poet that scribes poems as graffiti. Most of the poems are reflections of famous paintings. The poet's name is supposedly Georgie Bruno. No one knows the real identity of the poet. Georgie does not even post works online; a diligent band of admirers takes photos of the works and uploads them to social media. He or she has a huge following around the world. The reporter goes on to read a poem painted on the side of a train boxcar:

The Gulf Stream
The mast is broken
Stoic acceptance
Shift your weight
And right the broken ship
The main ship is on the horizon
Predators at reach
The monetary mandates,
even further out of sight

—G.B.

It is signed "G.B." Next to it, on another boxcar, is a graffiti-style painting of the famous painting.

Tyndall half listens to the report as he makes a toasted bagel with cream cheese and a turkey sandwich that he slides into a Baggie, then into his shoulder bag. The cream cheese bagel sits on a paper towel next to the coffee mug with the steaming cone on top of it. He grabs the keys, Yogi the dog instantly goes from slumbering to raging beast ready to go. He runs to the door and spins to his right and then to his left; he is in the way of Tyndall trying to pry the door open. Tyndall fetches the dog with a tennis ball. He throws the ball through a gap in the side flower garden into his neighbor's yard. Then he turns, jumps in the truck and starts it. The dog barks. Tyndall jumps out of the truck, which is parked on the street and warming up. "Don't bark, people are asleep," he says. "Here, bring the ball closer," he taps the ground at his feet. The dog obliges and flicks his head to toss the ball forward as he backs up looking intently at the ball and then up at Tyndall's face. There is a chill in the air, and the grass is wet from the morning dew. It will frost in a week or so he thinks. The apples on his tree will taste their best then.

Another school year has begun. Thank God those wretched meetings are over, he thought. There was so much anxiety and contention. Teachers had fits over the new schedule, wrought with disruptions from testing. Some teachers cried; the newbies just sat there and tried to figure out who was who and what was what. Most of them still don't have keys to their rooms or the building, even though it is now three weeks into the madness. The veterans were sitting back and waiting to get the last word in.

He remembers after leaving the meeting he walked down the hall with Scott Jay, the other science teacher. "Man, just a little honesty and a functioning infrastructure would go a long way."

Jay responded, "Yeah, we didn't even talk nuts and bolts for more than an hour."

"Five days of meetings, and that's it."

Maggie Gunter, the math teacher, walking behind them, interjected, "Yeah, at least you guys aren't changing your curriculum for the fourth time in ten years. It's the first week, and I'm already shopping for a new job."

Now the drive unfolds before his eyes. Pastoral, and open, just a few miles before the expressway, traffic and lights. Pink Floyd's "Have a Cigar" plays on the radio; Tyndall turns up the volume. Bump bump pa bump pa thumps the bass line; "Riding the gravy train…" moans the lyrics. He pulls the sun visor down and puts on his sunglasses. In the crisp autumn light, a giant water cannon irrigates a horse pasture to his left. The pivot head interrupts the stream in a rhythmic way. Water blasts hundreds of feet out and over two stories high. The perspective of the ranch house and the scattered horses adds a surreal feel. It is all backlit, white against the dark green grass and horses. In the near pasture, next to the road, is a small corral of dirt and two horses. They look with envy out to the larger pasture, grass and all. The guitar screams; he pulls the shade down further and sits up straight to block the light.

With his bag on his shoulder, hanging heavy, Tyndall unlocks the back door to the school. Sialia, Helen and James run over even before he gets the door open. Descending on him, they start to harry. "Do you have them?" Sialia says.

"Can we do it now?" Helen adds.

Fumbling with his keys and coffee mug, he tosses the keys to one of the boys. "It's the square one. I don't think there's enough time," he says, hounded.

"There's ten minutes. Come on," James says.

"Okay here." He sighs. "Cleanup and make sure the little one gets some." He hands Sialia a white styrofoam container with a symbol of fish on it and big red letters that say "EARTHWORMS." The kids scramble around the long aquarium with five large motionless frogs floating in the green water. There is a poster of stone-head statues on Easter Island to the side of the aquarium. James removes the aquarium top and the frogs start darting and lunging toward the surface.

Voraciously the African clawed frogs grab the worms and manipulate them in their large mouths with their tiny forelimbs in spastic motions. Two frogs grab one worm and tug each other around the tank. Two kids kneel on the counter while two others stand. Sialia has her hand on the back shoulder of her friend, Helen. Their heads pull back simultaneously, as the frogs devour worms in a violent, inefficient way. The frogs never blink, sit so still they seem inanimate, then they lunge powerfully, grasping for any quarry. One grabs the leg of another frog and won't let go. The struggle for what to them seems fleeting and brief. Another boy grabs a toy snake, made out of divided slatted wood, and startles Helen kneeling on the countertop. She screams, then rolls her eyes. Tyndall calmly looks on and smiles.

Once class has started and the kids are settled in, Tyndall—or as the kids call him, "Tynd"—explains the week's schedule to the blank faces staring back at him. He knows most of their names by now, but still has to peek at his seating chart to make sure he's right. He looks over to his right at the countertop next to the frog aquarium. It is a mess of black dirt, a dumped over white styrofoam container and a toy snake. The frogs float silently at the surface of the water, never blinking. He explains the testing this week. The kids moan and groan. The frogs stare on motionlessly, adrift. Water tumbles out of the filter, and the frogs float at the surface. They require more oxygen after such a big meal. Their small round eyes with small round pupils never blink; they breathe rhythmically in and out.

The frogs float at the surface, green and striped on top and pale white beneath. Their back legs are powerful and muscular all splayed out, webbing between their toes. Their mouths are huge, with a slight never-changing smirk, almost a smile. They never blink. Their white bellies and sides are distended and bloated. They would probably eat themselves to death, unable to come to the surface for air. If you look closely, you can see the worms withering in their guts, pushing to one side or the other. Occasionally a frog regurgitates a worm, fumbles it around in its small arms and devours it again. They float, adrift, never blinking. So full they can scarcely move.

4

AND SO IT BEGINS

The three senior boys—Hector, Ryan, and James—sit in Tyndall's room during River Watch class and remember the first day of school freshman year. They are loud and boisterous, almost obnoxious in their tone. Ryan and Hector plop down at the big table as James cruises to the back table to pick up his notebook that he cached the class before. Cussing and laughing, "No, no, no, the best was Mali and Ryan on the bus that first day," Hector says overtaking the others. James confidently walks back over to the table, tall and muscular now as a senior, a far cry from the scrawny little guy he was as a freshman.

James exclaims as he is sitting down and slamming his hand flat on the table, "Oh. That was so fucked up."

Tyndall pipes up, "Easy boys, I don't need to hear this," half as a statement and half as a question.

"No, this one's okay Tynd, you'll like it," James says, laughing and pushing his light-brown curly hair back.

Tyndall quickly adds, "Yeah right, Lord have mercy."

Sialia and Sandy from the table next to them drone out almost singing, "Oh yeah, what a great start."

Sandy sits there with all her materials out in front of her, the reading packet about aquatic insects, a picture book, a mayfly specimen in a petri dish, a hand lens, and a myriad of colored pencils all sharped to a fine exact point. "I wasn't there, but Sialia was pissed off that day when she got off the bus," she says.

Tyndall, sitting at his desk grading papers with his feet propped up says, "You boys impressing the ladies again, ay."

The girls laugh nodding in unison. "Oh yeah, oh so, so impressive," they say with a sassy overtone.

Tyndall, interested now, stops grading papers at his desk. He kicks and rolls his desk chair with wheels over to the table. He has a handful of almonds in one hand and coffee, now cold, in the other. "An inauspicious start to your journey here, imagine that," he says.

The boys start off all vying for position and talking at the same time and laughing so much no one can finish a sentence. James finally takes command of the story: "Yeah I get on the bus and Ryan is in one of the back seats. We've never gone to school together before, even though we've been friends since we were in Cub Scouts back in third grade. I remember it was humid and warm in the bus, and it smelled like vinyl." Pointing at Ryan he continues, "I sit down and you got this funny smirk on your face. High school here we go— then you pull out a bottle rocket from under your shirt."

James continues, "Me and Ryan talk it over. Ryan says to me, 'We'll light the fuse and you'll launch the bottle rocket out the window at traffic when we cross the light at Ogden Avenue.'" Ryan opens the window wide open, and the bus driver barks that he should put it halfway open. We argue that we can't do it now, 'cause the bus driver has us on his radar. I'm sitting there and Ryan's flicking the lighter sitting next to the window. I have a bottle rocket in my hand. The wind keeps blowing the lighter out. So, we lower the whole operation down below the seat. The fuse is lit and I'm trying to lunge over Ryan to cast it out the window. I'm fumbling away with it as it smokes a white acrid smoke, way more smoke than I anticipated. It wasn't going out the window and the stick breaks, not completely but is hanging there limp and the fuse is sparking away all this white smoke. And finally, we panic and try to extinguish the firework. I'm frantically stamping away on the bottle rocket on the bottom of the bus floor. There was this quick swishing sound and the bottle rocket flies straight up the aisle of the bus, slams into the front windshield and explodes."

And so it begins. Untethered and cast in the eddies and vortices of what may come—and here it comes. Sialia Torres is also there on the bus, sitting up front and flipping through an art book when she comes to *Nocturne in Black and Gold—Falling Rocket* by James Whistler. All at the very moment of sparks flying orange and radiating out against the inside bus window in a frozen moment of abstract time. They float there, floating suspended, orange and red, white smoke, blue, green and yellow on a bleak black-scape of the imagination; and then a startling bang. There is left of boom and then there is right of boom. And again, time begins anew, the slate was clean for only minutes; *panta rhei.*

The room is full of laughter and energy. James nodding his head, saying, "We were such little fucking punks then," smiling a big grin.

Ryan adds, "How'd we ever get out of that?"

Tyndall is laughing, rubbing his hair with his hand and his eyes are closed. Not a loud fall-down laugh, but a continuous low clacking sound. Sialia chimes in, "Oh it was so loud, and we were all coughing, and my clothes smelled all day."

"What punks," Ryan says. "Yeah we rode our bikes to school until Christmas that year. Then we got a new bus driver after break."

"Whatever happened?" Sandy asks.

"I don't know, we talked a lot with the driver, just talking away, asking forgiveness, tellin' him we wouldn't do it again. The guy said, 'Here's the deal. Don't show up on this bus again—and I won't report this.' He let us off the bus right there and we walked to school the rest of the way. Yeah, never got reported—I guess. We got a new bus driver after Christmas, anyway."

That morning, the bus continues to school. Immersed in her art book, Sialia slowly turns the page and looks at the abstract painting *Animal Destinies* by Franz Marc glowing vividly as the boys trudge toward school. Chaotic, distorted and contorted, blazing in movement and color; they tumble toward a fate that awaits them.

5

BOTTLE ROCKET RIPPLE

After school Hector and James meet out at the soccer field. They sit in the grass getting ready for soccer practice and reflect on their first day. "So, Mali, first day of high school," Hector says, looking down tying the laces on his soccer cleats. "How'd it go for you?"

James thinks back: Bottle rocket exploding on the inside bus window. Walking the rest of the way to school. Then 30 minutes late to first period class and scolded and ridiculed by that teacher. Then second period, sent out into the hallway to be yelled at by that teacher. Lunch, and getting on the radar of the assistant principal for throwing food. Then third period, could not find my assigned seat. Finally, last period class, and sent back out to the hallway to be reprimanded for something about leaping from tabletop to table-top. James looks over at Hector as he puts on his shin guards, and says, "Ah, well seems pretty much the same as middle school. Except there are bigger kids around and man are there some girls—mamma; woo...mamma. Yeah, it's all good, just a bunch of adults talking and then they talked some more; just the same old—same old."

James Malichite continues speaking with Hector, but there is something in his mind that he is really thinking about and that is the doors to the school, and pulling them open: He remembers listening to tunes on his headphones as he was walking up the hill and bopping through the parking lot. He floated in and around parked cars, tunes blaring a rambling, funky, bouncing beat with jumping and cutting lyrics. On up the main sidewalk, past people standing around, but scarcely noticing—yeah, whatever. The song closed gradually with a false ending; first fading, then becoming moderately stronger, then gradually stronger rhythms, and a reduction in tempo to an ascending melodious musical instrumental parade as he approached the main front doors. Oh, those magnificent huge doors of Elysium Hills High School, the Isle of the Blessed, the gilded bronze doors of the *Gates of Paradise* stand before him with their ten panels and numerous sidebar images all telling stories of some continuous narrative, but you never just start at the beginning, each panel is a story to wander through, and you can look at any one and the story stands on its own, vivid and dimensional, and study each with its dynamic characters all blended into a flowing story, and the doors are massive, interconnected stories and so heavy to swing open, a strong wind blows out of the doors, entering a mythological world of familiarity, contingencies and mystery, pulling on those doors and looking down the hallway at *The Circus*, with all its fanciful movement and color, wheeling about the various rings of activity and entertainment flashing under a high top roof within a large round atrium that is nowhere, in a misty imagined and realized dreamscape, and there line up all the paintings, and the animals, and the history and step back and look at it, and remember.

Hector asks, "Anything about the fireworks in the bus?"

James blinks with a long slow closing of his eyes and reopening and says, "No, can't figure it out, I kept thinking they'd call us to the office but nothing."

"How the fuck did that happen?"

"I don't know. But Ryan and I are gonna be ridin' our bikes tomorrow, and... Probably for a while."

"Does coach know?"

James, looking over at Hector, shrugs. Then a big whistle and the boys jog in and coach barks "Malachite." James thinks—oh here it comes. Coach continues, "You and Hector gather up the balls, set them up here for passing drills," pointing to the quadrant in front of the goal. Hector looks hard at James as they run off to the fence line to gather the soccer balls.

"All day it's been like this; then nothing," James says.

Panta rhei.

6

SPIDERLINGS BALLOONING

How I entered there I cannot truly say,
I had become so sleepy at the moment
when I first strayed, leaving the path of truth; ...

I raised my head and saw the hilltop shawled
in the morning rays of light sent from the planet
that leads men straight ahead on every road.

—Dante Alighieri *(Inferno canto I.12-18)*

A Pilgrim has a destination, a point of completion to somehow attain. To circle the pyramidal peak jutting out of the Tibetan plane; prostrate, then to knees, feet, hands clap together, only to fall forward again and again. The path is worn to bare rock, prayer flags snap in the cold wind, tattered and frayed, colorful and meaningful in the stark frozen Asian steppe. But for the most part it really is not that well-defined. To find the path at a time and space when each sway of the breeze sets a new course.

Sialia sits at the table outside the backdoor to Tyndall's classroom. It is a late morning in September; she looks east into the warm morning sun. She watches as gossamer threads fly on the southwest breeze as the warmth of the day begins. Each thread is a spiderling ballooning on the rising heat of the day. Each baby spider clambers up to the top of a branch on the small cotton-wood tree. There, at the apex of a branch its spinnerets shoot out a short web that then catches the warming breeze of the day, and it lets go. Off it flies on a tiny shining parachute of silk.

Waves of glittering light undulate as the web rides the air movement and static electrical charges to propel itself planktonic on the wind. The glistening webs fly over the basketball court and back door and over the roof of the building. Each thread has a single lone spiderling dispersing into the greater world. Sialia is mesmerized by the gleam of the webs and the waves of light. Silver-white on the deep morning blue, setting in motion a journey unknown. Some individuals will land on the school, some in town, some will ride the jet stream for hundreds or even thousands of miles. Aeroplankton adrift upon greater currents that determine their position in time and space. Each individual has let go. Set upon the path, separate from the wheel. To let go, let go of the constraints that bind it. Free to fly. To see the angle of the light, not attached, but free—absolutely free.

Sialia calls for Tyndall: "Tynd, Tynd, come quick." Tyndall turns from the board, where he was writing something, and strolls slowly to the open back door. He stands in the door; the sunlight is warm. He raises his arms above his head and grasps the doorframe at the top and feels the wind blow out from the building moving his untucked shirt. Sialia is seated with the morning light on her face and her braid of long black hair gleams in the light. She is bending and contorting her body to the side holding her phone out trying to video something. "Look! Look at the spiderwebs flying from the tree," she says, pointing with one hand while holding her phone with the other. "The tree is casting out a thousand webs, and they fly in the light. My camera cannot catch it." Tyndall stands transfixed as the rainbows of glistening webs ripple off into the growing breeze. It is warm, Sialia's' hair shines, she points. Tyndall smiles. Sialia asks, "What is it?"

Tyndall says in a slow almost drawl as his arms stretch across the door frame in the warm sun. "It is spiderlings parachuting, they fly—fly to a New World." He starts the lecture about animal dispersal but stops himself. He knows Sialia is a creative spirit. He stops midsentence, and just says, "Isn't it beautiful. So beautiful."

"I can't get it on video," she exclaims.

"Just see it, see the beauty, the light is just right," Tyndall says.

He laughs and says, "Wee, wee—be free little ones—go," in a goofy voice while folding his arms inward, wrists limp in exclamation. "Go, be free, wee!"

"Stop it Mr. Tyndall."

"But it's beautiful."

Sialia drops her phone on the table, raises her hands up and smiles at the warmth, the breeze, the free flight of the spiderlings. Silently, both hands open to the sky, she sits and smiles.

Tyndall smiles and says, "Shouldn't you be in class?"

Sialia gets up, smiles at Tyndall and says, "Yeah, can I get a pass please."

"Ah, I guess, it really was a lesson."

In front of his desk she stands there, flower print shirt, cut-off blue jean shorts and smiles, looking at him with big brown eyes.

Tyndall says, "What am I to do?"

"Thanks Mr. Tyndall, you're the best," she says in an exuberant voice.

The pass is scribbled on a yellow sticky note with a big S and an arrow to whatever the teacher's last name is, with a big overlaid T and the time— 09:52. Sialia smiles, whisks this sticky note out of his hand and floats into the hall, as if flying.

Light revealed in a tiny thread of silver light captured. Reflected, unattached, set free to move on the waves and forces, it is but a dancing, glistening, momentary flash across the sky.

7

HIGH FRUIT

It is Saturday late morning when Principal Dr. Jonathan Stufa, on his way to the high school, heads to Elysium Hills Middle School. On Saturdays the youth soccer league plays at the middle school fields in the morning. It is a cool crisp day; the golden leaves are just starting to fall off the cottonwood trees. On the way, he pulls off the highway into the new mall area with shops, restaurants and a new Starbucks, complete with a drive-up window. The slick new mall, called Gillette's, is about complete. A roundabout leads to narrow streets along neat brick buildings, parking and crosswalks. To enter the Starbucks drive-through, Stufa turns left and wraps around the corner of the building. He interfaces the small billboard and orders a tall double cappuccino, the same as he always orders. He then hooks left around the building to the sliding window, exchanges his card with the woman attendant, complete with green apron and a headset. She recites the order and finishes the exchange. She is actually reading verbatim from a large monitor screen that Stufa cannot see from his vehicle. A neat hermetically sealed representation of Neo-Americana strip mall. So perversely appealing and alluring.

Sialia is pouring cereal for her little sister at the table in her kitchen. Her mom says, "Make sure you pack a drink for your sister. Don't be late to the game. It is at the middle school and starts at ten."

"Yeah, yeah, mamma, we'll get there," Sialia says. She is flipping through social media and comes across a posting of a Georgie Bruno poem titled "The Oxbow." After reading the poem, she is quick to like and share the post.

Then she looks up the painting. The poem is scribed in neat curved yellow letters on a rusted gray girder under a bridge.

The Oxbow
The river turns back on itself
the natural repose of the land,
absorbs the water
Channelized
A levy, and a dike
Orderly and managed,
the improvement assures the flood
—G.B.

James Malachite rolls his bike out of the back door of the garage. It's an old red mountain bike with a black suspension fork. The bike sways back and forth with James in the saddle, then he has to stand up to pedal in a higher gear. He cuts off the walk along the side of the garage, and bounces across the corner of the neighbor's front yard. He rides down the sidewalk, cuts onto the street by jumping the curb and zips up the other curb onto the sidewalk on the other side of the street. He jogs left, strips the leaves off a tree branch with his left hand, and throws the shredded bunch over his shoulder. Then he heads down a narrow single path in the tall dry grass of a vacant lot. He then zips between the yards of two other houses, rolls into the driveway of one of the houses and back to his right down the sidewalk. He briefly lets go the handlebars and leans back and glides, as he pulls his cell phone out to look at it. He is heading into town to the middle school before he has to head up to the high school for his soccer game.

He rolls into the expanse of space between the Elysium Hills Elementary School and the Middle School. A small caravan of cars, station wagons and minivans are unloading giant net bags of soccer balls as kids in deep blue jerseys run off across the field. Several adults are putting up a net in the soccer goal in the field.

James rides across the baseball diamond; he swings his right leg over the seat while standing on the pedal with his left foot. He glides and drops his bike with a clang at the corner of the playground. He can see Sialia on the other side of a low chain-link fence where there is a long linear community garden with a path covered with woodchips that passes through a wooded corridor. An arbor bridges the walkway. Green and yellow palm-shaped leaves on grapevines hang down. The leaves are mottled brown with yellow veins; some leaves have finger-like blotches of green with yellow. The bright light shines through the leaves highlighting the pattern of veins in the colorful leaves. The flat paving stones directly underneath the arbor are wet, a roly-poly scampers along on the rock. The light is shining through the wet vegetation. In the distance a referee's whistle sounds, and they can hear the yelling of parents, as kids in bright soccer uniforms run for the ball.

The two of them meeting up is unexpected. Sialia says, "My little sister has a game. I thought you played soccer today?"

James says, "Yeah, but my game is at the high school in the late afternoon." They turn down the path toward the arbor, and on it is a hanging bunch of deep purple grapes. James shuffles his feet through the wet woodchips. Sialia fidgets her fingers while grasping the edge of the sleeves of her hoodie jacket. They walk silently. James bursts forward, leaps and swings for the grapes. He is well short of grabbing them. Impetuously James grabs the arbor, about to climb it.

Sialia yells, "No, you'll break it." She looks around and sees a plastic chair next to one of the classrooms at the middle school. Tapping his shoulder, she points. They run off to fetch the chair. Stufa pulls up to the empty faculty parking lot and pulls in a parking space. He lifts his coffee cup and sips the coffee through the opening in the plastic top. He sees James and Sialia off crossing the field, carrying the chair. The sun is bright, the blue sky so very clear now in October.

The grass is dry, almost crisp, but the light changes as they enter the wooded path of woodchips. James places the chair down, and Sialia puts her hand on James's shoulder as she steps onto the chair. Reaching on her tiptoes she grabs the bunch of dark purple grapes with her right hand, and balances with her other hand way out to the side. Sialia bounces down off the chair; they both laugh out loud and let out a sigh in unison. They each pop a grape into their mouths and open their eyes wide at each other. Juices that at first are sour, then sweet, explode into their mouths. "Wow. So good," says Sialia.

Dr. Jonathan Stufa walks over to the ball field to join the other adults watching the game.

"Hi there, Dr. Stufa."

"Oh, hi, Jo Anne. Is that Ryan's little brother?"

"Yes, they look so much alike." Mom raises her hand to her lips and looks out at the little ones running.

"We'll see you Tuesday night at the high school for the Parent Accountability meeting?"

"Yes."

"I'll email you the agenda Monday."

"Great, thanks Dr. Stufa."

Stufa continues to amble along the sideline visiting with parents. His phone rings and he answers while looking across the ball field at the community garden and James and Sialia with the blue chair. He smiles and waves at parents walking by, as he listens to his phone. He drops the phone in his pocket and sips the last of his coffee. Then he drops the empty cup in the nearby garbage can. He claps and smiles at the rumbling mass of children in bright colorful soccer shirts tumbling by. Lifting his hand in recognition, he smiles at another parent. "Yes, see you at the game at the high school this afternoon."

Stufa heads over to the garden. He ambles up, with a smile on his face. He points to the grape bunches hanging on the arbor. "Ms. Torres, what do we have here?"

Sialia smiles back, "It's grapes! They're so good—want one?" Looking down, she hands him a couple of grapes.

He smiles and pops the grapes into his mouth. "Oh, they have seeds—but they're good tasting." Looking over to James he says, "Now Mr. Malachite, let's put the chair back where it belongs." A stiff breeze blows through the leaves in the trees overhead. The walkway changed rapidly; the path is now dark and foreboding, almost cold in the shade.

James looks down at his phone, "I got a text from coach—he needs help putting up the goal nets. See you guys."

"See you at the game this afternoon."

"Great—thanks Dr. Stufa," James says with a smile. Stufa cheerfully smiles back.

On Monday morning, up the hill at Elysium High, Sialia stares out the window of her math class. A mile away at the middle school; the arbor and grapes hang dream-like in the autumn cool, foggy and wet. While math equations flash on the screen in the front of the class, Sialia sighs and looks down at the plastic desk top with the fake wood grain pattern on it. In pencil she doodles a flower on the corner of the desk.

8

EL SALVADOR IV

Miguel Angel sits in the back seat of his uncle's Ford pickup truck. It is early morning, the first week of September, and he is heading to his first day of high school. School had started the week before, but he was working for his uncle and did not attend. He sees another pickup truck dropping a student off in front of school. On the back bumper he sees a bumper sticker of a Mexican flag. He thinks, *I hate those motherfuckers.*

He thinks back to his first days of middle school just two years before. His mind continues to wander, as he thinks back to his last day in El Salvador. Standing in the hilltop field he could see the dust and the smog of the city below. Miguel remembers the plot of corn and beans that he and his father worked on the mountainside. He can see the image of the cemetery from that high perch; how it floated on the hilltop. He closes his eyes and sees the prominent huge *cieba* tree in the center of the slash and burn field. The ever-sprawling barrio below—a landscape of stone, steel roofs, razor wire and stone brick, with crisscrossing electrical wires and TV satellite dishes on rooftops. The steel wrought-iron gates of the cemetery with one slightly off-kilter crucifix on top. The rough rusty face of Jesus stared out in agony. The Jesus statue was held in place with an X-shaped wrapping of rusty bailing wire. The gash in Jesus's torso, from the Roman soldiers' sword was exposed just above the crisscrossing wire. Trucks without mufflers went brawling by. There was a garage-like building across the street where a man was sawing and hammering the wood planks for piles of coffins. Another carpenter was rhythmically sliding a hand plane across the wood planks, long curled wood shavings accumulated, in a pile, at his feet. It was hot and dusty. Everyone gathered at the corner along the gray brick wall down the street from the gate. He can see the bright pink cotton candy, as the vendor waved it in the dusty air. He remembers the boys, in gray blue denim pants, selling bottles of water at the gate entrance. They gestured that the water was cool, and you could clean the gravestones with it. Nothing was sacred, the commerce of death in a violent country. It all faded to ever-deepening hazy shades of orange, green, and purple.

9

MONOLITHIC

It is the beginning of biology class and Sialia sits at her desk and reads the following Georgie Bruno poem:

> **October**
> Libra and Scorpio high in the sky
> After the harvests, and the final tilling
> Sow the seeds
> Rake the land
> Overseen by the opulent landlords
> —G.B.

Tyndall stands in the hall doorway and greets the kids as they shuffle in for sophomore biology class. He turns and comes in the room and sees the gang all hanging out by his desk in the back of the room. Hector is seated in Tyndall's desk chair; the classroom is strangely silent and still.

He starts heading to the front of the room to begin class, stops and turns around and walks to his desk in the back of the room. James, Ryan and Hector are silent and not moving—something is up. As he approaches his chair he sees that Hector has his arms duct-taped to the armrests of the chair. Tyndall says, "Good idea; we should do this to all of you. Come on let's have a seat and start class." He turns leaving Hector there and starts class.

Once the class is reading, he walks back to his chair to release Hector.

He flicks his pocket knife open and says, "Now hold still this won't hurt a bit." Hectors eyes get big; the other kids in class laugh. "Now go have a seat and get started." Tyndall walks around class, as the students read, with the roll of duct tape in hand. He stops by James' seat. "This would fit nicely over your mouth. Um, now hold still." More laughter.

Tyndall starts up the lesson. "Okay you guys, let's review the reading we just did. What is cystic fibrosis? Now, no gene acts in isolation…"

After school, Tyndall sits back with his feet up on the corner of the desk. Stacks of magazines, papers, and books are arranged in separate piles. There is scarcely a square foot of space to write on or to eat lunch. The window counter is a mess of microscope slides, eyedroppers, and coverslips next to a microscope. Also, on the countertop is a stack of *Smithsonian* and *National Geographic* magazines.

Last summer his neighbor had dropped them off on his porch, note on top of them saying he was "hoping you could use these at school with your students." The magazines sit in a stack right where Tyndall had dropped them the week before school started. He perused the articles at leisure over the summer. He placed yellow sticky notes in articles he thought his students could enjoy. Terse little writing prompts written on some. He had envisioned using them in his science class with various units, or just as free-reading material for his students to enjoy. The cover photos and the photo essays within are so mesmerizing. Some of the articles even had nice online teaching resources.

All those grand plans, potential and real, were shattered on the first day at the before-school meetings. There he sat in the library, with all the teachers, sweat dripping down his back in the uncomfortable summer heat. Stufa explained how the school district had a new curriculum. The new material, adopted over the summer, was designed with new state standards for each grade. Principal Stufa introduced the educational consultant, Joel Haustoria. There was panic, dismay, even anger in the grumblings of teachers seated in a neat circle with the window shades closed.

Disheartened, Tyndall listened as Stufa and Haustoria explained how the students would now engage in higher-level thinking, with a focus on nonfiction writing. All this coordinated with the school district's quarterly tests for each subject and grade level. Meanwhile, a faculty training schedule had been established by the Spring Forward representative Master Teachers. Spring Forward was the name of the curriculum sold by the Bradmoor Publishing company, who designed and sold the new curriculum. There it was, three in-house training days in which he and other teachers would be pulled from the classrooms. Tyndall wondered who was footing the bill for this training. Money for all the travel costs, hotel accommodations, food, subs for those days; and for so many teachers.

Stufa elaborated, "We have a grant for this."

The old veteran teachers turned, did a wink-wink nod-nod with a wry smile. The ubiquitous quip they had heard thousand times out of the mouths of so many school administrators. Teachers are so easily placated into submission.

But there on top of one of the stacks, is the *National Geo* with the cover of an Easter Island statue head, known as *moai*. He had always taught a one-day lab lesson about Easter Island. But now he wanted to expand it into a full set of lessons with the Ecology Unit.

Oh yeah, that was the one, the one article that was the perfect lesson plan. Art, engineering, culture, geography, travel, history, environmental science—all in one; he thinks quietly to himself. Fuck it, I should do that lesson. It's all planned out. It's a couple weeks' worth of reading projects and some way cool engineering. Just that one, I had done so much work, even when *to do it. But if I do it then, I'll be two weeks behind all the other tenth grade teachers who stick to the new curriculum. It will most certainly show on the quarterly standardized tests given by the school district. My future pay scale is to be determined by how the kids do on those tests. But this is such a cool unit. I was excited by it.* Tyndall sinks into his chair feeling heavy and tired.

He opens the magazine. He unfolds the photo of the great expanses of green grass, huge statue heads familiar to all, dwarfing distant hikers on a single path. He stares over the top of the magazine to the green turf of the schoolyard, so dark green with the cooling autumn. The dandelions are flushing out again. He thinks about the environmental lessons within the pages on his lap. *No one heard the last tree fall. It just went from a forested island with big palm trees, to one with medium trees, to small trees, to shrubs, to open expanses of grassland. The clans fighting over the ever-limited resources. Each clan erecting monoliths of staggering size. Each monolith moved on miles of roads from distant quarries, using tree trunks from trees that no longer existed.*

In the schoolyard, a broken sprinkler head squirts water straight up in the air. At the back door, the school secretary hauls boxes on a dolly from a yellow van. Such a tiny woman with towering green and white boxes stacked. He wonders, Who is answering the phones?

That afternoon, before soccer practice, James walked off to play some basketball. No one heard the last basketball dribble rhythmically on the hardwood court. The ball was dropped, resonating a resounding echo from the hollow wood floor that faded with ever smaller and rapid beats. It bounced and rolled into the corner. There it sits, a deflated sentinel, looking over the expanse of space; waiting, looking, never blinking. It is a testament to a time long ago. Now the Auxiliary Gym's door handles are chained and locked. A Paleolithic madness engulfed and stripped their entire world; shrinking it to a treeless expanse of rock and isolation.

10

SIALIA'S FIRST DAY

On a humid spring morning in 1954, photographer Fan Ho is walking the streets of the Causeway Bay area of Hong Kong. He stops in the shade of a building to load 120 Tri-X black and white film into his Rolleiflex twin reflex camera. Looking down the viewfinder he sees the inverse upside-down image; he takes a couple of shots of the geometric lines of buildings. The lines are exquisite and the light is fantastic, giving him an exhilarating feeling. But despite the beautiful light and the various shadows on the walls something is missing—it needs a subject. Some opposite, a woman, form and beauty—yes. Ah, a woman, to stand in the light. Geometry and human form. He continues shooting, twelve shots at a time, before having to reload the camera with new film. The next morning, after preconceiving the shot, he meets his cousin and has her stand in the corner at the junction of two imposing walls. The walls rise, smoothly painted, with the left wall in the bright tropical morning light. She stands there in a black dress, erect and tall, with her head looking slightly down and her arms folded in back of her.

The next day in the darkroom Fan Ho makes the first test print. He sets the timer for a burst of light for two seconds while holding a piece of stiff paper over the photographic print paper. Then he slides the paper two inches to the right and does another two-second exposure. He continues until the entire eight-by-ten–inch print paper is exposed. What he ends up with is a test print with five bands of different exposures. He chooses the correct exposure of eight seconds. Then he lines up the square negative and crops out the left wall to make a rectangular print. After exposing the print paper, he drops the paper into the developing solution and rocks the tray with the liquid and the paper back and forth; in the soft red light he watches the image magically appear. All the while he is keeping an eye on the clock, then he drops it in the stop bath and into the fixer.

He emerges from the darkroom and drops the wet print into a tray in the sink and runs water on the print. His eyes adjust to the light as the water runs over the final print and the test print below it in the same tray. He lights a cigarette and watches the prints dance in the bubbles under the flowing water. After ten minutes he places both prints on the table and wipes the excess water away with a squeegee. In the silence of the room he stares out the window and takes the last draw of his cigarette. He looks back down at the prints, and smiles. A playful thought echoes through his mind and he reenters the darkroom.

The actual final print, titled *Approaching Shadow*, has a diagonal "shadow" line cutting it in half, with the young lady in the corner of light with the other half a perfect triangle of shadow. All added imaginatively in the darkroom. But to the viewer it is imposing, frozen time, held in a geometric space. Is the shadow moving in to engulf the woman, or is it moving out? Sun and shade upon the imagination, a captive soul held in a human space, projected upon the mind's eye, looking at it, out from within.

The yellow school bus pulls up to the designated stop on the east side of Elysium Hills High School. Sialia steps off the bus. She stands there on the sidewalk, in the cool morning, and looks down at her phone. Helen and Sandy come walking up as Sialia undoes her braided hair and reties it. She wears a printed shirt with loose long sleeves and a tall collar with her midriff slightly showing. Around her neck is a plastic beaded rosary with a bone white plastic crucifix. The girls stand and talk as Sialia again unties her braid and pulls her hair through her fingers. Her jet-black hair, wavy from being in a braid, hangs across half her face. The sun reflects off her hair as streaks of dazzling silver in the bright morning light.

As they walk up Helen says, "We just saw James and Ryan walking way back on Madison Street."

"Oh, you should've been there. Those shits lit a firecracker or something.

Smell my hair; ah, I hate those guys!"

"Yeah I saw a posted photo of the bus driver talking to them outside the bus."

Two senior boys walk up in their letter jackets. "Hi Helen; we'd be glad to show you around." The girls, looking down, laugh in unison, rolling their eyes. Sialia and Sandy look back up at Helen.

"No, no I'm fine, I'll see you around."

"Senior boys, already Helen?" Sandy says.

"What's your schedule?" Helen says, looking at her phone and pulling up her schedule. They walk outside, around to the huge gilded front doors and pull on the handles. A breeze, almost a gust of wind, blows out from the building. They step in.

Sialia sees a smoky vision of a thousand large spools of thread all lined up and stacked at six feet off the ground stretching down the length of the hallway. Below each a long thread of fiber stretches to the moving loom pumping up and down in long twenty-foot stretches. Large brass plates pack the elongated threads into a woven pattern of cloth, each spool spins clockwise one-half rotation, six inches of thread is pulled down, machine parts move in rhythmic thumping unison, slam down, slide, down the dusty hallway, girls in sooty gray dresses adjust knobs and replace empty spools of thread. The noise is deafening from the racket of steel and brass plates clanking together. The thread spools out as parts slide and produce pallets of coarse gray cotton sheets folded on scaffolding below the machine loom stretching down the hallway as far as the eye can see. Along the opposite wall young boys and girls open metal lockers that are full of stacked spools of thread, each spool is about eight inches tall with a six-inch circumference. The children grab the spools and pass them to a line of workers loading the massive loom stretching down the long hallway. Spools turn, sheets of gray cloth are folded, a rhythmic thumping symphony of sound bangs out resonating in the cavity of the mind, people stand shoulder to shoulder in small groups looking out as the girls walk by. A look and a thought. Processions of kids shuffle down the long hallway to a junction of another set of hallways to the left and right, so many looking on, looking from the side, all eyes, the weight of the gaze upon the mind, the girls turn left to numbered lockers and drop their packs and books in the lockers and each pulls out a giant spool of gray thread. Sialia holds the spool in her hand and looks down at the concentric overlaying layers of thread. In one section a bright sky-blue length of thread emerges from the monotonous overlay of gray threads. She smiles and looks down the hall at the room numbers by the doors of different classrooms.

"We're here: 122, Ms. Crowley, English Composition," she says. The girls smile at each other, enter and stand right next to each other, shoulders touching. Sialia drops the gray spool to the ground; the spool rolls away out the door, with a bright sky-blue thread extending out from her hand. She looks out at the classroom with 25 or so students in a big circle with the teacher standing in the middle orchestrating some first day activity. She thinks about the start of her day.

"Sialia, get some cereal out for your sister," her mom said.

"Yeah, yeah, I got it."

"So, get your sister to her stop, make sure she gets on the right bus."

"But mamma… can't you drive us?"

"No, no—we talked about this. Come on."

"But…"

"No—I've got work, and now you girls are on different buses."

"Yeah, yeah mamma, I got this—it's okay."

Sialia's thoughts are broken as the teacher starts up. "Okay, everyone have a seat, I'll assign seats next class, let's just get started here….I'm Ms. Crowley, and this is English composition…." It is the usual dos and don'ts, and the reading of the syllabus. The teacher proceeds to some inane, convoluted grading system. "So, the Spring Forward rubric…"

Sialia is quick to interject, "I don't understand, so if a kid hands in a paper late, then he or she gets graded as sixty-six percent, but if they then rewrite that paper they can get one hundred percent of the grade?"

"Yes, that's how it works."

"But why?"

"To motivate those students."

"And how's that fair to the kid who handed it in on time? Anyways, when does motivation become manipulation?" Sialia says.

The teacher, aghast, stands there frozen for a minute, with a perturbed look on her face. Then she proceeds, "Okay, now we're going to stand up and form a circle, then we'll break into groups for this introductory exercise." The teacher breaks them into groups of four students. Sialia thinks—*no, no, not with those guys, no—fucking Salvadorans. What are they doing here? They can't even speak Spanish or English. I hate them. It's hard enough here, being Mexican, and they have to ruin it.* She and the other three students stand in a small circle, avoiding eye contact. Sialia stands there with her arms folded in front of her. She thinks, *My friends are over there. I should be with them—that's where I belong. When does this class end?*

James walks in a half hour late. "Now, who are you? Why are you late?" the teacher says. Pointing, she says, "Now go join that group."

"Well, ah, some bus problems."

The kids laugh and Sialia smiles and shakes her head. She looks over at Sandy and silently mouths, "I told you." As James walks by, she puts her hand on his shoulder and smiles.

James walks by and smiles back and then joins Hector in a group standing in the corner. "Man, you made it," Hector says. "Are you in trouble?"

"No, nothing—yet."

Sialia looks down at the pattern in the carpet and in a daydream, she sees a bright painting dancing before her eyes. Marc Chagall's *I Am the Village* dances at her feet. A bright smiling goat is eye to eye with a smiling man holding a shining glittery tree of hope and peace; there is a circle of red over a green triangle, houses and people. *I like cows and goats and the lines of small houses, it reminds me of being a little girl in Mexico, before we all left…so, so long ago, a circle within the circle, hand tools working the land, and everybody walked. I'm friends with animals….* She looks across the room at Helen smiling and laughing with three boys vying for her attention. Helen stands there, tall, elegant and poised with straight arms clasping her crossed hands together, pinkie fingers up in front of her. She leans back and flashes a smile, as if she were standing in front of a calm ocean shining backlit; an expanse of water and sky with billowing clouds. In her mind's eye, Sialia can see the small church with the cross on the steeple atop the hill. She remembers walking hand-in-hand with her grandmother and her explaining, in soft musical Spanish, the history of the buildings on that street. *I hope my little sister is having fun in second grade.*

Wow, that was my first year here, that's when I made friends with Sandy and Helen. We had fun then. Now all this.

Sialia turns to the group in back of her and says, "Hi, JR. Did you have a good summer break?"

"Ah, hi, ah yeah," JR says, looking down at his phone smiling.

"Hey, do you have art today? I have it third block."

"Yeah, I'll see you there. Hope the teacher is cool."

"Yeah, we'll see."

JR's cool. Such a little guy. His straight brown hair hangs down to his eyes in a flat greasy way. No one likes him, kind of weird, but he's nice, doesn't act like a jerk. He was nice to me back in grade school. Looking across the room, she smiles looking at James and Hector. Both of them are on the floor having a one arm push-up contest, cussing and swearing. *Those guys, always goofing off, having fun, they don't even care who is looking. They just tumble along. I don't know why, but they're okay for such spazzes.*

Here it comes—the teacher, obviously annoyed, starts up—"What are you boys doing?"

Hector falls to the ground and lies there absolutely still, like a mouse under the gaze of a hawk. His head is on the floor with his cheek smashed against the carpet and he starts talking with his mouth in the carpet—something about a push-up contest. The whole class erupts in laughter. Arms splayed out, body absolutely frozen, Hector continues to mumble away face down. "Ah, we were just like doin' pushups. Ya know, it's important to stay in shape."

Smiling, Sialia stares out the window at three bluebirds on the split rail fence. She can see the half circle of green grass where the lawn sprinkler water hits, with an arc of brown grass enclosing it where the water misses. One of the bluebirds alights at the interface, grabs an insect and flies back up to the fence rail by its friends.

11

MORNING RIDE

The day after the bottle rocket incident, James and Ryan meet up at the corner. It is pretty much a straight ride up Madison Street to school. They approach the first hill. James drops his head, stands up and sways his bike left and then right sprinting up the hill.

Ryan catches up, "Dude, why do you do that at every hill?"

James, looking over to Ryan says, "There ain't no other way: it's just you gotta go hard, you know what I mean?"

"But it's a hill!"

"Come on, were going to be late," James says as he charges up the next hill. Ryan overtakes him at the top of the hill and looks to his right, smiling at James.

Panta rhei.

As the boys are riding their bikes up the hill to Elysium Hills High, Sialia exits the bus at school and strolls across the lawn to the front doors. She is looking for her friends Sandy and Helen. She looks back over her shoulder at a group of Latina girls watching her walk by. She flashes a quick look back with a scowl. Closer to the main entrance, a group of upperclassmen are talking and laughing in boisterous outbursts. The sound resonates. A mass of eyes casting envious looks at others. She looks down at her phone to break the weight of being watched. Everyone is the other. It feels more like a path through towering gray rocks and boulders, but then the way opens up to the doors. She walks up to the magnificent gilded doors, polished bright as flames.

The morning light reflected off the gleaming panels like golden sunlight on rippling water. The intensity of light bounces back upon her eyes, penetrating the mist to unveil within her a fierce determined exhilaration. She grabs the handle of the right-hand door, pulls the door ajar, and stops to gaze at the individual panels. There is a breath of wind coming out the cracked door. Five panels on the right door and another five on the left. She realizes each panel is a picture story on its own, like a chapter in a book. Carved into each panel, within the lines and relief, is sadness, joy and the tormenting gravity of the unfamiliar road ahead. The top left panel is the beginning and the bottom right the end. But she starts by staring at one of the middle stories, then her gaze jumps down to her left. It is all out of order, but it did not matter. Viewed this way it is more like a box of old photographs spilled on the floor. The very instant the door is pulled a myriad of brilliant colors flash, like a diamond being split.

12

SMOKY SPARKS FALL

It is the second day of high school; still no trouble from the bus incident. With relief James rolls his bike up to the soccer field, drops his pack, and leans his bike against the outside of the fence by the gate to the ballfield.

After practice James helps schlep the balls, in a big oversized mesh bag, back to the locker room. James asks, "Hey coach can I take a ball and go back to the soccer field? I'll give it back to you tomorrow."

"All right, take one of those Adidas gold and black ones; those are last year's balls."

As he walks back out to the ballfield; one of his teammates' moms rolls down the car window and says, "Hey James, you want a ride home?"

"Ahh—no thanks Ms. Stanley, I got my bike—I'm okay. Thanks."

Martin Schongauers engraving of *The Temptation of St. Anthony* flashes in all its agony with tormenting fantastical creatures pulling on the very existence of a man ripped and haggard while floating in the air.

The sun sets and most everyone has headed home. James Malachite remains; standing about ten feet from the goal, he kicks the ball as hard as he can into the center of the net. It flies and hits the net with a thwap, and rolls back out toward him. He strides forward and at the line of the goal he blasts the ball again straight into the center of the net. The ball bounces back, and he then dribbles the ball on his knees, then his feet. He thinks, *It would be so cool if I were good enough to play varsity as a freshman. I'm so skinny and small, I wish I weighed more and was all muscular.* Coach drives by looking up at the ballfield with one lone boy dribbling a soccer ball silhouetted against the deepening western sky that is fading into night.

The ball bounces off his foot careening to the left and rolling to the corner of the net. James drops down and does twenty-five push-ups. He can feel the cool grass each time his nose comes to the ground. It smells like earth and smashed green grass. His mind wanders to seeing the girls in the hallway: *Oh, that one in her white sweater, tight with no sleeves, midriff slightly showing. She turned and saw me checking her out, and with a quick scowl turned away to face her friends while looking down at the phone. Fuck, what an idiot I am.*

He sees a blue plastic chair by the gate and jogs over to grab it. He brings the chair over to the goal and places it in the center under the crossbar. Standing on the chair he jumps up to the goal crossbar and does ten chin-ups and then swings out to the right and drops down to the ground, letting out a coughing exhale. He leaps back up on the chair, jumps back up this time facing out from the goal, and brings his feet up to the bar and does ten leg lifts, grunting with each lift. He falls to the ground and rolls in agony from the exertion. He retrieves the ball in leaping strides and dribbles it out of the net, turns and blasts it past the chair back into the net. Then he drops and does more push-ups.

His mind races: *Fuck, I gotta start not fucking up at school. Got lucky with this bottle rocket incident.* He does some more chin-ups and leg lifts. He lies on his back on the cool ground, the cold sinks in through his sweat soaked shirt. He's breathing so hard, his chest rises and falls with each heaving breath. Lying there, he gazes at the first stars through the net at a sky that is not quite black but not blue either. Getting up he stumbles to his bike, rips off his wet shirt, puts on his hoodie and pulls the hood up over his head. He wipes the sweat off his face with his shirt. He then stashes his cleats and the ball behind the maintenance shed. He drops his sweat soaked shirt into his empty pack and zips it up.

On the ride home he sits up, leaning back, gliding down the hills with his arms out. His mind wanders again: *I probably have to make my own dinner again tonight. Mom will be just sitting there, frozen, staring at a flickering TV, in the small dark side room. Just can't make it right. Fucking mom, trouble, trouble finds you, gotta not get in trouble—it finds you. Where's my phone?* He thinks it's in the small pocket of his pack. *Don't know. Fuck it—there'd only be trouble on it anyways. Getting cold now, I better find some gloves for the ride tomorrow morning. Fuck, God dammit why? Why does it find me?*

13

DRAGONFLY PERCEPTION

Gustav Klimt's oil painting, *The Kiss,* depicts two lovers embracing in an elaborately patterned blanket. They are kneeling together in a grassy field of colorful flowers. The added silver and gold gilding make the entire painting glow.

It is the second week of school, Tyndall strolls into his science room at 07:30. The usual grand putzing around the room: cleaning up old lunch food wrappers, straightening twenty-nine desks into rows, finding the seating charts for the day's classes. He pushes his tattered desk chair from the front of his room to his desk at the back of the room; the wheels squeak as they roll on the white linoleum floor. Back at the front of the classroom, Tyndall stands on a yellow plastic chair fixing the schedule on the four-foot by four-foot white board in the front corner of the room.

Here it is only a couple of weeks past Labor Day and the schedule has to be changed because of some unannounced assembly last week. He teaches four sections of biology to sophomores, one section of AP-Biology, and one section of River Watch. He is thankful for the latter two classes because they have mostly seniors. The school has a block schedule so he sees the kids every other day. He outlines a schedule for each class for about a three-week period on this board. He then cruises over to the sink by the windows and fills up a pitcher of water and then waters the plants on the light table; a set of shelves on wheels at the front of the class. Then he fills his coffee cup with water for hot tea and puts it in the small microwave on the back table by the hall door.

Early on things are very regimented, formal, and disciplined. On the tall demonstration table at the front of the class his computer is open and the materials are out for the day's lab, papers stacked, tea hot and ready to go.

The girls come floating in from the hall. They have hot cups of drinks from Starbucks in their hands, and they plop down in various desks and tables. Sialia says in a cheerful voice, "Good morning, Mr. Tyndall."

"Hey Sialia, how's it going?" Tyndall says while standing on the plastic chair writing the schedule.

"What are we doing today?" Sandy says while looking down at her cell phone.

"We got a lab, I think you'll like it. Hey can you guys close the blinds for me, thanks."

Sandy and Helen are looking down at their phones, the persistent whisper of some algorithm feeding on their psyche. They blink and say, "Ah, sure," and get up and stroll over to the east-facing windows and close the six blinds.

One of the blinds closes only to the top of the large aquarium with frogs in it. Tyndall says, "Yeah, don't worry about that one, it does not close all the way."

The morning light comes streaming in a warm and inviting way. Sitting at the large stone-top lab table by the windows, Sialia spins around in a blue plastic chair. She sees the rainbow of color projected onto the counter top by the sunlight shining through the corner of the aquarium. She gets up and passes her hand through the colorful light, twisting and turning her hand. "Wouldn't be cool if we could see like this with everything?"

Standing on the chair Tyndall pipes in, "Well we do, that's why the chair is blue, or yellow."

It will be hot today in the school. Tyndall has on long khaki pants and a white T-shirt with a long-sleeved button-down Oxford formal shirt with no tie. He wears running shoes because his feet and shins just kill him from standing on the concrete floor all day. This past summer they finally reroofed the building after years of having a constantly leaking ceiling every time it rained or the snow melted. But as usual, the lowest bid got the contract. So, the new roof is black asphalt, which replaced the old silver-white colored roof. These hot late-summer days bake the roof, which heats the space above the drop ceiling. For air circulation, the forced air is blowing out of the vents. But the air ducts in the ceiling heat up and make the rooms in the school a blast furnace. There is no direct thermostat; it is just on. The actual thermostat for the room is 100 miles away in Denver.

Out Tyndall's back outside door, across the grassy courtyard, is the "The Yard." It is a large fenced-in area in back of the cafeteria. There is a large flat expanse of concrete with two basketball courts and a small grassy quadrant with two small kid-sized soccer goals. Interspersed in the area are seven picnic tables. At lunch on this hot day boys are playing basketball; on the grass a soccer game is proceeding. A wall-ball game, with half a dozen boys, is sandwiched in-between the two basketball games right at the edge of the grass and concrete. Kids are seated and milling about with lunch trays in and amongst the various games. A couple walks hand in hand, out the cafeteria doors, all googly-eyed, looking at each other laughing and smiling. They walk together oblivious through the commotion of games, players, and balls flying. They proceed leisurely, making their way under the basketball hoop as boys fly around them for a rebound. The tennis ball bounces off the wall in front of them and is quickly caught and thrown back against the wall in back of them. As they exit the gate a soccer ball slams into the chain-linked fence right next to them. They do not even flinch or break eye contact and continue to glide across the grassy courtyard into Tyndall's open door just as the lunch bell rings.

The afternoon class is sweltering. Kids, with red flushed faces, are collapsed in their desks. The windows are open, the back door is open, the hall door is open, and the door to the building outside in the hallway is open. Sweat rolls down Tyndall's sideburns. Standing at the front of the room, he leans heavily to his right against the tall front demonstration table. His eyes cheat over to the seating chart. A boy in the third row in front of him is checking his phone hidden under his backpack on the desk. Tyndall is quick to call out his name, "Jack! You want to lose that phone?" he barks out with authority. It's not that Tyndall doesn't know the kids' names, or their personalities, it's just using the individual names early and assertively brings the students to attention.

Tyndall is just finishing up the lab instructions for the day's activity. He takes a lab drawing example, and a magnet, and puts the drawing up on the whiteboard in back of him. Just then a large six-inch blue dragonfly comes flying in through the open back outside door. It cruises and hovers just below the ceiling, effortlessly and speedily cruises across the heads of the seated students. Here we go. Kids start screaming, a girl is crouching and puts her notebook over her head. Another smaller boy, Johnny, has bounded in one clear leap, to the top of the desk and is swinging a textbook at the insect. It deftly dodges as the boy leaps from desk to desk frantically swinging away.

The dragonfly sees the room, the humans, and perhaps just a little bit more than that. Each rounded bulbous eye is really an array of hundreds of hexagonal eyes or facets. Each facet captures and projects its very own image to a suite of neurons and sends the visual signal to a pinhead of a cerebral ganglion in the beast's head. Small bristly hairs stick out between some of the facets and perceive additional information as its head swivels around. Together this visual system can perceive an angle of view four times what a human set of eyes can. The visual field of each facet overlap with superimposed high-resolution images reflected in its visual core. It sees in multiple wavelengths of light, including ultraviolet and infrared, as well as visible light.

The radiant light indicates a room that is rectangular and is forty feet by thirty feet with six large six-foot by six-foot windows. Every other window has a screen and the window can swing open from a hinge at the top. The outside wall with the windows also has the open door from the courtyard it entered through. Below the windows there is a countertop with cabinets and drawers below it and a sink in the corner. At the back door the flag of the U.S. hangs at an odd angle over the end of the counter. Tyndall's scattered desk and another plastic and metal folded table sit in front of the outside door forming a little alcove.

The back wall has a door to the adjacent science room of Mr. Jay and a short countertop with a sink and cabinets above and below. Also, in back, just below the ceiling, there is a large two-inch yellow pipe that extends for about three feet and has a large round showerhead at the end with a big pulldown handle. There is a metallic bowl-shaped eyewash at the height of the sink counter just below the shower. There is no drain in the floor below the giant showerhead. The hall side wall has a countertop with cabinets above and below. By the hall door, in the corner, is another folding table with a pile of books and papers and a small household microwave. Another large, very old, boxy microwave sits on the countertop. There are three large stone top sturdy lab tables by the windows. The ceiling is a patchwork of drop tiles and fluorescent lights, some of which have no bulbs.

Johnny and another boy are leaping across desktops chasing the drag-onfly. As the desks slide out from under them, books fall to the ground. Johnny is finally standing on top of the big black stone-top lab table as the dragonfly, facing the window, rhythmically flies swaying back and forth. Tyn-dall yells, "Okay chill out, it's just a dragonfly. Johnny stop!—stop!—be still! Turn off the lights, turn off the projector," he says pointing to the projector hanging from the ceiling. Through five hundred and twenty hexagonal facets the dragonfly sees the geography of the room with twenty seven kids, one adult, twenty nine seats—all these images are beyond the field of vision of a human. The colors are completely different. As the fluorescent lights go off, all the colors of the multiple images change in the new light. It darts for the projector screen. When the projector light goes off, all the colors change again. Through its eyes, a triangular piece of pizza, splattered on the floor, glows pur-ple with fluorescent green. It can see through the shirt of a girl and see her bra is not the rose red humans would see through her thin off-white t-shirt, but instead it is a blazing yellow orange. The rocks, inert on top of Tyndall's desk, glow and flicker an unknown brilliance. It sees the pipe beneath the linoleum floor, under the concrete, that was supposed to be hooked up to a drain that is not there below the flower-like showerhead. It hovers strangely above a lu-minous prism on Tyndall's desk as if attached by a string above it, wavering back and forth.

Tyndall jumps toward his desk and in a couple of quick bounds lunges for the butterfly net leaning on the wall by the filing cabinets next to his desk. He turns and swipes the net, just missing a girl's head, as she swings her head to the side quickly and her long blond ponytail whacks across the face of a boy, making him fall to the ground backwards. The dragonfly is now in the bottom of the net, flapping and clacking its wings. Tyndall, hot and sweating, a little irritated, but trying not to laugh, takes a quick assessment of the situ-ation. He backs up away from the windows and his desk and sits down in one of the back seats, all while sliding his hand down the net on the outside to pin the dragonfly down through the mesh fabric of the net. He can feel the vibrating of the animal's wings. He then reaches in and extracts the six-inch mottled dragonfly and grabs it on the back of its thorax carefully to keep its biting jaws from getting him. He starts up, "It's a blue darner dragonfly—these are beneficial insects." Some kids can't get close enough to see, as they hang over one another's backs and shoulders, others can't get far enough away and stand in the hallway looking through the door. Five-hundred and twenty facets look back at the human faces, as it turns its head frantically, jaws lashing and flapping its stiff wings. It even vibrates its entire body. Many of the kids have their cell phones out and are photographing or videoing the insect now in Tyndall's hand.

"Here, put your finger here," Tyndall says to the boy next to him. "Feel that?"

"Whoa."

"It's called stridulating."

The critter looks back at them. And it could see. See the angle of the light, the photons streaming into multiple prismatic hexagons, the light reflected and refracted into a spectrum beyond comprehension. A celestial light-show of electromagnetic energy ripples around the room as seen through the dragonfly's eyes. In the ice-filled purple plastic water bottle, it could see the two-masted ship with its crew stranded in the frozen ice of a polar sea; the light illuminating the large aquarium on the windowsill and the never blinking eyes of the floating frogs; on the back cover of a textbook, splayed on the ground; the emblem of Bradmoor Publishing glowing with pseudo-gilded gold and silver, embossed above a limestone pyramid with black smoke; the thick green oil flowing below the white linoleum floor; the facade of the school entrance; the stain on the skin of the cheek from where the tear rolled down earlier in the day; the fear, the joy, and the anxious tremble in the voice rolling on the waves of light; right through the three blue plastic cups with the ball underneath one of them; into the eyes of each child, glistening moist and clear, and open; the screens glowing and flickering with a plethora of halo images; and the light fades in the eyes of all who stared into the electronic devices; into the lenses of each camera devise to the photo plate; and to every photo, every text, email, website; each individual secret reflected off the photo plate from electrons then back to photons. The glitter sparkle on the cheek of a boy, from a hug he received by a girl in the hallway before class. *God, she smelled so good and was warm.* Streaming light, hexagonal, inverted, all coming at the speed of light; revealing, revealing a hidden world glowing with a myriad of projected images superimposed on a frenetic moment in a hot classroom some-time after lunch.

The mass of students and Tyndall step outside into the courtyard to re-lease the dragonfly. One kid asks, "Aren't you going to keep it for your insect collection Tynd?"

"No—it will fade in color, it's too beautiful. Besides there's still a couple more weeks of summer left for this guy."

The dragonfly is a brilliant mottled blue and gray on what seems to be an almost translucent body. Its stiff wings, with prominent veins, vibrate and flap.

"Here, Helen." She looks over at Tyndall; she has long straight dark hair, bright frosty blue eyes with fine dark eyebrows. "Here reach out your hands flat, don't be scared, it'll feel scratchy but will be gone in a second."

She reaches out; holds still. Tyndall gently places the insect in her hand. It grasps her fingers with its six legs, looks around one more time and then alights into the ether.

14

BIRDS IN THE ART ROOM

Tyndall walks up to Stufa at the beginning of the day, "Hey Jon, my room has not been mopped for a couple of weeks now," he says. Besides his feet sticking to the floor, and the visible grime, he knows because he wrote, with water-soluble ink, a date on the floor. If the room had been mopped, it would be gone.

Stufa responds, "Oh, okay. We have a new guy. I'll talk with him. It's so hard to train these guys."

At every school, there are numerous safe places. Unintended, natural spots for a student to sit, wait, visit and think. These places precipitate out of the matrix of the chaos and commotion. The jovial English teacher's room is one such place. It is here the kids come to eat lunch; they use his microwave oven behind his desk in the corner, with impunity. He laughs with them as they explain the antics of the morning bus ride.

In the art room Sialia sits with an art book in her lap. She sees fantastical birds with blue feet, blue feet? Birds with blue feet? Yellow and orange birds with their heads arched back as spiders dropped down silk lines into their mouths. There are birds flying upside down, wings folded, so unnatural. Insects, flowers and berries permeate the paintings. The weight of the large book, the musty smell of the old paper, the sound of turning pages complete the moment.

She turns the pages of the book to *Duck Hawk,* Plate 16, and *Mourning Dove,* Plate 17, on adjoining pages. As she opens the book to the page her head goes back in a startled manner, and her hand reaches out to touch the duck, dead in the talons of the hawk. Plate 16 transfixes her. The hawk on the left stares straight back at her, its open talons so yellow and black on the rock. There is a dead duck under its body with green wings, folded and limp. But the second hawk, on the carcass of another gray striped duck, takes her breath away. Blue beak dripping pink-purple blood, mouth agape, over the torn carcass, feathers strewn and talons clutched. Her hand reaches out and touches the head of the dead, mangled duck on the page. A tandem of violence and vitality on a tandem of inanimate death—a feather in the air floats between the two hawks and their quarry.

On the adjacent page, Plate 17 is the mourning dove. It presents a contrast with the cannibalistic blood dripping down the beak of the predator on the previous page. Here, on this plate, was the union of two pairs of doves in a flowering tree. One dove arches downward to presumably feed the female sitting on the nest. Meanwhile another dove pair is perched above them, one bird reaching to touch the other bird. The painting holds tender gestures of love and softness. There is a tangled ensemble of white flowers that cradles a breath of warmth.

The back of Sialia's chair jolts as James barges over and exclaims, "Cool— look at that blood." Then he rushes across the room to the door with two other boys in tow.

Sandy comes over and puts her hand on Sialia's shoulder and says, "Such jerks. Couldn't stand still if they had to." Transfixed on the doves she says to Sialia, "Don't you wish a boy could be so..." Together their eyes look to the left in revolt and disgust, then to the right in hope of such a world. How could a person paint such things? It is a simultaneous exhale and inhale.

"Who paints such things? says Sandy in a mournful sigh.

Sialia does not move and says, "Well..."

She silently flips the pages back. Plate 7, *Purple Grackle.* Yellow beak overflowing with corn kernels, corncobs stripped in gluttony. Plate 6 on the left page, *Wild Turkey,* a mamma with baby birds at her feet, one young bird knocked over on its back as the adult bird runs forward.

Sialia says, "She's moving and has somewhere to go," the babies tumble along feeding—"Look!"

Sandy pushes her glasses up her nose. "These guys are mean," she says pointing to the yellow-eyed blackbirds in the purple grackle painting.

Sialia says, "We grew corn last summer. It tasted so good. Look at the babies, scurrying to keep up."

Sandy says, "They're feeding—look."

Sialia touches the pink orange tassel on the corn; remembering the cool silky feel of the hairs from when she and her mom cleaned the corn on the back porch last summer.

Sialia flips back to the title of the book: *The Birds of America* by John James Audubon.

The next class period begins, it is biology with Mr. Tyndall. Sialia plops down in a desk chair. It is so constrained, hard folded cold steel and plastic with a fake wood desktop. There is masking tape, with the number on it, in the upper right-hand corner of the desk. The class is doing a lab making DNA models. On the board is the daily class objective. In numerous professional trainings, teachers have been told to write this on the board. This is because when the admin is assessing learning in a teacher's class, the admin often asks kids what they are learning. So, most of the teachers have advised and taught the kids that when asked by some strange adult who enters the room what they are doing, just read whatever it says on the board. On the far-right hand side of the board it says: DNA and…structure….Now Tyndall knows the admin is walking around and visiting various classrooms because Mr. Jay walked by his door and tossed a shiny purple folder into his room; it skidded across the linoleum floor. "Purple folder" is a warning that a "walk through" is probably going to happen, so Tyndall is prepared. As he picks the folder up, three administrators from different schools enter the room and sit down around the room. He smiles as they enter and knows that this is part of his official evaluation. James and Hector are sitting at the side table with scattered colored plastic bead-like parts being assembled into a double helix of DNA. One of the visiting admins leans forward over the shoulders of the boys and asks, "So, what are you boys learning today?"

Hector looks up at the left-hand side of the board, the wrong side, where funny jokes and ridiculous kid statements are posted, such as "No Phun, Tyndlandia," *et cetera*. He reads, then says, "Ah, we're learning about Sasquatches on the backs of flying mastodons." Everybody at the table erupts into laughter. You can hear the reverberating echo of children, in each classroom, as they blindly read what is on the board as they have been instructed to do.

Tyndall walks out with the other adults. Standing in the hallway, Tyndall can hear one of the administrators say, "Now all our data has been compromised. These kids aren't taking this seriously." Tyndall silently thinks about data collection and science. He recollects about his internship at the hospital cancer research center he did back in college. Tyndall, standing in the hallway looking at the administrators, points over his shoulder gesturing that he has to get back to class. Quickly he says, as he steps back into his room, "What background do you have in data collection and analysis anyway?" He almost lunges back into his room before they can answer him. Sialia looks hard at Tyndall, knowing he is in trouble, and then she kicks Hector and gestures to James.

At the end of the day, Stufa walks up to the janitor and says, "Hey, Mr. Tyndall's room needs mopping. I know you are really busy. Just mop it, then get back to your regular routine. He's kind of a whiny, bitchy teacher, anyway. We are so appreciative for the hard work you do." Stufa knows the rooms don't get cleaned, because he is the one that cut the number of cleaning staff years ago.

15

PARENT TEACHER NIGHT

Ancient of Days
A caliper to measure with
So mighty from above
A great metric
In which to rule with
The angle ever increases,
as the distance increases
And with both,
the accuracy is lost
Neo-phrenology

—G.B.

It is two weeks into the school year and Tyndall is shuffling around at the end of lunch, trying to get ready for the next class. He hears a loud ruckus in the hall just outside his door. He thinks, *Now what?* He stands in the frame of his door and watches James running a couple steps, launching himself in the air, legs kicking and flailing away, and landing hard on his butt on the thin carpet in the hallway. A roar of laughter comes from the other boys. Tyndall stands perplexed. Hector does the same, landing on his back. He rolls in pain on the floor, obviously having just knocked the wind out of himself. Sialia and her friends stand looking on with their arms folded in front of them. She throws her head back with her eyes closed and laughs.

Tyndall thinks, *Who are these freshmen?* And asks, "What are you boys doing?"

"We're kicking ourselves in the balls—watch."

Tyndall smiles then laughs, all the while at a complete loss for words.

James launches. "Dude—ah, you almost had it," Ryan says.

Tyndall says, "Dude this is so wrong—oh." As he watches, another boy lands splayed out on the floor. He laughs, and thinks, *Fucking freshman boys.* "Are these your lockers?"

"Yeah."

"Bonehead Central, that's what we'll call it."

"Yeah, we're in Bonehead Central."

Mr. Jay steps out into the hallway. "What's all the commotion?"

"Oh, someone just pithed the freshman boys; they're trying to kick themselves in the nuts." Jay smiles and just stands there silent and watches.

Finally, Tyndall pipes up, "All righty guys, let's get to class." He thinks, *It's going to be long day, with Parent Teacher Night tonight.*

James' mom pulls up to the school parking lot, walks up to the east side door, pulls and finds that it is locked. Looking through the door's window down the long hallway she can see a small crowd of people gathering in the open atrium. She walks down the lawn to the main front door entrance.

She pulls on the small, round bronze handles to the enormous gilded doors and enters the half-circle atrium, with a high ceiling, joining a couple of dozen parents and students milling around. James's mom looks back down the hall to her left, the shiny linoleum tile floor with the trophy cases on one side. She sees other people pulling on the locked door at the end of the long hallway. She is annoyed after a long day of work, the traffic, wishing there was some coffee to find. *You'd think they'd have the door unlocked,* she thinks.

The principal, Dr. Jonathan Stufa, and the assistant principal, George Combe, stand uncomfortably next to each other by a podium. Combe is younger than Stufa, tall and thin, with wispy brown hair parted strongly to one side. The wood podium seems out of place in the half-circle hallway atrium. Young boys blast out the entrance door with a football, oblivious to all the people. A banner hangs from the ceiling with some Governor's Choice Award for top schools in the state. Painted papier-mâché masks are partially covered by the banner, which was obviously hung only recently for the event tonight. Behind the principals on the wall there is a large framed Mission Statement. Down the hall in the first glass display case to the left is a shelf with small, six- to eight-inch roughly carved statue heads that stare blankly out. Dr. Stufa starts his speech, "Welcome to Elysium Hills High School. Tonight, we'll have you visit with your son's or daughter's teachers in the gym." His hands wave in the air, "We have put out tables for you and the teachers by departments." Parents and kids stand silently as Dr. Stufa points out the banner and the Mission Statement.

Sialia and Sandy stand in the back next to each other. Their shoulders are so close that they touch every once in a while. Sandy says to Sialia, "I hope we go out for pizza after this. You should join us."

Sialia says, "That would be great! I'll see if I can talk my mom into it— school night and all." The girls stare over the backs of the parents and the other students at the Principal standing at the podium. His hands wave in a circular motion as he babbles on about the new schedule and how it maximizes learning. The words hang in the air. *He makes no sense when he talks,* Sialia thinks. He exclaims something about the art classes and all the wonderful things going on. Shadows of dancing bears flicker on a cave wall, somewhere in the back of the parents' eyes; illuminated by an unseen light. They are spellbound by a perception of a flickering reality.

The girls turn to each other and look into each other's eyes. Sialia's eyes are dark chocolate brown, Sandy's hazel green. Sialia puts her left hand on Sandy's right shoulder, leans over, and says, "Yeah, when we really have art class. Last time we only took tests," she proclaims in a sturdy assertive tone.

"Yeah, that's what we do now."

Sialia goes on bitterly, "We didn't even get to paint. Ms. Rayleigh said we had to write a paper, so we didn't have time. Practicing for something—its fucking art class!"

Sialia thinks about the art book she was thumbing through before class that day; soft eyes blink as she turns the page. *Quail-like Bobwhite scatter under the talons of a descending hawk. Such brutality displayed in what you'd think would be a happy painting of birds.* The dancing shadows on the cave wall, behind the flickering flames of the fire, are quite different for her.

16

THE VIEW FROM ABOVE

Sialia sits in history class and opens the webpage to the document about the history of the conquest of the Americas by the Spaniards. The document she is about to read has excerpts from Bartolome de las Casas' *Short Account of the Destruction of the Indies.* The opening page has a horrific woodcut print. The print shows in black and white lines a conquistador throwing a baby who was held upside down by its foot, into a large open fire burning the bodies of hanging captive Native Americans. It is the last day of class before Thanksgiving break.

Over Thanksgiving break, James and his family are on vacation in Veracruz, Mexico. A large oblong coppery-green rock washes back and forth at their feet on the beach. He and his little brother are flying a four-bladed remote-control drone helicopter with a video camera. As the small craft rises up above the half-moon bay, a magnificent frigatebird soars with it. The bird goes across then under the aerial vehicle. Its black wings obscure the view. Its thin long head with an ominous hooked beak peers sideways up into the camera. This individual bird has been flying continuously for the past 180 days; it even sleeps on the wing. Always flying, always moving. James's little brother at the controls panics and the vehicle plummets, then rights itself. On the laptop computer screen the boys observe the bird's eye view of the tropical beach, turquoise blue-green Caribbean to the right, and lush tropical mountains to the left. For a moment, as the vehicle flies under the bird and control is lost, the whole scene flickers on and off on the computer screen. Scenes of smoke, fire, and the movement of thousands of people flash on the screen for a second. The computer freezes; James reaches over his brother's shoulder and frantically hits the buttons on the keypad of the laptop. In the pack on his back is a large chunk of black obsidian. James had found the rock the day before. The black volcanic glass also flickers smoky images from the depths.

For that quick second, the view on the computer screen is of an April day in 1519. The conquistador, Hernan Cortez, and his small armada of ships are anchored in the bay. Five hundred and twenty-plus men have just finished their first battle to secure a holding on the mainland of what is now central Mexico. Caravans and lines of men return to the busy beehive of activity at the bay. Native villages for miles around are burning. The air hangs heavy with an acrid smell. From the surrounding villages, armored men on horses are leading hundreds of captive natives bound to each other by ropes and chains.

On the northern shore, the largest village is now a pile of smoldering ash and burning stumps. The road here is wide enough for three horses side-by-side. The main center of the village has a central plaza about 100 square feet in size. A large stone rectangular slab sits in the center. It is covered with brilliant white plaster with red patterns painted on it. There are sinuous reliefs of snakes around the stone altar. A Catholic priest stands, gesturing as he blesses the altar. A boy stands next to him in a white robe holding a gold cross on the end of a very long pole.

Inland as the view widens, a long linear arroyo runs down from the mountain. Within the canyon a huge fire burns. On the road next to the cavernous canyon, the men of Castile sit around a fire pit with a dog carcass roasting on a spit while other small dogs, some of them with little or no fur, circle around the group of men. One of the conquistadors throws a bone, from the roasted dog, to the dogs slinking around. Processions of native slaves, bound and shackled on one ankle to a thick leather belt around their waists, proceed by. The clinking sound of chains resonates next to the crackling sound of the flames. Some slaves pick up and drag dead bodies to the cliff and throw them into the flames. Other pairs of slaves follow with large tree branches and trunks to feed the fire in the canyon below.

Farther inland, about a mile from the northern village's central plaza and altar, are fields of corn maize, granaries, and rows of rocks for grinding the hard seeds. Outside a thatched hut stands one Spanish soldier; another is on the ground lying on his back. Inside the hut a third soldier is naked on top of a young native girl. She cries and screams; the man laughs and grins. Both of his hands are on her breasts while her arms are bound with a loose leather strap over her head. The female warrior's gold-plated copper breastplate, with large pointed breasts, lies next to the native girl. It lies there so silently. The men outside harass and tease the man inside with the young native girl: "Better than those Moorish whores in the battle on your birthday."

"Oh, I remember that one." Laughing, and then a final moan emanates from the hut.

The men outside continue, "Oh, Antonio you go." Inside the hut, the native girl extracts a six-inch obsidian blade from the throat of her captor. She escapes silently, rolling under the thatched woven palm leaves of the hut wall, black stone knife dripping with blood in one hand. In her other hand is a puma skin cloak, loosely slung over her shoulder. The tail of the animal hangs down and sways with her every movement. She silently slips into the lush green vegetation in back of the hut.

Inside the hut Antonio cannot speak. Bright red blood squirts rhythmically out of his neck, as his legs thrust up and down skidding on the floor. The red blood mixes with the spilled grain; the yellow, tan and purple seeds as the ever-thickening blood coagulates around the grain and cobs on the floor of the hut.

James and his brother continue to argue on the beach about who is at the controls of the drone flying overhead. The video feed comes back. The green rounded mountains, the beach, the blue Caribbean all come back into view. James stops looking at the screen and picks up the oblong green knobble rock exposed by the receding wave. Unknown to him, the rock is a large one-pound chunk of copper with just a trace of gold.

17

FUN IN THE SNOW

After lunch, the art teacher, Ms. Rayleigh, sits at her desk, reviewing art pieces to share with her class that afternoon. She is going to introduce a new unit for her Art 2 class, called Emulations. The project involves reproducing another artist's painting as accurately as they can. She flips through her slide presentation and stops at one image. It is Winslow Homer's painting called *Snap the Whip*. In the painting, a group of young boys are involved in some schoolyard game. But she knows from past years that the kids now don't understand the game being played and are always distracted by the clothes the boys wear and that they have no shoes on. But the important part is not that, but the way Homer was able to capture the action, the very essence of the activity, a genuine early Americana snapshot. The next slide is of Audubon's *Carolina Parakeet*. Seven brightly colored green, yellow and red birds are displayed. Each bird is in a highly animated pose, not a calm quiet painting, but a noisy and boisterous one. She tries to remember, she thinks, *Yeah, the carolina parakeet is extinct.*

Mr. Brown, the gym teacher, and Tyndall step out the back door into the frozen courtyard, with Brown's after-lunch class. Each kid has a pair of snowshoes in their hands, and the commotion of the awkward ordeal of putting snowshoes on for the first time begins. The teachers each strap on their snowshoes and stare in wonder at how teenagers will struggle away and just not help one another. Tyndall pipes up, "Josue, help Davi put his snowshoe on," pointing at Davi. Girls, arms entangled together, laughing so hard that they fall over in the snow, getting their now-ungloved hands all wet and cold. The first snowball is lofted in a gentle arc over the girls and hits Josue as he tries to help Davi.

Brown turns to Tyndall and says, "Thanks for helping with the outing."

"Beats grading." Tyndall looks over as Davi chases Josue into the soft, deep, unpacked January snow. Davi's left snowshoe falls off, and he does an exaggerated face plant in the soft snow. "Besides, this a brilliant idea to take the puppies out for a romp," Tyndall says pointing to the antics of the boys.

Tyndall asks Brown, "Hey, were you at the meeting yesterday after school?"

"Yeah. Were you there?"

"No, I had a crown fall off my tooth. What a pain in the ass to try and get in to the dentist and get it fixed."

"Why do you ask? You didn't miss anything."

"Ah, it's just that Stufa came up and said something about how people were asking where I was, and how they missed my contribution."

"Huh, I was there from the beginning and no one even noticed or said anything."

"Hmm, go figure."

Tyndall looks across the snowy courtyard and shakes his head at the antics of Josue. He is an immigrant kid from El Salvador. He moved to the area when he was eleven, along with two older brothers, an older sister, and his mom. The previous year Tyndall had him in Basic Science class for English language learners. The two of them had established their relationship that year. Josue was a big, strong kid, who played soccer, or football, as he called it. But like so many in his position he struggled to stay on the school team because of academic eligibility. He spoke English in a slow, halting manner with a deep voice. When he spoke, he enunciated each word completely, giving it an almost formal quality. His command of the English language was very good while speaking; writing was a much different story. He wrote at a third- or fourth-grade level. Now in his sophomore year, things were going well, as good as can be expected. He came to school, stayed out of any real trouble, and passed most of his classes. He hung out with his friends, other rowdy, wild, fun immigrant kids from Mexico, El Salvador, and Brazil. That group of Latino boys most certainly had a wild exuberance to them. They were loud and talkative, quite rowdy at times.

The whole class and the two adults head up the hill in back of school, packing a new trail as they went. The group turn up a gully and loop around a big round clump of gambles oak. There the group catch their breath and then start back down to the school, except for Josue, Davi from Brazil, Gabriel from El Salvador, and Victor from Mexico. They just charge up the gully. Tyndall looks up at them and smiles at their reckless exuberance. He thinks to himself, *They'll tire soon enough and see us heading down the hill, then catch up with us.* But no, the boys just keep heading up the gully as it got steeper and narrower. The young ones wrestle their way up. Each would grab the trunk of a Douglas fir tree above them and pull themselves up and then swing their snowshoes to the top of the trunk. And up they proceed. Cursing and swearing in broken English, Mexican Spanish, Salvadoran Spanish, and Brazilian Portuguese. Tyndall and Brown both have a last-period class and have to get back. They stop at the back outside door looking and listening for the boys and wondering what to do.

Tyndall says, "Ah, I wonder who will eat who tonight?"

Brown quipped. "Brazil Davi is too skinny, no one would eat him"

"Yeah, but Victor is pretty scrappy, and would eat 'em all."

"Yeah. I suppose we'll lose our jobs over this."

"Yeah, those things happen. Well, it was nice working with you. I got a last hour class, I'll check in with you after that." Brown says, with a wry smile.

They left it at that: Wait an hour or two and see if the boys show up. Sure enough, Tyndall steps outside while his last-hour class is reading and stands in the frozen courtyard looking up. In the distance he can hear hooting and hollering as the four boys descend from the high ridge. Tyndall shivers as he stands there now that the sun is behind the ridge. Twenty minutes later the boys appear, smiling and yelling, all amped up from their adventure. They are there standing at Tyndall's back door removing their snowshoes and laughing and cannot stop talking about what fun they had. Steam is rising from Josue's sweat-covered fleece jacket. Tyndall starts scolding the boys, but can't stop smiling, and actually is quite relieved they are okay. The boys, with all their boundless energy, are so happy and excited. They enthusiastically exclaim about the top of the ridge, the view of the high mountains with the town and the school so small below them.

18

PRISM

Tyndall enters school early in the morning. The hall lights are still off and a strange green glow comes from the emergency light fixture just below the ceiling. A few kids are sitting on the floor of the hall either curled up and asleep or aglow from the light emanating from their electronic screens. He enters his room and notices the heat is out—again. He ambles down the hall to inform someone to call maintenance. Dr. Stufa is standing in the office doorway. Talking to him is like approaching a crack in the earth and looking down; you approach cautiously with your arms held out, as a vaporous miasma rises from a fissure. "Hey Jon, the heat is out in my room."

"Oh, I'll call that in."

"Thanks."

Back in his room Tyndall sits at his desk feeling the first light stream in through the window and warm his shoulders. He holds a large glass prism in his left hand. It is slightly smaller than his fist and fits nicely within the cup of his hand. He recalls extracting it from an old broken dissecting microscope his first year of teaching. It is not the perfectly shaped symmetrical triangle prism but has a large flat bottom with two angled sides of different angles and a flat top painted flat black. The two sides are also painted black. One black side has a faded white stamp that says, "Made out of crystal optics Sep 22, 1959 1067 IP. American Optical Corp." It is a right-angle prism called a Dove prism; the triangular apex is absent. The Dove prism does not deviate or displace the image, but it can either invert or reverse the image. Because it is a near perfect reflector, it can replace mirrors in a microscope.

Tyndall holds it in his hand with the small side down and turns left, then right, in his swivel desk chair. He is trying to catch the morning light as it comes through the glass door behind his desk. On the white drop-down ceiling tiles, a small rainbow is projected, a bright ten-inch long by two-inch wide splay of brilliant color. He swivels in the chair ever so slightly; the colored light dances thinner and blurred, and then sharp and in focus.

It reveals what is there, but cannot be seen, reflected and refracted, from the palm of the hand slightly twisted in the long morning light. The rainbow on the ceiling dances left and right with the slightest twist of the chair. The chipped and scratched crystal glass gleams silver white in his hand. Looking into the prism itself reveals a microcosm of small blurred rainbows repeating in waves of cloudlike bands of color. His wrist tires from the weight of the chunk glass. In the shadow of his desk it is inert and reveals nothing. It must be examined and played with to reveal the unseen. No formula or directions required. Just pick it up, be curious; look and see.

The long school bus rumbles down the road. Snow is flying off its roof and eddies down to the cold dry black asphalt and wisps around dancing on the surface. A blue minivan follows the bus with a sixteen-year-old driver anxiously watched by mom in the passenger seat. She is nervously flexing her right leg, like she is stepping on an imaginary pedal, as the vehicle comes to a stop at the light. When they pull up to the school, the young driver lowers the back window. Her curly-haired dog sticks his head out the window. She exits the vehicle and the girl pets the dog's head and scratches his ears with both hands. She kisses the dog between the eyes, turns and heads in to school. Mom sits absolutely still in the passenger seat, gazing straight ahead as if transfixed on a floating object.

James walks into Tyndall's room as he does most every morning. Quiet and mellow without his comrades in terror. Tyndall tells James to hold out his hand. "Here, sit here and turn it in your hand. I gotta go make copies." James plops down in Tyndall's desk chair; Tyndall places the prism in the boys' hand in a way that the morning light can be captured and projected. James swivels around in a full circle holding the prism in his hand. Then like a eureka of insight, the moment, the angle of the light, and the colored rainbow is projected on the ceiling. With every subtle movement of his hand he observes the colors on the ceiling and also inside the crystal prism in his hand.

He thinks about his day. *Oh yeah, I have to do my math homework. I hope Ms. Jones has that tight skirt on revealing some sweet thong straps underneath, she must do that on purpose…* He can see the lesson on angles and tangents and hear her say, "Follow the line to the intercept," but all he can see is her thin cotton tan and white skirt with some amazing lingerie that shows two straps that hug her small ass and disappear into—whoa. *I hope the girls come soon and have food for me. How am I going to get to town for lunch? When do I leave for the game?*

Walking back to his room, Tyndall passes the assistant principal, Combe, who is speaking in Spanish with Miguel Angel and Josue. Tyndall says, "Hi", and continues down the hall. Combe waves a hello, straightens his tie and pushes his parted hair to the right, then with long strides ambles down the hall in the other direction.

The boys continue speaking in low hushed Spanish. Josue turns to Miguel Angel and says, "I can't stand the way he talks in Spanish, so formal and stuck up."

Miguel Angel responds, "Yeah, like we can even understand that kind of Spanish. What a fucking idiot, thinks we even respect that."

Tyndall returns to his room with just James sitting there at his desk. As he is putting down the tests he just made copies of on the desk, James asks, "So Tynd, um ya know when you get in trouble, how do you stop getting in trouble?"

Tyndall stands there silent for a good while then says, "Well, do you realize you're in trouble?"

"Um, yeah."

"Well, then I think you'll be okay, You're okay, right?

"Oh yeah, I'm okay."

"Some people say we are who we are."

"But what if you want to change that?"

"We are set upon the wheel Mali; I guess you have to know that."

"But…"

Just then the girls come into the room. "I got your text wanting food—

here." Sialia says in a sarcastic way.

Tyndall walks to his desk and gestures to James to get out of his chair. As James stands Tyndall puts his hand on James' shoulder and says, "First you got to see it."

Sialia plops a bagel and a cup of coffee down for James.

Smiling at Sialia he says, "Thanks, you saved me."

The kids exit with a wave and bouncing energy. Tyndall sits at his desk, pensive. The room is strangely empty and quiet just fifteen minutes before class begins. The prism is on the desktop amongst the piles of papers. He shuffles the tests he has just copied and places them in a red folder and slides it into his desk drawer. He picks up the crystal glass and places it, like a paperweight, on top of a pamphlet from the latest curriculum training. Through wavy ripples of color, images are projected. Tyndall stands up, and as he is walking away from his desk, looks at the multiple dancing images. He blinks, then walks away to the front of the room.

The prism sits atop the pamphlet with the Bradmoor Publishing emblem of a limestone pyramid. The perfect reflection and the bent light reveal a distorted image of a monstrous two-headed figure with two hands waving frantically. The beast is moving, with its blue hand, bright yellow corn kernels into the open mouth of a serpent in a cave. The very weight of the site, standing in witness. Revealed. At his front demonstration table, Tyndall checks his email. He sees that there is a new training with Bradmoor, the same company that makes the standardized curriculum and also makes the standardized tests. Kids start to shuffle in, and Tyndall closes his email. Color images continue to ripple under the prism crystal on his desk.

19

EL SALVADOR I

Juan Miguel Lopez and his twelve-year-old son Miguel Angel stand on a steep hillside in the mountains forty kilometers northeast of the city of Santa Ana, El Salvador. It is the dry season; fires burn and smoke hugs the hillsides. The sound of a machete resounds on hard tropical wood. The first swing of the machete exposes the white wood under the green acacia bark, burned black on the outside. Another couple of swings exposes the red heartwood. A giant *ceiba* tree, a hundred and twenty feet tall, stands sentinel, overlooking a semi-pastoral landscape. The tree is sacred in the minds of the local people. It has stood for millennia watching the forest landscape grow, burned and plowed, and then back again. Looking to the west, the valley rolls in a broken landscape of agriculture and small towns. It eventually gives way to a sea of roofed houses; all one story with angry electrical lines crisscrossing red and gray corrugated metal roofs. The sun is shining through a dirty-crimson ring of smoke and dust.

Juan has brown muscular arms and a weathered red brown face. He is wearing rubber boots and holds a machete. The machete falls hard at a downward angle on the yagrumo tree trunk. Half the tree's branches and leaves are charred; the other half is still alive and green. The large palmate leaves are like a weather vane, which lets you know how the wind is blowing. The leaves lift and blow as the first wind of the day begins. The leaves are dark green on the top side and silver-white on the bottom. They flap and wave, alternating in the wind from green to silver-white. The tree falls, twisting from the uneven weight of burned and living branches. Life weighs so much more. The green and silver leaves lie on the ground like folded flags. His son, Miguel Angel, stands uphill wiping his face with a rag. The hillside vegetation is now cleared; exposing the view of the valley and the town below. On a rounded hillside facing the town is the cemetery.

Miguel Angel remembers standing in the cemetery just the week before. How his family and his uncles and aunts all talked about leaving. He could see the cemetery, the gated steel fence, the rusted cross, the white dress his sister was wearing. There were the boys selling water. Also, someone was selling bright pink cotton candy wrapped in clear shiny cellophane.

"Papa, why is the big tree there?" Miguel Angel says pointing to the big tree left standing while all the others had been cut down.

"It is a *ceiba* tree. What is left from long before—left over from—the old indigenous ones say the roots are connected deep to all that lives and was. To remove the tree, would cut the tether that holds us all to the earth and keeps us alive. Even if the tree dies, it is left in place. Do not cut the branches until they fall—then you make fence posts out of them."

Miguel Angel interjects, "You mean the *Indios* that sit on the steps of the church and speak the native language?"

"Do not use that term to describe them. Their fate is their own; they are born into it."

"Sorry, Papa."

"The tree is there so that we never forget and remain connected. It is our past."

Miguel Angel stares out down the broken hillside to the lone *ceiba* tree, then continues his gaze on down to the cemetery. He swings the machete in his hand with unexpected force; the ash around the tree trunk flies upward and chokes him. His eyes water.

Miguel Angel opens his eyes and looks up at the white board in his English II class. He has been in the United States now for four years. He is perplexed at the lesson and is struggling to understand what is going on. The teacher is going on about something related to some Hero's Journey and *Star Wars*. He knows *Star Wars* is a movie and that's about it.

Mr. Klinger is clearing his throat as he often does. "So, we are here with the example of Luke Skywalker meeting Yoda. Now what is the relationship of this modern story to classical Greek stories?"

Sialia looks over at Miguel, sees that he is lost and reaches over and turns the outline page for him and points, *"Aqui."*

Sandy raises her hand and goes on about the classic Greek stories that have some guru type that emerges to help the hero in their journey.

"Excellent, so what is the role of Yoda with Luke Skywalker?"

Mr. Klinger calls on Miguel Angel.

"Ah, he needs guidance, so Yoda helps him."

"How so?"

Sialia helps Miguel Angel, "Like ya know, he teaches him The Force."

Class continues and Klinger is writing an essay prompt on the board.

Sialia raises her hand. "No, no this is unrealistic and bullshit. Where is this Little Green Guy with big ears? Seen him, I have not!"

"Now Sialia, don't use language like that. He is The Guru who guides The Hero."

Sialia is quick to respond, "But we have no guide in the real world. Here and now it does not work that way—so it is bullshit."

Klinger continues, "He teaches Luke Skywalker The Force."

"But really? Come on; there is no magic. There are no gurus."

20

HISTORY AND GEOLOGY

Sialia looks down at Rembrandt's *Self-Portrait with Two Circles*. It shows the famous painter boldly looking out, perhaps even defiant, with painting paraphernalia in hand. Two half circles on blank canvas are half shown in the background. She looks up and peers at her own reflection in the window. Low gray clouds whip across a heavy sky, like a monotonous moving conveyer belt.

James tumbles into Tyndall's room a little before biology class begins. "Hey Tynd, I got some cool specimens for you on vacation down in Mexico," James says as he unpacks his pack at his desk.

"Well, let's see what you got."

"Check out this green rock, it's like a pound." James hands Tyndall an oblong rough green rock with craters and holes in it.

"Wow it's heavy. Where'd you get this?"

"Mexico, on the beach, down at a resort outside of Veracruz."

"Huh, copper oxidizes—that is rust like this. Let's check this out with some acid, here." Tyndall says carrying the rock to the back sink and reaching up into the cabinet for a plastic bottle of hydrochloric acid. In the sink he pours the acid over a corner of the rock. Bright green liquid flows out in the dirty stainless-steel sink.

"Now it's just a browner-green."

"Here, let's file it, get the file out of that tool drawer." James files a knobby corner, and sure enough, it is a big chunk of copper.

"So, is this man-made Tynd?"

"Maybe. Well, not necessarily; copper can be found elementally in nature—that's why it was one of the first metals to be utilized by humans."

"I also found this up in the mountains when we went birdwatching and toured a coffee plantation."

"Wow, cool! That's a big chunk of obsidian."

James gets a kick out of how enthusiastic Tyndall gets when someone brings him something. James smiles standing there and thinks about his trip to Mexico. He can see the tour jeep pulling up to the clearing in the forests, as mist rolled over the top of the ridge. A dozen gringo tourist filed out, some were serious birdwatchers, others just touring around. The guide stepped out and pointed to the clearing with some sparse little bushes under a few remaining trees. In eloquent formal English, with a thick Spanish accent he says, "Over there is the coffee and you can see on that ridge some chocolate trees. Our next stop will be to see vanilla growing."

"Hey, mom there's no cell service," he remembers saying. He and his younger brother, exasperated, stay in the vehicle.

"Just come out and see how green and lush it is. Come on, we're all the way down here. You boys spend too much time anyways looking at those electronic devices. Come on."

"Okay, okay I'm coming, yeah," he says. He kicks around the gravel along the stream bed, periodically looking at his phone, when he sees a shiny black rock at the edge of the water and the gravel bar. He picks it up, turns it in the light, and observes the greenish tinge and the tiny uniform directional streaks of white in the rock. The color changes as he turns the rock in his hand, as he is reaching for his phone. He turns it against the sun and snaps several photos, he hears the melodious descending trill-like song of a bird. It is an echo. Light flickers inside of the dark rock.

Light dances in waves in the dark volcanic glass as Tyndall turns the obsidian chunk in his hand. "Wow, it's so smooth and convex on this side, and all chipped here." When Tyndall looks up to talk with James, the obsidian rock continues to flicker. In it are images of an Aztec high priest gazing into an obsidian mirror while hearing a bird calling in the mists. The ancient shaman sees monstrous figures in painted glyphs. The next vision is of a Spanish conquistador, steel blade in hand, on a horse; the Spaniard digs his spurs into the bloodstained flanks of the spotted Appaloosa stallion. Dancing in the ripples of the dark glass he sees a green and red glyph of a z-shaped serpent poking a scepter into a bat-faced monster standing on a rabbit.

"Yeah, it's almost green sometimes, then smoky colored, then jet black," James says.

"Glass has such cool properties," Tyndall says as he places both rock specimens on his desk. "Nice find, James." He looks up at the students filing into the classroom. In the sunlit green water of the aquarium the biggest frog floats at the surface and spits out a worm; then lunges and shoves it back into his mouth and ingests it again.

Sialia comes into the room and plops down in her desk. She's quiet, keeps to herself and pulls out her drawing notepad and is doodling away. As class proceeds, Tyndall looks over and sees that she is not doing the assignment. It is quite clear that she is upset. He thinks, *Aah, leave her alone, she is a good student. Anyway, is it cell phone problems, boy trouble or did someone die? You never know with sixteen-year-old girls.*

Sialia continues to draw and fill up the page with flowing disparate nonsensical drawings. In her head she is stewing about what Juana said to her in the hallway. She recalls Juana saying, "Yo, why are you such a soft white pastry? Hanging out with those gringas. Have some Chicana pride—be brown, girl."

Sialia responds quickly in Spanish, "Hey at least I got friends, don't have to hate everyone and everything, all the time."

Juana flares back, "Just saying. Ya know. What the fuck!" Other kids in the hallway step back and out of the way. People turn and stare from their lockers.

"Fucking live here, not there, come on. Why do you always gotta be judgin' anyway?"

"Hey, I was just sayin'."

Sialia, emphatically gesturing with her hands over her head says, "I know both worlds; I remember." Like a firecracker exploding in the hallway, it is over; the kids move on and dissipate like smoke

To exist in-between; to know. But it rings in her head; so intense. Again, and again, it bounces off the cliff wall of her mind. Long after the bell is struck, there is a deep resonating sound reverberating, scarcely audible but for a low hum in the bones. On the next page of her notebook she draws a picture of the back of her own head, down her arm to her hand holding a pen on an open page in a notebook. It is drawn, in red ballpoint pen, with hard bold lines. It shows her braid, blazing red with rounded exaggerated curves. The side of her cheek and the back of her shoulder and arm flow off to the corner of the page. She colors in blue pen the background in harsh lines. Even between her woven hair is blue, blue on red, red on blue, screaming out in radical lines, embracing a feeling torn from her soul.

21

CONQUISTADOR II

The educational consultant, Haustoria, is driving away from Elysium Hills High in his black BMW sedan. He is putting his sunglasses on as he talks on the phone with an executive from Bradmoor. Reflected in the dark sunglasses are the images of Spanish conquistadors. An armored Spaniard eyes the native upper class with a particular curious contempt and jealousy. He is in awe of the fine cotton clothes with gold woven into them. He is particularly taken by the bright red and purple dyed clothes; the color of royalty worn by monarchs and clergy in Europa. Such wonder and splendor in the woven cloth. He turns his head to look at a heap of gold icons and jewelry in a pile. Then he leers at naked captive women tied to a long line strung between two trees. A look of want is in his eyes.

The images flicker. In the encampment on the beach, native slaves cast gold items into the smelter. Firewood is put in on the far side. Golden earrings, rings, hair ties, pins, necklaces are put in on the near side. The entire head of a native with gold jewelry is cast into the fire. Every gold motif and statue, an entire culture is being melted down. Black smoke billows out of the top chimney hole. Orange-red molten gold flows out a narrow gutter at the bottom. The gold flows into chambers of clay forms to make an ingot. Each is then stamped with the Royal Seal of Spain. A large hammer swings and strikes the stamp held in the hand of a Spaniard. The muscular forearm of a black North African Moorish slave swings the hammer. A Dominican monk blesses the small pieces of metal as they enter the smelter and flames. He then blesses all the stacked ingots of gold on a pallet. All the gold, including a giant golden wheel-like relief from an altar, is melted down into ingots. The pallets of ingots are then loaded onto one barge and taken to one ship that is anchored in the harbor.

Several miles inland a Spaniard extracts his foot from the stirrup of his horse, which is lying on its side. Multiple arrows stick in the dying horse's neck, bloody foam bubbles out of the its mouth. Arrows fly by him as the Spaniard lifts the cloth bag with gold icons in it. A crossbow is in his other hand. He runs, an arrow deflects off his steel armor. The obsidian point shatters on the shiny metal. Behind him a procession of native warriors descends. They are dressed in bright feathers and spotted fur. The bag is so very heavy. The veins in his arm bulge out as his muscles flex. He runs.

22

PARIAH (NOWHERE TO GO)

The painting *Airborne* by Andrew Wyeth shows a grand seaside landscape. But its most prominent features are the feathers in the foreground, floating before an expansive green lawn with a big house and pond in the distance. The feathers float, haunt the imagination, caught in a dynamism of movement, never to remain in one place. Elements so familiar, suspended in ephemeral time, frozen in space. Stop and stare.

It is Friday evening; James walks home after lacrosse practice. He checks his cell phone. There is a strange silence. No texts, no Snapchat, and no Instagram. He checks again, nothing. Checks the service, all is okay. It's as if the world and everyone he knows has stopped to take a breath. They all have simultaneously dropped their cell phones to the ground. Some kind of complete sincerity of release; the hand goes limp and the device slides out of each hand. As if it were ergonomically designed to slide and fall—free. Eyes blink, a breath is drawn in. The sky opens up, the sun and stars appear; a deeper blue to purple then to black and back again. All. It is the Grand Silence. Once a day for a moment, humanity blinks, takes a breath, and is. No one knows. Who would ever believe it anyways?.

But after that moment the chatter grew thick. Norma had a line on some cheeseburgers for the weekend. Norma was a code name for Ryan's dealer cousin. Cheeseburger was slang for weed. Norma's was the diner near the railroad tracks where the boys sometimes ate breakfast. All of it—the texts and talking—looked like and sounded like typical teenage boy talk.

So, it was on. Go home, have dinner and shower. James takes a deep breath and drops his head, looking off to the house to his left. He knows he could cut through the yard of that house and end up in his own backyard. He momentarily steps to his left then hesitates. That's how he always went as a kid; cut through the side yard and the back lot and into his own backyard. But now it is uninviting. So he continues down the street to the corner and turns left, then down the block, turns left and half a block later turns left again into his driveway. He drops his pack and lacrosse stick at the door of the back porch. A pall hangs heavy over the very essence of the space in that house. Even though he just finished lacrosse practice, he does a hundred pushups. Twenty-five regular pushups, then fifty sit-ups, twenty-five wide-arm, twenty-five diamond hands together, another fifty sit-ups, then twenty-five more regular pushups. Then, just for fun, ten pushups clapping in the air. Out the back porch to the door frame to do three sets of ten pull-ups. Then shower and dinner.

Ryan comes over and they sit on the back porch and talk with his mom. Things would be better for a moment; James thinks, *This is almost normal, just hanging out with Ryan and his mom on the back porch.* Joey-dog lays on the small couch next to James's mom, while she runs her hands through his thick soft fur. The boys text each other sitting there, so nonchalant. The sweet fragrant odor of the apple tree, in bloom, hangs in the cool, damp spring air. Whitish-pink petals litter the ground below the tree. All that James notices at the time is a robin bathing in the dog's round metal water bowl under the apple tree. The robin half opens its wings, dips, and flutters. Small droplets of water fly in the air, catching the light at the apex. And the bird jumps up to the rim and stands tall, then jumps around and faces out. It then turns and faces in, orange breast-feathers fluffed out, making the bird appear larger. Then it hesitates and jumps back in the bowl. It flutters, dances and shakes again. Then hops to the rim and takes off, with heavy flight, to the nearest branch of the apple tree.

James looks up at Ryan. They sit there babbling pleasantries with his mother. He looks down at his phone then back at Ryan. James, having been transfixed by the bird, realizes it is time to extricate his buddy from the clutches of his mother and her over-exuberance for human company. The immeasurable weight of loneliness.

Tonight, hopefully it would all come together. It was the first warmish night of the year. The boys ride their bikes to the designated meeting point at Woodfield Park. The park is at the corner of town where the railroad tracks and interstate highway meet. It has a playground and baseball fields with lights that are rarely turned on. In the southeast corner of the park the lawn gives way to broken shrubs of buckthorn and Siberian elm. The tracks are elevated on a steep berm of soil and rock. On the other side of the tracks is a long stretch of sewage lagoons with linear waterways with various levels of stench. It is a secret hinterland, in an endless blob of suburban Americana.

Like any Friday night everyone was driving around texting, hoping something might open up—a place, anyplace where they can go. Rumors, clues, and innuendoes evaporate in the electronic ether. The boys read and listen to the chatter as they ride their bikes on down to the park where they meet the rest of the outcasts. They climb up the berm of loose rock and backfill to the tracks then take a sharp left to the concrete pad. Below the sloping slabs of concrete is a giant culvert taking water to the river on the other side of the highway. To their backs, the interstate is humming with semi-trucks and cars. To their left railroad tracks, a river, and a huge expanse of sludge pits and wastewater treatment runways. A no-man's land, void of definition; here they meet in the long angular light cast from the interstate lights. The group of boys smoke some weed. They stand in a small circle and pass around the blue and pink flower-patterned pipe.

Sandy is driving, and she and Sialia pick up Helen and drive off. "How about we go by and get coffee?" Sandy says.

"Hey, there's supposed to be a party out on Countyline Road," Sialia says.

"Does the text say the address?"

"No. But let's drive out there after we get our drinks." So, the girls float down the undulating road, cell service fading in and out.

"Ahh! No service," Helen says.

Sialia continues, "We've been driving all over; we should just go hang with James and the guys."

"It's gotta be just up ahead," Sandy says.

Looking down at her phone and exasperated, Sialia says, "We spend our whole life racing ahead, thinking how it'll be—why can't this be it, just this?"

Beer cans float below in the stagnant water at the bottom of the sloping concrete pad. Clouds of steam rise from the water. Ryan drops an empty beer can. It echoes a metallic clanking sound as it bounces down the concrete, falling silent in the still water. A car turns at the far corner of the park throwing light and shadow for a moment. James gazes sadly at the red and white cans floating below, but he remains silent.

James looks up from his phone, "Hey, looks like the girls are going to join us."

"Do they got a car tonight?"

"It looks like it."

"Hey, remind 'em not to park too close; if the cops come, they won't get back to the car."

Sialia, Sandy, and Helen, having parked a block away, are walking through one of the ballfields of the park toward the railroad tracks and the embankment. Sialia says, "We must've driven twenty miles in circles looking for a party that never was going on."

Helen adds in, "Yeah I can't believe how many people were driving around in circles."

Just then the cops show up. All show, no substance. The police cars race across the grass of the ballfields of the park. One of the cop cars veers off and drives up to the girls. The other car races to the bottom of the steep embankment, spotlights on. Everyone stands frozen for a second; then scatters or hits the ground. Head spinning, a bit drunk and stoned, James and Hector hit the ground, while Ryan runs off down the tracks. James is laughing, Hector grabs his arm. James violently shrugs it off. Ryan is down the tracks about 100 feet looking back. Turning to Hector, James says, "We're okay man. The cops are fools, they won't come up here. Hopefully everyone knows where to leave their cars and bikes or they'll be busted." Now crouching, they look over and see the girls in the ball field with a cop car next to them. The cop is out of his car talking to the girls. Sialia assertively steps forward in front of Sandy and Helen and is talking away.

Looking over at James, Hector says, "Fuck, the girls are screwed."

Suddenly James stands and starts jumping up and down and yelling. Hector was on the ground grabbing his pant leg, "What the fuck you doin'; man?" The spotlight from the cop car hits him.

James turns quickly and drops his pants and starts mooning the cops while yelling between his legs. Hector figures it out, jumps up, turns and drops his pants while yelling and jumping up and down. The boys are hooting and hollering. They moon the cops while the spotlights from the cop cars are on them. There is a discernible agitation in the voices of the police rising from below. The cop talking to the girls quickly jumps back in his car and drives up to the embankment. James jumps up and down, pointing for the girls to get the hell out of there. James and Hector are both laughing hard with their boxers around their ankles, trying to pull their pants up, and flipping the cops off in the bright, sharp, narrow light of the cop car searchlight. The boys then jump over a couple of sets of tracks and slide down the loose rock on the far side of the tracks. They land at the flat bottom of rock and weeds. From there they navigate a labyrinth of sewage ponds with mechanical skimmers and round aerators.

About a half mile down, Hector and James climb back up to the tracks. Tonight, they abandon their bikes and start walking home. They are joined by Ryan who was waiting there for them. Ryan says, "Fuck, that was really close."

"Yeah, that was brilliant to start mooning the cops," Hector says.

"You could hear how pissed off they were."

Yeah, you know, fucked up sideways."

"Yeah man, those fuckers can take that back home; we got away."

"Yeah, oh, I got a text from Sialia—they got back to their car."

"Yeah, fuckin'-A, got away!"

They cruise the tracks past a long line of parked coal cars full of coal. Each car has coal slightly mounded at the top. Hundreds of coal cars, with black coal in mounded piles in black cars; black on black. "Come on we'll cut over here; let's take Washington Street back home. Nobody ever drives it. And, we can see cars from a long way off and hide," Ryan says.

The boys drop down to the street just as the first creaking sound emanates from the tracks behind them. They stop and stand below the tracks and listen intently, staring up at the black coal cars. James is standing behind Hector and he leans forward with both hands on Hector's right shoulder. Ryan stands next to Hector with his right arm across Hector's shoulders and his hand grasping the collar of James' hoodie-jacket. A good half mile down the tracks, to their right, they hear the clang followed immediately by another metallic clanging sound, and then the double bang resonating down toward them, as the front and then back of the coupler joints between cars hit, metal on metal. The wheels squeak and creak as they start slowly rolling. And the ripple of double clang continues past them to their left. Coal train car ripple.

With almost a laugh Ryan says, "Whoa, man."

"Fucking what!" James says.

Hector adds, "Yeah, it's the coupler joints hitting front, then back at the junction of each car."

James says, "That's so cool. It just rippled for like a mile." The boys stand transfixed by the sound and try and understand what just happened. Motion, sound and parts; mass and steel hitting steel. They turn and proceed down Washington Street, with the creaking clacking sound emanating behind them, pushing them home.

James is looking at all the trees bent over the street, tunnel-like, silhouetted against the dark orange clouds aglow from the sodium street lights. He's still all amped up from running from the cops; he does a couple of lunging steps and kicks a can on the side of the road. It rattles and bounces along the curb. He looks over at the front yard of a house with a soccer ball and a couple of bicycles lying on their side. Then he just starts talking, fast and emphatic. "God dammit, you ever notice how, like, nobody wants us around anymore. We can't even walk down the fucking sidewalk; people just turn and cross the street. We have to walk in the middle of the street. Remember how we used to cut through yards, down secret paths, to get to each other's houses. Now if you do, they just stop and stare, they look so hard. They look right through you. Always someone lookin'. Drive around and ride our bikes, talking about places to go. What the fuck! Nowhere to go. You can't even go to the store to get food, everyone stands far away. You see the moms grab the little kids and pull them away. You just turn and look down at your phone, even though you know there's nothing on there. But you know, if you look up, look at them looking at you. Ya know ya don't even belong in the line at the grocery store. Just want to get some fucking food. Can't even walk home the way we used to. Fucking no place to go. Being hunted down. Look where we hang out— at the edges of sewage pits, highway, river, can't even hang out in the park where we played as kids."

They walk, silent, not looking at their phones, down the middle of the street. The oldest street in town, with the huge trees on either side.

23

EL SALVADOR II

Miguel Angel immigrated to the United States late one night. He and his mother and younger sister huddled in the desert heat in the weak shade of a creosote bush. The sun blazed, the hot ground burned his knees through his denim jeans. Previously, they had been riding in the back of dark semi-trucks for a week. Before that they rode La Bestia, the train north through Mexico. All throughout Guatemala and Mexico the local people scorned them. Somewhere in Oaxaca, a man spit on them. Even when his father was present, men came up and advanced on his mother. She carried his little sister, Lolita, like a shield to dissuade the rude men. Somewhere just north of Mazatlán, his father departed to try to make the almond harvest in California. He wanted to secure a little money. Miguel never saw his father again.

A week later, at night he and his little sister crawled through a tunnel into California. That night, they were without their mother for several hours. A tiny older woman, with one plastic grocery bag, took his hand and led him and his sister away from the tunnel. Miguel Angel kept looking back as the woman tugged on his arm. In a used-car parking lot they sat and waited. The older woman stayed with the twelve-year-old boy and his five-year-old sister. Miguel squatted, Lolita wrapped around him, as he cried silently. The tears fell slowly down his cheeks. He took the jacket from around his waist and laid Lolita down on it, as she grumbled a little. He gazed, blurry eyed through the tears, at the far streetlight. White lights, on rows of wires, hung above the cars so tightly parked. Everything was bright white, smeared on black. Black asphalt, black bricks, gray cinder blocks turned black. Streaks of light reflected off the hoods of the cars. His mother emerged from the darkness of the empty lot on the far side of the streetlight. She wavered shimmering in the light, looking frantically to her left then to her right. Miguel called out to her, called to the silhouette. The old lady lifted her hand from the back of his shoulder, he ran out and crashed into her. His little sister slept. His Mom and the elderly lady clasped hands for a second over the resting body of the little girl. His mother said, *"Gracias."* She put her hand on Miguel's shoulders and told him, "You did good."

Three weeks later Miguel Angel, his sister and mother moved in with his uncle and cousins in Colorado. It was August 15, exactly two months after they left the rugged mountains east of San Salvador, El Salvador. Two months before that, he was standing in the slash-and-burn field looking down on the cemetery.

24

DILLIGAF FOR THE CHILDREN

Sialia comes walking into Mr. Tyndall's room on this cold winter day, as snow is blowing and the shadows are long in the afternoon. "Hey, Mr. Tyndall, what are we doing today? Let's not do anything, it's Friday."

"Oh, don't worry, today's a pretty easy day, we're just doing some water chemistry."

"Cool, I liked doin' the chemistry." Sialia studies the life-size head sculpture on the back counter by the sink. It is a sculpture made of modeling clay with exquisite facial features, showing a somber and anguished look. It has a hollow open brain cavity with fingerlike projections sticking up, and one black onyx pupil. The other eye's pupil is gone; and there is a hollow socket where a round smooth rock once was. The statue stares out at the classroom; some kids had picked some sunflowers in the fall and placed them in the hollow head, along with a long pheasant tail feather. The flowers are now dry and hang over the braincase limp. "Who made this sculpture?"

"It was made by a student years ago. He was an incredibly productive art student, went to some art school in New York City. He'd whip up projects like that really quick; that probably only took him a day or two."

"Where's his eyeball?"

"It fell out a couple years ago."

Sialia is picking through a bowl of acorns that Mr. Tyndall collected for a lesson about variation in a population. "Hey Mr. Tyndall, why don't we put one of these acorns in the eye socket—so he can see a little better."

"Sure, why not. See if you can find one close to the size of the other pupil. There's some glue up in the cabinet above you."

Sialia finds a small acorn with a cap on it, and places it, with a dab of glue, in the eye socket where the pupil goes. It is perfect and round and a nice complement to the round black onyx pupil in the other eye. She steps back and admires the statue, now looking a little more symmetrical with two complete eyes, each with a unique pupil. She places the bowl of acorns back on the counter top, swirling her fingers around and looking at all the green, tan, and brown acorns of different sizes. She makes an observation, that there are little white maggot-like grubs crawling around in the bottom of the bowl below the acorns.

"Hey there's little worms in the bottom of the bowl, where'd they come from?"

Mr. Tyndall is now standing at the board writing an outline for the day's lab. He looks back and says, "Oh yeah, those are the larva of some beetle that lays its eggs inside the acorns. Look and see how some of the acorns have a little hole where the critter crawled out. In the natural environment, those guys eat the meat of the acorn nut and then crawl under the leaves, pupate, and overwinter. They're a little disoriented being in the bowl, and they just crawl in circles on the bottom."

Tyndall, wearing a down vest, has a seat at his desk in back of the room. The heat is out, again. The room has finally warmed up by late afternoon. The cookie ovens in the corner have been humming away all day, and there is a pleasant burnt cookie smell in the room. The students are off and running with the day's lab; doing three different titrations for the water chemistry analysis that the River Watch class does once each month.

Tyndall has just finished making his afternoon coffee; it is the usual commotion-filled start to the lab. Tyndall, sitting in his chair, coffee cup in hand and a piece of dark chocolate in the other hand, scoots his desk chair to the big center lab table. All the while chairs and lab stools are being moved around and kids are fetching different beakers and flasks for the analysis today. Tyndall turns and looks to his left, and says, "Not that size Erlenmeyer flask, you'll need the big one for that analysis."

"Yeah, oh yeah," the student says.

Tyndall, pointing to his eyes, gestures to Sialia and says, "Goggles."

Sialia pulls the goggles off the top of her head and puts them on.

Turning to his right, while sipping his coffee he says to Hector, "Now clear the burette. Remember?"

"Yeah, okay," Hector says.

Now, late in the first semester, the students have done this lab analysis many times. So, Tyndall just strategically places himself in the center of the action and relaxes, sits back, and sips black coffee while giving a few reminders here and there.

James says, "Tynd when you gonna get the heat fixed?" as he rinses out the flask at the sink by the window. There is a cart with two cookie ovens on it, both turned on, with the doors ajar to release the heat.

"I don't know I put in a request a couple of days ago. Good thing it's sunny today, so the room warms up by afternoon."

James says, "This heating system is so ghetto, only at Elysium Hills," as he opens and closes the oven door.

There in the corner by the sink is a cart with two boxy silver colored metal cookie ovens. Each oven is about two feet square. and about a foot tall and has room for two cookie trays. These are used mostly by various school clubs to bake cookies to raise money. A couple of years ago, when the heat broke, Tyndall commandeered these to heat the room. He plugs both ovens in, turns them on, lets them heat up and then cracks the door open and places a small fan on the countertop behind the ovens. In the morning the room is quite cold; kids wear their jackets and Tyndall teaches wearing his winter wool cap. The ovens give the room a pleasant burnt sweet smell, and kids stand by the oven doors and warm their hands.

James then adds, "Hey can we cook some cookies?"

"Yeah you bring in the cookie dough and we'll cook'em up."

"Next class?"

"Sure," Tyndall says, then continues, "Hey James unplug those ovens and turn off the fan; the room is warm enough for today."

Different lab groups of three to four kids are rotating into the equipment as the first groups finish their analysis at the lab tables. Tyndall asks, "Okay, who's on deck for hardness chemistry?" as he swivels his chair around toward the center of the classroom.

"That'd be us, Tynd."

"Okay, remember goggles and rinse with DI water."

"Yeah, we got it."

Sialia and her group have just finished with their analysis and Tyndall swivels in his chair and says, "Sialia, can you draw a drain under the shower for me? There are a couple of sharpies in my desk drawer."

"Oh yeah, safety for the children," she says with a wry smile and a nod to Tyndall.

In the back of the room is the large shower attached to a prominent yellow two-inch pipe sticking out of the wall just below the ceiling. But below the shower there is no drain. There are just white square linoleum tiles on concrete. Below the concrete slab is a pipe that goes straight down to a 90° fitting and a pipe that runs underneath the building. It runs for fifty feet out into the center of the courtyard and abruptly ends, not connected to any water system whatsoever. Inside of the drainage pipe in the court yard, under the apple tree that Tyndall planted, is a ground squirrel curled up and hibernating. Somebody didn't read the directions.

Each year, Tyndall has drawn in permanent sharpie a pretend drain under the shower head. And around the circular "drain," written "Safety for the Children." Sialia, grabbing her phone, turns to Helen and says, "All right, here, look up a photo of a floor drain," then hands Helen her phone.

Class is almost over; it's Friday and all the students in River Watch are seniors. So, some students have checked out saying they had to print out a paper at the library or something—but they're just heading home early. It is just Tyndall and about a dozen other students hanging out, joking around. Helen and Sialia are finishing up coloring in the drain and are carefully, in neat handwriting, writing "Safety for the Children." James and Hector are playing chess as Ryan looks on. Tyndall, standing by Sialia and Helen as they sit on the floor, says to the boys, "Hey guys, can you grab those burettes and chemicals and put them away in the chemistry box. And Ryan, get those beakers and rinse them out."

Ryan, standing at the back sink rinsing the beakers says to Tyndall,

"What was it you called the heating system. Some military acronym—something all messed up?"

Tyndall smiles, "Yeah ah—SNAFU—Situation Normal All Fucked Up."

"Yeah, I'd say that's the heating system here at EHHS," Ryan says as he pulls out his phone and starts scrolling. "Look, there's a military acronym website. Check this out."

"I'm sure there are a lot of appropriate things for us to learn about," Tyndall quips while shaking his head.

James, moves a chess piece while looking up at Hector and says, "Yeah what's the other one you taught us sophomore year?"

"FUBAR," Tyndall says as he gestures to Ryan.

Ryan, smiling and scrolling on his phone says: "FUBAR—Fucked Up Beyond All Recognition."

Sialia says, "Now the heating system is a SNAFU not a FUBAR. FUBAR is a completely different thing."

Laughing, Tyndall says, "Excellent you guys have learnt so much."

Ryan, looking down at the drain and scrolling through acronyms, says, "Hey you spelled "safety" wrong."

Sialia, sitting on the floor looking up, says, "Tynd, sorry, now what?"

"No problem," as he reaches into the cabinet above the sink and grabs a plastic bottle labeled EtOH. "Here, this ethyl alcohol will wipe the permanent ink clean. It'll feel cold but it won't hurt you."

Sialia is wiping SAFTY out as Ryan says "DILLIGAF" and smiles.

Tyndall says, "I don't know that one."

"Does It Look Like I Give a Fuck?"

Sialia says, "Maybe we should replace safety with that?" she looks up at Tyndall.

"It fits," and with a long sigh and a sideways smile Tyndall continues, "Go ahead."

So, there on the white linoleum floor is the pseudo-drain below the large shower head. In permanent ink, with neat handwriting, are the words encircling the drain: "DILLIGAF for the Children." And the statue of the head with the eyes stares out looking over the back of the classroom toward the front. Inside the eye pupil made from an acorn, a small white worm crawls around endlessly in the hollow eye socket made from modeling clay. Forever trapped.

25

CORTEZ'S SPEECH

Stufa, Combe and Haustoria are walking around in the hallway, talking and looking into various classrooms. As they pass by Tyndall's science room, the obsidian on his desk flickers as light scatters within the dark volcanic glass; it shines for a brief second. Shimmering waves of color, emitted in pure optical resonance bouncing off the darkness.

In Mexico, at the conquistador's beach encampment, stands a young native slave, Cualli. He is under the watchful eyes of the oldest Spaniard, Fernando, and the youngest, Salvador. Sal beats him at regular intervals, the lowest ranking individual always being the cruelest. Here, at camp, he does as he is ordered to do by individuals too old or young to participate in the battles. Most of the time he is not bound and shadows Sal in his duties.

For a week now, Captain Cortez was retired either in his tent cabana on the shore or on one ship. His slave girl interpreter was nowhere to be seen. The monks were scattered about. Food was brought only to that ship. No servants stayed, nor the working soldiers; only the captain and a handful of officers. On the shore the regular soldiers observed in silence how the officers and captain would not speak to each other. Only their eyes would meet; to them something was familiar and known. The orders that were given were utilitarian, busy, task-like, almost common place. Suddenly twenty-five Spanish soldiers and two officers were dispatched to that one ship. They sailed out with all the gold, twenty-five native slave men and twenty captive girls as concubines.

A pall fell heavily on the camp. The armaments were readied, the food amassed, slaves housed, fed and watered. All the slaves were bound to long lines of shackles, in open long houses with thatched roofs. No fires burned that entire day. The men stirred, gazed around, and fell silent. The sun set over the mountains, the bay was still, a deeper blue-green with a slight hint of orange. Clouds far off on the horizon started to turn orange against the purple-blue sky.

The order was called out, "Light the central fire and call the men. Leave the slaves; all must come." The horses shuffled and Cualli stood next to Sal and Fernando. He kept looking at them. Fernando gazed back screaming silently with his eyes to have them both be still and quiet. The moment had come.

El Capitan strode out of his tent. He was in full battle regalia, sword at his side. His officers followed him. On the beach, the central fire was lit; it began to glow underneath the pyre. It started orange-red underneath, with the flames snaking around the wood. Four rowboats went out to the remaining four ships; each with one Spaniard and two slaves rowing. A deepening purple sky hung over the bay. The rhythmic sound of the small waves came at the stroke of each oar. The central beach fire crackled. The men shifted their weight from foot to foot. All stood, silent, and waited. Salvador kept looking at Fernando. "Be still you fool, or I'll run you through myself," Fernando said under his breath. His hand was out from his side with fingers gesturing – be still and silent.

Cortez spoke. "We have come in the name of Christ our Lord, the King and the Queen, and all their majesty for which we are good men of God and Spain. Our mission here is to save the savage infidels; free them by the hand of The Lord. As good Christians, all of you, and the blessed King our Majesty of Spain. We have come to secure these lands for New Spain. God has granted you Majesty over all these lands for the blessed crown of Spain. Your oath to God and country is to save all, and secure commerce for all of Spain. What awaits you is God's glory, for her Majesty in Spain."

The captain nodded to his officers, who then each waved a torch and threw it in the central fire. Silently they looked at each other, their eyes shifting left then to the right. Then each man stopped looking at the others around them and was transfixed by the fires burning before them. A torch lit the bow of each remaining ship anchored in the bay. At that moment the ships, all set afire, started to blaze. The men stirred, gasped, held their hands over their mouths. Cualli was standing next to Salvador. Salvador started to speak. Fernando grabbed him by the shoulder and dug his fingers into the boy's collarbone, making him drop to his knees.

All watched with horror as the four ships burned, the small rowboats returning. Murmurs, then shouts, all quelled as El Capitan spoke again. "God and Spain have granted all of you this land to be secured. Lands so rich with people innumerable, all waiting for you." At that moment Cortez threw the breastplate from the female warrior into the fire. The men watched the flames envelope the two large pointy breasts. The reflection of the dark bay, with the burning ships in their eyes. The golden tits gleamed in the flames, the female shape danced out. The last light of day illuminated the billowing orange clouds out on the horizon over the sea.

Cortez continued, "This, this is yours to have. Each of you, all that you can carry. All for God, the savages you will save in his name." Reflected in their eyes was the gold breastplate glowing in the fire. Anger and fear welled up. "Each of you will stay as governor and ruler of more land and gold – all that is here. Here for you in the name of God." The hammer falls on the stamp – a flash of light. The mind's eye sees the ingot of gold. The seal of Spain flashes on the gold ingot in the red orange of the fire. A gold cross flashes on the next blow. A woman, naked, has one hand out to her side, open and inviting. A crucifix flashes; Christ, limp under his own earthly weight. The captain's green eyes shine in the fire as a young girl drops her whole dress for him. The stamp reverberates; a clanging sound with pictures of roads and canal causeways, golden Native American icons melt and flow out. The cannons fire at the next hammer swing and the natives drop. The hammer strikes; the stone blades shatter. The gold ingots are stacked with a clanking sound as wooden shields, covered in bright green and blue feathers, crack in the arcing swing behind a steel blade.

The men stood still, frozen, tears flowed down their cheeks as the captain continued. "The path is forward in the New World. This is yours, all of it." Round plump breasts lift, heave and arch up; the small of the back of a bronze woman lifts off the ground. A cross is waved over the fire. The hammer strikes the stamp; the moan of a woman. The weight of a gold ingot in the hand; muscles flexed in the forearm of the Spaniard, veins popping as the muscles contract at the sound. Flex. Smoldering flesh pops in the fire. The pox and pus of disease on the skin of a writhing native under an animal skin blanket. The clanking sound of metal, as the sweat pours off the face of the native gasping for air.

"On that plateau is El Dorado. All the gold, riches innumerable, gems the size of your fists." The hammer strikes; the juice of tropical fruit spills down the face and over the pointy beard of a Spaniard. An obsidian blade slices a girl's throat; as she silently succumbs, blood flows over the iconographic hieroglyphs on the gold platter-like altar. The hammer falls: The Royal Seal of Spain. The hammer falls; a spent Spaniard falls off to the side of a naked native girl. The breastplate melted into the fire. An orange glowing silhouette of breasts shimmered in the blazing coals. The hammer falls; spurs dig into the side of the horse. A cross flashes and native motifs of wood and plaster are burned. The hammer swings; a round stone grinds corn into bread that is baked on a flat stone by the fire. Brown hands, wrinkled and knotted, flip the corn flatbread. The bread is bitten into by the mouth of a scared face conquistador.

In terror, the eyes of the men stared on. Cualli dropped back, looking at the reflection of the burning ships in the bay, the central fire, and the Captain speaking. Conquistadors were dropping to their knees, crying. The men were shouting to the saints and God for salvation and courage to free this land. They pounded their chests with one hand, flogging themselves, for Christ, in his mercy to bless them in this new land.

Cualli continued to retreat. Silent and catlike he retreated into the vegetation. *Why can't they see me?* Past rows of slaves, his own kind, tethered. He dropped the cotton-like dress given to him by the Spaniards. Naked, he retreated inland to the interior. Animal-like, he silently glided through the green tropical vegetation.

26

SHELL GAME

The painting *The Conjurer* by Hieronymus Bosch has a showman entertaining, all the while a pickpocket is robbing members of the audience. The ball moves, flat dull-faces mesmerized, misdirection and money made.

It is early May, sophomore year, and the boys are sitting around in Tyndall's room eating lunch. Ryan says looking down at his phone, "Hey look—the Pope is coming to Denver on Wednesday."

"What?" James says.

Hector pipes up, "Hey we should head down tomorrow and go see him."

James says, "Why?"

"Because, it will be like a parade with people and a party."

"But I'm not even Catholic. Won't I go to hell or something?"

"Ahh, it don't matter."

"Maybe it will help in the end, given all you've done."

Laughter, as they look at Hector quietly sitting with a slight smile on his face.

"Ryan, looking around at the boys at the table, says, "Yeah we all can use whatever help we can get."

"I havta be back for lacrosse practice."

"Yeah, and I've got work."

"What time—4 o'clock?"

"No problem, man."

The boys board the light rail and ride it into downtown Denver on

Wednesday morning. They buy their tickets at the electronic kiosk. The train is so crowded, that it is standing room only, except for one seat. The boys make a ruckus wrestling over the seat. Hector finally wins the seat from James. James stands up next to him, turns and slugs a punch into Hector's shoulder. It draws the attention of nearby passengers with scowls and dismay on their faces. The train is a mix of the usual business crowd in suits and ties. They are unable to read their papers in the overcrowded situation; with the tourist-like passengers out to see the event.

At the next stop a young mother boards the train with two young girls in tow. The girls have bright pink and white dresses, with dark blue leggings and sneakers with lights that blink in the heels. The little girls cling to their mom's dress and the hanging strap of her backpack. James kicks Hector's foot. Hector looks up from staring at his phone, readying himself to cuss and punch James. James gestures to his left at the mom and the girls, while lifting his hand. Hector sighs, takes one last look at his phone and drops the phone into the cargo pocket of his khaki shorts. He waves to the mother to take his seat as he stands. She plops down; the girls climb on her like she was a set of monkey bars at the park.

The train arrives at Union Station downtown Denver. The tarmac is smooth gray concrete, with arching girders with gleaming glass. The automatic doors open, a metallic, terse, automated voice commands people to exit and clear the tracks. The atmosphere feels hurried; but many of the passengers are gazing about taking an assessment of the situation. It is all automated, the number of passengers and the crowded situation are not factored into the algorithm that runs the train. There are no conductors or train employees in sight. But despite all the extra people, the tarmac absorbs the extra bodies as they bump and jostle out into the bright spring light.

The boys make their way into the tunnel-like central train station and then continue on out and emerge onto the street. James blinks as he peers out to the east at a sea of humanity. There are tens of thousands of people all walking south toward Capital Park. Car traffic is nonexistent as they approach within six blocks of the park. It is just people shoulder to shoulder stretched between the towering city buildings. They are all moving slowly, steadily to the park. By the time the boys reach the park, 150,000 plus spectators are already there. The streets in all directions spill out a constant stream of humanity toward the park.

"Whoa man, check this out, James says." He has his phone over his head as he videos the scene as he is jostled forward into the mass of people. Hector is taking selfies and uploading them to social media.

Hector is quick to add, "No one will believe this is real. I'm not sure I believe this is real."

All around them is a human sea of variety. As they enter the edge of the park, from the northwest, they crest a small hill. To their left is a church choir singing with a conductor leading them. Nuns in black and white shuffle past them; wood crosses hang on long necklaces that sway back and forth. A woman pushes an elderly man in a wheelchair, wood cane in his hand.

At the bottom of a hillock is a man under a tree with a four by four-foot folding card table. The man is about thirty years old with long shoulder length wavy jet-black hair. He has a long thin nose, dark brown eyes and a thick curved mustache with a large patch of thick black hair below his lip. His complexion is dark, almost greenish. He wears a faded blue button-down shirt with a frayed edge to the collar. The top snap buttons are undone and black chest hair curls out. He has a thin leather necklace with a green-yellow stone pendant hanging loose on his chest. The three boys make their way down the hill as the crowd mostly heads off to the right of the table and the tree.

James points and says to Ryan, "Hey, check out the Dudare-Man." They veer left to observe the Dudare talking away, looking straight ahead as his hands move at waist level. With his hands he is sliding three bright blue plastic sixteen-ounce beer cups. The boys stop and watch from about seven feet away, observing the people around the table pointing to the cups. The man lifts the cup with his right hand, then lifts the cup in his left hand. Under that cup is a small ping-pong sized ball. The person throws his head back, turns and walks away. A small pile of money, at the corner of the table, is scooped up by the Dudare-Man's hands. All the while he's looking straight ahead, jabbering away with a deep guttural voice. The boys stand in front of the table. The man saw them as they crested the hill. He jabbers away, "So keep your eye on the ball," as he shuffles the ball between just two cups. He lifts the edge of the cup to reveal the ball. He turns the cup open to reveal the inside, empty. He dumps the ball into James's hand. Ryan is smiling. The man continues, "Here, you're a quick young man, just watch." The Dudare-Man continues, "Follow the ball. Now it's in this cup…."

Before he can finish the sentence, James points and says, "That one."

The Dudare-Man says, "Okay, keep it up now."

James points, "That one."

"You got it." All the while the man looks straight ahead shifting the gaze of his dark eyes to each boy as they stand there. Hector has both hands draped on James's left shoulder. Smiling he says, "Yeah James, slower than a lacrosse ball." James shifts his weight back and forth, left then right.

"Just a dollar. Put it there." The Dudare-Man places a one-dollar bill under a small rock on the table and then goes back to skidding the cups back and forth with the ball rolling between them. Seen then not seen, the boys stand transfixed. James reaches into his right back pocket extracts his wallet and puts a dollar bill down under the rock on top of the other dollar. Ryan rolls his eyes and smiles. The boys erupt into laughter and jive James, egging him on.

Ryan says, "No problem, you got this."

Hector pipes up, "No, you can't win."

"Oh yeah?" says James, with a cocky sharpness in his voice. "Oh, look at this," as he grabs the two one-dollar bills from under the rock. James is smiling and shaking his hands with straight arms like he's trying to dry them off. Two dollars go down under the rock, the cups scrape and shuffle, the ball bounces between them and then is engulfed like a Pac-Man. The Dudare is talking and looking straight ahead back and forth between the boys. James wins four dollars.

"Come on, let's go," Ryan says.

"No, I got this." James extracts a five-dollar bill from his wallet. He loses it quickly. "No, I got this." Then James puts another five-dollar bill down, with five one-dollar bills. The Dudare places ten dollars on top of that, and then the rock. James wins twenty bucks. Then boom!—twenty dollars on top of twenty dollars. James shakes his hands out and the jiving continues. The thick mustache just keeps moving with incessant babble about the ball, the cups. How quick the young man is in the prime of his abilities. His black coal eyes look around down to the cups, exposing the ball in his left-hand cup, then shuffles the cups and stops. James points and says, "That one." The Dudare lifts the blue plastic cup. Empty—in an instant gone.

"What!" James shouts. "No!"

The forty dollars is quickly scooped up and placed in the blue shirt pocket. James starts cussing and swearing. "What the fuck, you mother fucker," Hector grabs James and starts to pull him away.

Ryan cracks a joke about what the Pope would say to James and the Dudare-man. "The Lord giveth and the Lord taketh away." With the growing attention and the commotion, the Dudare-man folds up the table and picks up the cups and ball and drifts away counter to the flow of the stream of people cresting the hill.

James is livid, still cussing at it all. He looks at Ryan, "How much did I lose?"

"Man, you made two, lost five, then made five, lost ten, then lost twenty—you're fucked. Remember that guy does that for a living."

Hector, with a quizzical look on his face, says, "Da ball is weighted, not a ping-pong ball. So, it moves faster."

"But how?" James says looking around. "He's not faster than me."

"No, he's not, but he's the one movin' the ball," Ryan says.

"So, he let me win, then he changed it up," James hisses.

"Yeah—it's the same every time—you're the target, he reels you in and lets you fumble, then be successful. Then he changes it up when the money matters. Then he reels in another, same pattern," Hector says.

"It's a blessed business plan," Ryan says as he looks at a collared priest walking by.

27

TAX MONEY

It is sometime around midnight on a cold April night, somewhere in Iowa. The poet artist is standing on an aluminum ladder propped up against a railroad car. The cold metal penetrates the artist's hand, making it ache. In the other hand is a spray paint can that hisses away into the shadowy darkness. Yellow paint scribes the following poem onto the dark gray metal of the boxcar:

The Tribute Money
There—a gesture of grace
Where does it come from?
Where does it go?
Who gave the command?
What good does it serve?
What evil?
Who is profiting?
Can you follow it?

—G.B.

On the windowsill of the science room the water in the aquarium is a glowing light green color, as light illuminates it from behind. A fat frog floats to the surface and breathes, slowly drifting from the left to the right.

"Early release today," Tyndall says.

James says, "Yeah, I know, but I thought I'd look through the microscope before lacrosse practice." He looks at the tank and says to Tyndall, "Your room is starting to look like a swamp," as he motions to the green aquarium.

"Yeah we've got to clean that later this week," Tyndall says.

As a senior, James knows how to set up the microscope and prepare the slide for viewing. "So Tynd, which aquarium will have the most animals?"

"Oh, get a sample from that sunny tank. It is water from the pond down in town and is full of critters. Reach in and extract some of the muck down in the corner. Use a depression slide so the critters can swim around."

James sets up the slide with the mucky drop of pond water, as Tyndall fumbles around making coffee for the afternoon meeting. "Hey Tynd, check this out, it's one of those…ah…that we saw in lab at the beginning of the year. Ya know, the whirly thing."

"Oh, you got a rotifer? They're the coolest!"

Tyndall walks over and looks through the eyepiece of the microscope. Clearly in view is a rotifer; at one end is a set of two whirling cilia-fringed, "wheels," that appear to be spinning. These structures create a vortex; water and debris are visibly being sucked into the mouth of the little animalcule. A rainbow of color is created by the cilia as these hair-like structures move at the apex of the animal. As the cilia move, they suck in little green algal cells and tiny specs of material. A vortex randomly engulfing. Sucking it all in.

As Tyndall exits the room, James pushes his curly brown hair to the side and looks down through the eyepiece of the microscope. To his right, an African clawed frog floats silently in the current of light green water in the aquarium. From the surface, the big mottled green frog stares out at James.

Tyndall heads down the hall to the weekly teachers' meeting. His mind is occupied with the copies he has to make and the essays he has to grade. Principal Stufa walks in with a green and white box that says Bradmoor Publishing on the side. It has a tight, yellow, quarter-inch plastic strap around it. Stufa wrestles with the strap, and someone runs off to get scissors to cut it. When cut, the strap makes a sharp snapping sound as it flies back and the pressure is released. Principal Stufa extracts a stack of booklets wrapped in clear plastic shrink wrap. He goes on to explain that these are the direction books for the first round of the state tests to be given next week. The man is clearly uptight; he takes deep breaths between quick statements. His eyes are small and dart back and forth when he speaks. "These booklets are assigned to each of you, do not lose them. It is important that we are very clear on the directions," he says. The teachers moan, and chatter.

Mrs. Verde says, "Yeah like we need directions on how to read out loud verbatim."

Stufa continues, waving his right hand in front of the booklet, now turn to page...Now the state will be overseeing...As a staff...Stufa's mouth continues to move as The Beatles song "I Am the Walrus" plays: The thumping repetitive orchestra blares away—Waa waaa waaa—All so recognizable, gazing into the looking glass as nonsensical words, albeit familiar, ring in the teachers' ears as the band plays on—Bumm, bum, bee, buma, load-thumping descending baseline with overlaid rising strings repeat over again as the woodwinds vibrate with an overlaid deep cello, the books are passed out, overdubbed stereo lyrics resonate with the uprising increasing beat, they all get sucked down the rabbit hole as the mellotron strings vibrate in a hollow box, and famous poets pounce on Edgar Allen Poe with the familiar nonwords echoing: ummpa—Koo goo k'joo!

On the other side of the school, Sialia sits in her comfy chair in Ms. Rayleigh's art room with an art book in her lap. She is looking at a painting of Jesus standing with a crowd around him. The Italian Renaissance clothes being worn are unexpected and odd—but that does not really matter. He is gesturing. The title is *The Tribute Money*. She thinks: *No. The explanation of the painting, in the text, is wrong. In the corner of the fresco painting is the disciple Peter extracting a coin from a fish's mouth. The coin is the tax being asked for by the Roman guard. It is more than just a tribute to enter the Temple, it is an insult, by Jesus—here is a slimy worthless coin for the great Caesar. He is mocking the Roman overlords.* Follow the tax money into The Temple that is now a marketplace for commerce and profit. God is Caesar first, for what is owed first—taxes.

The frog drifts in the green watery current, as James peers through the microscope. Water tumbles by its own weight out of the filter and splashes at the surface. Bright silver streaks of air bubbles descend, then rise to the top. Microscopic critters scurry by in the drop of pond water.

The African clawed frog, *Xenopus laevis,* is named for its unique feet—their hind feet webbed with prominent claws. They are green and mottled on top, with a pale white underbelly. This is the classic bicolor of a predator. Although they appear so inefficient at everything. They have small eyes; tiny flimsy forelimbs and they are nearly blind.

You can observe them in the aquarium; they sit so still you'd think they were dead, adrift and motionless. Then they lunge haplessly at any movement. They miss their prey, such as a worm or fish, most of the time. Yet they eventually catch and shove the prey into their great big mouths, with their tiny weak hands. The goldfish swims by, the frog lunges out. The scales of the goldfish float off in a reflective shiny puff, like silvery-orange smoke dissipating, as the tail fin sticks out the frog's mouth.

Despite their meager appearance, the African clawed frog is considered an invasive pest in states with warmer climates. It is illegal to possess them or ship them in certain states. In those places, when released in the local ponds, they ravage the aquatic food webs. They devour all the native frogs and their tadpoles. They compete with the fish for every available invertebrate, as well as small vertebrate prey. They even devour their own eggs and tadpoles. Also, these frogs are the vector of a chytrid fungal pathogen responsible for the decline of amphibians worldwide.

So African. There is a certain vitality, virulence and destructiveness for what has evolved in Africa. A predatory tidal wave engulfing all it can. They are so indicative of Africa. Our hominin ancestors walked out of Africa, upright, hands free, eyes forward—a hapless predator. Weak, slow, hairless and formidable.

28

THE CODEX

The girls sit at the big stone-top table in Tyndall's room. The dark tabletop is warm from the sunlight streaming through the window. Helen sprawls her arms across the warm tabletop, while looking to her side at her phone in one hand. Sandy, with multicolored pens, dutifully does her math homework. Sialia peruses the internet for ideas for a new painting, and searches images of Spanish conquistadors. She scrolls through page after page of small thumbnail images, including new paintings, modern tattoos, and centuries-old wood-block prints. She is struck by a hieroglyphic-like, stylized image of a two-faced beast blazing in green and red. The glyph is a facsimile from an Aztec codex available through the Vatican Archives.

The blazing yellow, red and green colored glyph floats like a hologram. The picture is square and framed by small, numerous square paintings of various animals. Thirteen round red circles line the top and bottom of the image. In the center is a monstrous looking figure with two different beast-like faces on one oversized head. One animal face is that of a deer, the other is the face of a bat. One hand is holding a spotted scepter and the other a bone scepter. The long fingernails on the hands are painted blue and red and are held at highly articulated angles as if gesturing. An elaborate headdress, huge rounded eyes and additional appendages and animal-like figures surround the monster. The glyph below that is of a snake eating colored dashes and circles. Sialia reaches into her pack for her notebook, and turns to Sandy and says, "Hey, can I borrow your color pen set?"

On Tyndall's desk, the obsidian rock phosphoresces an image of Stufa on the phone in his office. He is talking with a sales representative from Bradmoor Publishing. "Yes, I can assure you that the curriculum adoption is going according to plan. One more school board meeting, and it is a done deal." The rock continues to glow; the image of a bright green bird zooms across the smooth rock surface, while deep in the smoky-green glass is the image of a terror-stricken face of a young Native American as he turns his head to look over his shoulder. In a burning village, the young woman warrior and Cualli meet; both are fleeing the conquistadors.

Cualli says, "You run also, but you are a warrior—right?"

"And why do you run, slave?"

"I was captured and enslaved by the newcomers."

"Ah, a slave of one; then the slave of another."

"That is my fate—for now."

"That is all," she says, holding her hand up. "I do not speak to your kind."

"But our new enemy is the same and so is our fear—and our destinies, ever intertwined here and now."

"I fear nothing! Careful or I will send you to the afterlife," the warrior says reaching for her blade.

"I relent. But what is your name, and where do you run?"

"Go!" she says, as if to an errant dog lagging on her heels. "Go!" Now pointing.

Cualli stops and watches her march on, the long tail of her puma cloak swaying rhythmically as she runs. Then she stops abruptly and turns and looks hard at Cualli. He is bent over and breathing hard on the trailside. He says, "No, do not send me away. Not today, for I just run, run like you."

"I will not harm you. Come. You will run, here, behind me—boy."

"I am Cualli, from Xalqutl on the coast."

Standing tall and proud she says, "Do not speak to me."

"But we run together."

Exasperated, the warrior turns and says, "I am Anci-Ihuicatl of the Warrior-Class in training, from south of your village. Now we go to speak to the High Priest of my order."

They stand there together looking at one another. The momentary silence is broken when a green jay, with a bright blue and black head and rich green wings and body, flies across the trail. It flashes emerald light and disappears into the vibrant, glowing jungle, giving a raucous rash-rassh-rassh call.

"But where do we go?"

"We now have no place and must inform our kind of the coming storm."

"Those men are like gods, and they have skin they put on that cannot be pierced."

"Come, you have seen much, and can inform the priests. So, they are men underneath."

"But I do not belong."

Arriving ahead of the Spaniards, the two young natives come to a set of plazas on a hilltop. For several days they inform the priests of what they know of the Spaniards. They are then given the Codex. The Codex contains the story of the "Two-Handed Monster" and the "Overlord of the Underworld." The high priest hands them the Codex, taken from a vault-like chamber under a sliding stone. They are instructed to bring it to the Plaza at the Field of Black Birds. Follow the setting moon, and then turn north in the broad flat valley; the steaming snow-covered volcanos will shine to your left. The high priest says, "Go there, and inform the priest from the three tribes of the coming of terror. And you must deliver, at all costs, the Codex for safekeeping. All must know what comes from the rising sun. And the story here, in the Codex, will inform us on what we are dealing with."

The Codex is a "book," about twelve inches square. It is folded accordion-style, thirty-one pages, each richly illustrated on two sides for a total of sixty-two pages. The pages are made of deerskin worked thin into a fine vellum. Each page is illustrated with a glyph or many glyphs, all elaborately drawn in varying shades of green, red, blue, ochre-brown and black. The lone high priest places the block-like Codex in a leather pack made from the hides of four coati. Two of the animals' ringed tails extend down while two go up to form shoulder straps. The fur is still on the long snouts with the stiff whiskers. The eyes of the animals are of blue turquoise beads that stare out. The rest of the pack is elaborately covered with intricate blue and green feather work. The feathers undulate and wave with each subtle movement. The priest says to

Anci and Cualli, "The key to the coming storm is in the Codex. Keep it safe. Both of you know what is real, for mythologies are emerging like the mist pouring over the ridgetops. Know what is, and what is imagined. That is the key. The High Order will understand the Two-Handed Monster."

Turning to Anci, he says, "Before you arrive give the sacred rights on the flank of the great volcano." They are given the fine cotton clothes of nobles embroidered with gold. Also, Cualli is given a wolf skin cloak.

29

VITALITY

Embarkation of the Queen Sheba
The mind's eye paints a world
Of serene beauty—
And function

—G.B.

Tyndall tumbles out of the car, shoulder bag on his right arm, lunch bag hanging from the same hand. His left hand fumbles with the keys and phone simultaneously. He scoops another plastic grocery bag with a free finger. It is heavier than he thought. Thank goodness James and Sialia saw him lumbering up to the door and opened it for him.

On the floor of the hallway, by his door, a girl is lying on her back with her feet up on the lockers and a notebook held over her head. Her golden hair is splayed out on the gray carpet, like fireworks exploding in the darkening sky.

During homeroom, Tyndall pulls a basketball size puffball mushroom out of the plastic grocery bag. "Check this out," he says emphatically.

"Whoa, no way! What is it?" Ryan says.

As the class gathers around, Tyndall explains that it is a giant puffball mushroom that he found this past weekend while hiking with his dog. The kids pass it around.

"Oh, it stinks! Is it solid? It's so heavy," Hector announces.

Tyndall motions over his shoulder to Sialia for her to fetch the scale out of the cabinet.

She walks over, extracts the balance scale and yells, "This one?"

"No, the flat one—there," Tyndall says, pointing to the lower shelf in the cabinet. He places the big off-white blob on the scale. "Okay, four point two kilos or seven point two pounds."

One kid yells, "No way! Can we break it open?"

"Not yet, I want to show it to my classes," Tyndall says.

Sialia explains that the students will not be around tomorrow. "We have district tests all morning," she says. He is disheartened at the disruption—again. Tyndall thinks, the specimen won't last that long, I'll get in trouble for sure if I stick it in the staff fridge.

On the board he explains the world of fungi. "Out there," he says, as he gestures outwardly with both arms, and goes on to explain there is a hidden underground world with miles of hair-like threads called hyphae spread through the soil. Some individual fungi are immense in size, such as one in the Upper Peninsula of Michigan which measures one and a half square miles in size. It is one of the largest organisms ever measured. Almost all of it is underground and unseen. The bell rings and the moment is lost, scattered. The rambling, tumbling exuberance evaporates like falling rain in the desert sky. What a mess. My hands stink, he thinks.

His mind wanders back to college and Jason Lindquist's Plant Ecology Class. It was so captivating, real and genuine. All that, yet it was just a guy with chalk and a blackboard. What was that experiment? He thinks. It's in *Ravens Botany Book*, where is that. It has a painting on the book cover. Here it is. Who painted this? Monet? Van Gogh? He finds the book on his shelf and inside the cover it says *Farm Garden with Sunflowers* by Gustav Klimt. Never heard of it, but I remember the book because of it. He looks through the index. Where is it? Mycorhiza? Mycrorhyzal?—There, mycorrhizae. Oh yeah, the white pine seedling experiment. These forest trees, if grown in sterile soil, even with nutrients added, and transferred to prairie soil are small and stunted. But if the seedlings are exposed for just a few weeks to forest soil and then transplanted to prairie soil they grow vigorously. The trees apparently cannot grow without the foundation of their fungal mycorrhizae symbiosis.

There is a photograph of two groups of pine seedlings next to each other. One group is small and wimpy looking; the other group is four times larger with long, numerous roots.

The Germans were the first to observe this. In such Germanic fashion, they set out to put order to the forests. Greater efficiency, more product, *das ist sehr gut. Nein.* Seedlings that were grown in containers and transplanted to neat rows of trees in the forests, exactly measured, predetermined, mass-produced, contrived order, to maximize production. It was supposed to be a Bavarian conveyor belt of pine and spruce lumber. A commodity to be produced and used. But all the grand plans and schemes do not work in nature. The seedlings would not thrive in the containers. They germinated and grew, then they would stagnate. Only if unsterile soil from an intact, unorderly forest was added to the container did the seedlings grow to a sapling that could be transplanted. Miles of fungal hyphae, hair-like mycorrhizae, wrapped around every root tip in a mass exchange of water, nutrients, and minerals. Essential and unseen—the foundation of vitality.

Meanwhile, Elysium's administrators have canceled the last class of the day, to give a motivational speech about the importance of tomorrow's tests. The barber pole twirls in rhythmic concentric circles, giving an illusion of forever turning. The Barber Surgeon distributes the blue-mass pill, a deep cure in the hand.

In the hallway, the girls join up with James and Ryan and drift with the current down to the meeting. Standing at the junction of the hallways is JR who is playing a big red and pink electric bass. He is wearing light blue jeans, cut off at the knees; his long hair hangs down as he rocks back and forth with the deep sound. His long, thin, pale arms flex under the weight of the big instrument as his thumb and fingers pluck away on the thick vibrating strings. From the amplifier, a hollow sound echoes a strange primal rhythmic thumping. Miguel Angel and Hector, loudly laughing, kick a soccer ball off the wall past the eddy where JR is grooving. As Sialia passes by, she looks over and smiles; no one else notices, the precession flows onward.

They sit on the floor of the Commons as other tenth graders shuffle in. The Commons, as the new cafeteria/assembly area is called, is like the Primate House at the zoo. It is a large open area, slightly lower than ground level, with huge windows looking in from the hallway. The only thing missing is a big tree with vines in the center of the room. Assistant Principal Combe steps up to the podium and says, "As you know…"

Then he is followed by Principal Stufa. Dr. Stufa stands at the podium addressing the students. "Tomorrow you all will be taking the Formative Assessments for the new Spring Forward Curriculum. It is important that you do your best…" His hands wave in the air.

Hector turns to James and says, "What's an assessment?"

"A test."

"Why don't they just say that?"

Ryan then turns and says, "What's formative?"

James, looking up from his phone, shrugs his shoulders.

"Is it a rubric?"

"No, that's a different thing," James says as he sniffs his hand and smells the earthy soil-like odor of the puffball mushroom.

In the hallway, JR continues to thump away on the bass. In the Commons, the kids sit in chairs and on the floor; they rhythmically rock back and forth to the thumping, dancing sound of the bass line. The principal spoke, the children rocked back and forth; a strange comfort in the familiar rhythmic call.

30

MACHO IS REAL

In the corner of the art room, JR quietly paints away at his copy of Katsushika Hokusai's *The Great Wave of Kanagawa*. Sialia looks over and explains, "Did you know that was not a painting, but a woodblock print?" She points to the almost indiscernible boats in the water and starts talking about them.

JR, dabbing blue paint and pushing his long straight hair out of his eyes, looks hard and says, "Whoa, I didn't even see that, wow. That actually changes everything."

Josue comes into Tyndall's room and plops down on a desk with his head down. Junior year is very different for Josue. Tyndall does not have him as a student now, but he leaves math class most days to visit Tyndall during his planning period after lunch. Here, the very weight of another's world is felt by Tyndall. It is a precarious balance of what to do, what not to do? Good and bad, right and wrong.

Josue comes to Tyndall and explains how it is at work, a restaurant about twenty miles away in the next town. He works in the kitchen, as a prep cook, with other Latinos. There he is manipulated and run by one of the cooks, whose name is also Josue, to deal cocaine to the ski tourist. In short, halting sentences Josue explains how the deal is done: "They come in for the shit. You know, in paper packet. We sit at a table, a booth; we do everything under the table with hand signals. This man, he pays me good. More than I make at the restaurant. But it's so bad. I am a bad person. I hate myself for doing this. He gives me the keys to his car, big black car, a real nice ride. I talk to the girls in it."

It starts to make sense to Tyndall. The clothes Josue wears, the new kicks, best smartphone, Beats headphones. All the possessions valuable to a teenager.

For weeks, and then months, Tyndall hears Josue's confessions. He drops all his work to sit and talk with him. He talks to the school counselor, who refers Tyndall to professional psychiatrists. But ultimately, they decide that Tyndall will talk to the boy. The school's resource officer says that it's not his jurisdiction, but he will let the police up there know. Tyndall protests, "But the kid has the same name as the real dealer." About a week later the local police do a mock raid walking through the restaurant, but they just end up scattering the illegal help for a day or two.

They sit face to face on the desktops. Tyndall asks, "Do you talk to your older brothers?"

"No, I only talk with you," Josue says in a low soft voice.

"Did you work last night?"

"Yeah, but I was good; I didn't deal the shit. I think I can stay away, and not do it."

Looking hard at Josue Tyndall says, "Are you getting high?"

"No. Can't sell and do that. It's business. I'll be good, I know I can." The class period ends and students start shuffling in. Josue and Tyndall sit on the desktops, their feet on the chairs, look each other straight in the eye, and say nothing. In the nearby aquarium the frogs sit motionless and look on.

The next day Josue is not in school. Tyndall decides to go to Josue's house at lunch. He drives down the narrow streets of mixed small houses and doublewide trailers. Certainly, Tyndall is pushing the boundaries of what to do, as he knocks on the door. A tiny elderly Latina woman, who speaks little to no English, answers the door. She looks hard at Tyndall standing there. "Josue, teacher from school," she says in broken Spanish and English. "Josue, Josue, Jo-ito, Ito." She turns and calls at the closed bedroom door. Josue opens the door and looks up surprised at Tyndall standing there. All the while explaining to the elderly woman in fast incomprehensible Spanish that this is my teacher, everything is okay.

To Tyndall's surprise they stay in his room and talk. Josue shows Tyndall photos of the street and house where he grew up in San Salvador, El Salvador. He shows more photos of him and his friends during a slumber party. The boys are walking in the snow in just their underwear, all barefoot and cold, doing crazy sleepover antics. He grabs the bulletin from church that past Sunday and explains the sermon to Tyndall. They talk for an hour, as if it were normal for Tyndall to show up at his door and knock. Tyndall drives Josue back to school, stopping for a burger and fries on the way.

At school, Josue sheepishly turns to Tyndall, with the hamburger bag in his hand and says, "I'm going to go eat with my friends now."

Tyndall smiles, gesturing with his hand—go—without saying a word.

And so, it continues, good days and weeks, followed by intense guilt and sadness. Tyndall and Josue continue to sit face-to-face on the desktops. Tyndall is weary from losing sleep. Josue cries sometimes. The frogs look on, but do not blink.

Tyndall runs into Orlando, who works at several schools as a cultural liaison. "How's it going with Josue and your project?"

"Oh, he's a project all right," Tyndall says, straining to not complain. The two of them have worked together for years and there is a mutual trust, almost admiration for each other. They stand close to each other in the hall, outside Tyndall's door, while kids shuffle by and slam lockers all around them. They keep talking even after class has started. As they stand in the hallway Tyndall knows that in his room, kids are goofing off, probably starting a fire. But it does not matter, what is going on with Josue is of greater importance. Down the way, Stufa stands at the junction of the hallway, awkwardly joking with the last straggling students late to class.

Orlando turns and looks down the hall, and then at Tyndall and says, "Look, these guys are from another world. You have to demand from them that they stop being boys and be men. Only by being a man can Josue stand up to this other man. It is the world, I did not make it. He sees in you that you are a man—that is why he comes to you."

Tyndall looks down the hallway at Stufa standing at the junction. In all these months he has never spoken to Stufa or Combe, the assistant principal. No shallow recourse or protocol could help in this case. He has talked to doctors, psychiatrists, PhDs, counselors, police and others. Besides, he feels that these manic swings by Josue can only end in disaster.

On the windowsill, the frogs float silently in the aquarium, not blinking and looking on at Josue and Tyndall as they sit face-to-face again. The picture is now getting ever more distorted, through the bubbling water and the green algae on the glass of the aquarium. It is worse. Josue explains how he wants to get a gun and kill himself. How he can't stand it, that he is bad. How he is a toy to this man, the dealer, and with his hand he gestures a puppet on a string.

Tyndall knows it has come to a head. He knows machismo from having worked in Mexico and Puerto Rico. How it is even different from the blue-collar labor he had done. It is macho, and it is real. Josue is starting to cry.

Tyndall does what he was not supposed to do, but goes there nonetheless. He lunges up and reaches across the chair and desk and grabs Josue by the shirt.

"You listen here now! You're going to be a man," pulling Josue's sobbing face into his. "You're going to stand up to this motherfucker, god dammit. Do you hear me? You are a man; tell this other man no, you're not going to do it anymore. Do you hear me! Men don't cry—stand up."

Push against evil, the weight and mass of evil. It's like a large, soft, giant ball, it just squishes in. You throw your shoulder into it and push and lean, but it's so heavy and it just bubbles in. The pride, greed, want, and possessions. Possessions to a teenage boy from poverty. The weight of the car, the mass of the smart phone, the tunes, the shoes, the shirt and belt, the money and paper packets under the table. A mass so heavy, immovable, your arms just push, veins bulging, knees flexed, head down, and it all just folds and bends and goes nowhere. The weight of a freight train car of mush; the evil of possessions and money. The stack of bills in the boy's hand, inches thick, flicking through his dexterous fingers.

Josue is crying now uncontrollably, with Tyndall shaking him by the shirt. "You must be a man. Fuck. Stand up." The weight. Tyndall yells, "Stand!" Tyndall wants to thrust him on his shoulder and carry him, confront the dealer himself, shield the boy from evil. But the want and greed swallow it all—all that is. Just then class ends and students start shuffling in. Josue fights to stop the tears.

Standing, Tyndall puts his arm around Josue and walks him into the hallway. They walk down the hall together to the junction, the busiest place in the school. Josue rubs tears from his cheeks with his shirt sleeve. Tyndall pulls Josue's ear to his mouth and says, "Look, look around you, look at all this, the girls, the smiles, and the tag games." He gestures, pointing to the pretty girls and the games, "Look there, all this will be gone if you're not a man."

And with one motion Tyndall shoves Josue into the fray of the busy hallway, with all the resounding energy of the teenage world: girls holding boy's hands, soccer balls flying, games, beautiful girls, laughter—real laughter. He chucks him into the river, and with the powerful current he goes. It flows strong, and you cannot go back. It is swift and so very fast. Tyndall is almost in tears himself. *Fuck, what have I done? I just killed that boy. I'll never see him again.* He walks down the hallway, limp and exhausted, to another large class of thirty kids.   Only it is an afternoon class, with students full of energy, that he has to teach, somehow.

The weight, it is so very soft, soft and heavy. It does not move; money, possessions, poverty. To be a man standing alone next to what will not move. Like a soft cold rubber ball that just inverts on itself. The weight—the weight of evil. To push, push against it—push. The river is mighty and the water muddy, a liquid slip that envelops everything, filling in and sealing the cracks around humanity. Like a big log bobbing in a giant river, Josue appears and disappears as he rides the waves meandering down the hallway.

Sialia stands in the corner of the library, leaning on a low bookcase, looking down at her computer screen. She is supposed to be listening to her English teacher give directions, but instead is scrolling through artwork on her screen. The Canadian painter Alex Colville's painting *Horse and Train* freezes Sialia as she stands there in the corner of the library. A shiver runs down her spine, she shudders and looks around for her sweater.

31

YOGI TAKES A DUMP

As summer comes to an end, Tyndall, like so many teachers, starts to do a little schoolwork. So, one hot summer afternoon, about a week before it all begins, he heads in to school. It is hot, and he comes to school with Yogi. Now Yogi, like any dog, just loves to go places. He has been to school many times and knows the territory.

They come in the back door, the hallway is dark, some classroom doors are open as the janitorial crew strips and waxes the floors. Most of the paraphernalia from various rooms is out in the hallway. There are piles of desks, chairs, tables, and filing cabinets. Yogi bursts into the school and bounds down the hall, as Tyndall turns to his right to his room. Tyndall immediately swings around, hand on the door jam, and whistles and says, "Hey—in here." Yogi stops and trots back, tongue hanging out, strolls in the room and looks up at Tyndall. Like any good dog he knows what his human wants, and also how to push the boundaries. Tyndall kicks the empty recycling bin in front of the door to keep the dog in the room.

The floor is freshly waxed, but all the desks and chairs are piled in a haphazard way around the room. It is great the room has been cleaned, but also a hassle to put it all back together again. But it is just part of the routine of getting started again. Tyndall's tradition is to come in and set up the physical space—the geography of the room. Then he essentially sets up the first six weeks of his classes, which is about two units each. All set up—photocopies made, slide presentations done, electronic links, electronic quizzes, and paper tests, all done before school starts. Yogi lies on the cool linoleum floor watching his human move around the place. He knows the routine.

Later, Tyndall and the dog head on down to the office to make copies. Along the way they stop in the social studies room, where the janitors are cleaning, and visit. As they enter Roberta yells, "Yogiiii!" The dog runs up, running through her legs in a figure eight pattern, as she scratches his back. Yogi loves Roberta. It is interesting how he is so particular with people; some he just loves, others he won't let touch him. His golden-brown eyes flash as he looks up and back as Roberta scratches his back, right on top of the base of his tail. His hind end pushes to his left and then right.

Down in the office, Yogi and Tyndall greet the secretaries and one of the counselors. The office space is a square of hallways with one "hallway" being the copy and supply room. This is a typical start to it all, stopping and visiting with everyone and getting very little actual work done. But it is all part of it.

Tyndall loses track of Yogi for a while. He comes running in and flies by Tyndall with an unusual bounce, who is standing at the copy machine.

"What are you up to? Have you been causing trouble?" Tyndall says to Yogi as he straightens a stack of papers on the countertop. Yogi play bows as he plops down on the carpet, wagging his tail and looking playful. The dog lets out a guttural trill and looks at Tyndall.

Tyndall, who has been facing the copy machine, looks sideways and says, "What?" He turns to his left, away from Yogi and the copy machine, and heads out to the main office. Yogi lays there staring at Tyndall. He looks back at the dog, then at the now-empty office area. He thinks, what is that dog up to? He continues into the office area down the hall toward the principal's office. As he turns the corner Yogi bolts out from behind him, flies by him in the hallway, looking back and up at Tyndall. With almost a sigh Tyndall says, "You're a dog; what are you up to? Beast."

Principal Stufa's office is open but he's not there. But right there in the center of his office is a big steaming pile of shit. A gift from Yogi. Yogi is in the hall, head dropped down, ears up and tail wagging. Not like he's a bad dog, but more like—hey I dropped the tennis ball in front of you, look let's play.

"Ahh, fuck, Yogi, ahh," Tyndall groans. He looks frantically in all directions searching for a way to quickly clean this up and get out before anyone notices. "Ahh, fucking dog—beast."

Quickly he grabs the small garbage can in the office and scrounges around for a discarded lunch bag. He picks up the poop and drops it in the garbage can, then extracts the plastic garbage bag and ties it in a knot. He quickly stands up to exit the office, stops in the doorway and looks hard at the carpet. Only a slight stain, no one should notice. It smells like shit, not too bad, more like someone had stepped in it. Just then Stufa appears down the hall.

"Mr. Tyndall how's your summer been?" he says. Tyndall lowers the bag to his left back hip. Yogi moves by Stufa, ducking his head to avoid being petted by him. Then Yogi lies down at the junction of the main hallway, tongue hanging out, smiling, looking back at Tyndall exchanging pleasantries with his boss. All the while Tyndall is holding the small opaque garbage bag hanging heavy with the big dog dump in it.

32

EASTER ISLAND

In art class, JR turns to Sialia and says, "Hey, what you painting?" Sialia responds, "It's the scene that we read about in biology last class, you know the *National Geo* article."

"Oh yeah, the ancestor's story of the island—ahh Easter Island."

Ms. Rayleigh chimes in, "Now Sialia, aren't you supposed to be working on your emulation painting?"

"Oh, don't worry I can do these both."

Rayleigh says, "You are just your own bird, you fly where you want."

The copy of the magazine article is open next to Sialia as she paints. The article starts with these words: "Grandfather, tell me again the story of how the ancestors came here. I love that story.

"Ah, in the enormous outrigger canoes, each with all the extended families, sailed and paddled across the vast mother ocean. A face was carved into the front bow of the canoe, and the white waves spoke as a song in the rhythmic beat of the heart. The cry went out from the lead canoe, as Chief Apololan, pointed to a great gathering of porpoises. The families, one and all, grabbed their paddles and turned with the waves and wind in set pursuit.

"As they approached, the brother porpoises joined them and rode on the wave at the front of the boat. This brought such great joy that it was no longer a hunt, but a joined celebration of movement with the waves shining silver in the sun. And all leaned forward together on the paddles, and moved as one, with smiles deep in their hearts. For they had joined in union with their brothers. Never has a canoe moved with such speed, and every wave turned in front. And the great silver and white porpoises leapt high into the air, spinning and splashing water on the smiling faces. And when the festival of movement was done, the clouds on the horizon spoke of a green emerald in the ocean, under stars unknown. *Rapa nui*—home."

Later that day, Tyndall stands in front of his tenth grade Biology class and goes over the lesson. "Alright guys, last class we read about and discussed two readings about Easter Island. So now why don't you get those readings out, and we'll review."

A student raises his hand, "I wasn't here."

"Okay, here you go." Tyndall says handing the kid the readings.

"So, anyone else absent last class? Also, make sure you get the notes from another student." After the normal herky-jerky start to it all, the day's activities get outlined. "So, before we get started, someone give me a description of the environment today on Easter island." Sandy is quick to raise her hand and he knows he'll get a complete answer from her. She sits at her desk overly prepared: white water bottle with a black cap, floral pattern notebook open to a blank page, and a color pen set in a plastic case propped open with twelve colors arranged from yellow to black. He calls on Sandy.

Sandy jumps right in with an exuberant presumptive tone, "Easter Island is super remote and has open grasslands with no trees, but there were once trees there."

"Excellent—now what evidence do they have that there were once trees there?"

"Pollen records in mud from a lake."

"Excellent, now someone explain the statues. Helen"?

"Well there are these huge statues."

"And what are they called?" Helen fumbles through her papers and quickly says, *moai.*"

"And Johnny how big are they?"

Johnny says, "Ya know, um, big." Everyone laughs.

"Come on."

"Ah, like, um ya know, oh here—up to ninety metric tons."

"Okay this is not directly in the reading. Do you think the statues required a lot of time, energy and resources?"

"Well, yeah."

"How so?" Sandy is quick to raise her hand, but Tyndall does not call on her. The lesson continues. After teasing out the answers from the kids Tyndall turns around to the whiteboard and writes down: "(1) limited resources, (2) carrying capacity and (3) quarry, carve, and move."

"Now, write that down. All right, we have our basic overview, so now we'll do a lab activity."

Sialia interjects, "But it's more than just resources, it's how they acted."

"How so?"

"Yeah, they all started out cooperating, ya know, crossing the biggest chunk of ocean; then they used it all up and ruined it by being all tribal."

"Ah, I hadn't thought about it that way."

Tyndall continues. "Excellent Sialia. We'll get back to this after the lab. So, you're goanna have finite resources and you have to choose what to do with these resources. Each group will get thirty goldfish crackers to 'spend'. Now you can do several things with these. Trade them for a canoe. Or you can spend them building a statue. Or you can eat them. Or trade them for chickens or obtain weapons. I know from past labs, this is going to get kind of crazy and loud as all ten groups are at it. And don't just shove these into your mouths, but actually follow along and trade and build and barter away. Also, for our little experiment, the island will have only a thousand trees in which to build canoes, make rope and move statues." Tyndall hands out the goldfish to each group, steps back and says, "Go!"

"We don't have to be fair or nice, right?"

"No."

"We just have to get goldfish, trees, or statues to win, right?"

And with both hands in the air, sitting on the big front table Tyndall says—"Yeah go!"

He sits back and watches absolute mayhem unfold. Goldfish are flying, kids are arguing, scrambling, hoarding and cheating. He thinks to himself. *Holy shit, I hate this lab and love it. Every time it just gets crazier; but the lessons of limited resources and expensive monuments plays out so well.* After it is all done, Tyndall does his best to rein in the class and try to make some conclusions.

"So, what did we end up with?"

"All the goldfish ended up in the hands of only a few groups, and all the trees are gone."

Hector says, "Yeah now we all can pray to the statues for a juicy cheeseburger and fries." He drops to his knees and pays homage to one of the groups with all the goldfish. "Oh, please may I have another."

Sialia tosses a goldfish in the air and Hector catches it in his mouth while clapping his hands like a circus sea lion begging. Everyone laughs.

"So, what happens to the basics, like goldfish, if you build only statues?"

"Yeah end up with no trees and no goldfish—but a lot of statues."

"I think you guys get the idea of limited resources, carrying capacity, in a closed environment. Now what I want you to do is log on to the following website to take a virtual tour of the island. Also, they show a new hypothesis for the way that the statues were moved from the quarry to their pedestals overlooking the ocean. One last thing to outline, now write this down: 'The goldfish represent resources.' Now let's list out the resources, plus cultural things of value. Remember these are inextricably linked." The class continues to outline things about food such as: fish, shellfish, porpoises, chickens, crops like sweet potato and bananas. They also list out trees, in particular the big palm trees. The list continues: Statues, shelter, water, and weapons.

"Another student adds: "Remember the rats that were introduced, and their impact on the palm trees."

"Excellent. And what is the cost of a *moai*?" Time in years, labor, resources like trees for timber and rope."

Sialia said, "But the statues cost the most in resources."

"How so?" Then she answers, straining to convince others of what she can see and understand.

All for belief, a want and a desire; for peace, food, trees, a canoe, and water. It represented something in the mind, a mystical connection to a greater something. Why look out, look out at the sea, the vastness; a never-quiet place resonating with the sound of the surf, wind, and waves on the shore. As if waiting. Symbolic of a desire; to be in a clan, a group, and to place one's belief in a stone—so literal, so definitive. To go out and look at it, look out at what it might see. To see through the eyes of a deity. To know something by mere representation, a sentinel looking, and to believe in the never-blinking eye in the mind of a stone; a lithic permanence, penetrating the horizon, a place you can never go, from where your ancestors came from, ever connected to the ancestors, and you know, know how from a boat they came, a boat more powerful, a tool, and the igneous rock face that can only look out. Something to float your desires upon, inside the gaze of a rock. The pounding waves, the ever- penetrating cold of the mist that cools the stone-face of the rock dripping wet.

Quarry, carve, and move. Look out and see. See through the eyes. Eyes that never blink. Eyes that always see. What was it like to patch up the last outrigger? The last vessel to obtain food from the ocean. The canoe must have become less and less utilitarian and more and more symbolic. The last canoe had a face carved into it. The front of the canoe was erected and then directed as an outreaching cry to the waves that would never touch it. And when the rain and wind, and warring clans commandeered the last of the wood. Only giant stone faces could withstand the elements and the cultural upheaval. A stronger mystical sediment in the derived mind of someone who could actually see. It's all you got left. The inequalities created by the squeeze on the resources. The last rope. How they unwind all the broken little pieces of rope to try to make one last functional rope. The wet twisted fibers. To try and move the *moai*. The sound of the rope stretching, creaking, snapping. The sound of the *moai* hitting the ground. The despair to leave it on the side of the road. How could it then look out? Lying there, on its side. There, in-between, and the empty rock pedestal with no face to place on it, no eyes to look out at the surf crashing and the mist rolling in. The cool droplets, barely perceivable, but for the chill in your bones as the incessant wind howls past the prostrate face that was once a rock. Sun, moon and stars, and in the pitch-black—staring out. Soundless, next to the ever-humming ocean vastness.

A multiplicity of determinants; actions and reactions. Imagined, contrived and pre-presented in the symbolic mind that supersedes the material world. So germane to some purpose within the dreamland with mystic undertones, to evoke a recognition of meaning. To perceive and express in hidden tribal platitudes that shaped the driving force of applied validity. A treasure in the soft tuff stone, an edifice, imposing, iconic, manifested in belief, stronger than reason, emerging from temporal things. Distinguishing itself within the very rock looking out.

And to sit with the *moai*, upon the rock pedestal, overlooking the ocean and see a pod of a thousand porpoises swimming by, as the statue and a lone observer watches, touching the stone, feeling a more complete whole; the silver water, white waves, the aerial breaching, splashing, spinning, moving unencumbered with powerful thrusts of the tail. And no canoe to join them, and swim, and fly and breach the surface and splash—to be free.

33

EL SALVADOR III

In the late afternoon, Miguel Angel's father, Juan, and his little brother, Juanito, left the hardware store in Santa Ana, El Salvador, a dusty bustling hub of a city on the Pan-American highway. They had just purchased a shovel, a new pic handle and some fifty meters of twelve-centimeter plastic piping in a roll about one meter across, plus a couple of twenty-kilogram bags of corn. While driving out of town, they picked up a couple of men hitchhiking. The men rode in the back of the pickup truck with the piping and the tools. They had about twenty kilometers of mountain roads to drive. Cars and trucks, without mufflers, noisily zipped past them.

At about 5 p.m. the truck's tire exploded with a bang, and they stopped on the side of the road. The hitchhiking men departed. On the side of a curve, in a rocky flat spot, Juan and Juanito stopped to change the tire. It was a flat, rocky, packed-down area about the size of a baseball diamond. A roadside palapa bar stood at the uphill side; next to the bar were several three-sided shacks with thatched roofs. A mango tree, laden with fruit, grew between the bar and the empty roadside shacks. Juan sent the boy up to gather mangoes while he changed the flat tire.

"Don't get ones that are too ripe or bruised."

"How many, Papa?"

"What you can carry, no problem." With a gesture of his hand he said, "Go."

Juan did not like this place. It was quiet now, but come nightfall it was not a place to be. He cranked down hard on the lug nuts with grunting noises. The boy picked up a mango, turned it in his hand, then dropped it. Every other one or so he stuck in his T-shirt which he pulled out from his belly as a makeshift pack to carry the oblong sweet-smelling fruit. Outside the palapa bar was an old dark blue Toyota pickup and a parked ATV. Two other trucks pulled up and parked by the side of the bar. They were new, shiny Ford half-ton pickups, music blaring out the open windows. Both trucks spun around and backed into a space on the far side of the bar. The big boxy hood of each pickup truck stuck out ominously. Juan had the spare tire on and was tightening the nuts down. Squinting in the long light of the setting sun, he called and waved with his hand for his son to come back to the truck.

"Just one more, Papa."

"No, that is good." With his shirt stretched out, the boy carried the mangoes back to the truck.

34

RAVEN KILLING

The painting *Abbey in an Oak Forest* haunts and glows in ominous starkness. Stout bare-leaved trees, a ruined church, and gravestones emerge from a somber fog.

James comes bumbling into Tyndall's room, bumping and banging his duffel bag with a couple lacrosse sticks bulging out one end. "Hey Tynd, can I leave this in here until I leave for the game?"

"Yeah, no worries, just slide it under the table by my desk." Tyndall is sipping tea, at the front table, and opening his laptop to start up the day's slide presentation on gel electrophoresis. James's hair is more curly than usual with the rain and accompanying humidity. They both silently look out the window at the breaking clouds. The day hangs still for a moment, caught in the netherworld between a rainy day and a dry one.

"Where's your game?"

"It's up in Vail."

"When do you leave?"

"Noon, or something." James looks down at his phone, scrolling for some text saying when and where. Sandy and Sialia float in. Sandy plops down at Tyndall's desk and starts rummaging through the drawers. Her long blond hair hangs down around her head into the open desk drawer. This always annoys Tyndall, but he knows it is quite harmless. One more lost pen or pencil—or breath mint.

Sialia pipes up, "Hey Tynd, can I make some coffee?—I'm so tired."

James, squatting, shoves his jacket into his athletic duffle bag and closes it, leaving his crocheted winter cap on, brown curls hanging out in all directions. He exclaims loudly about the gruesome sight he witnessed the day before. "Tynd, you should've seen it—it was brutal. I was at the dog park, you know, over at the far end by the irrigation ditch and the rows of trees and shrubs. It was late and the sun was going down."

Sialia asks, "Was it with Joey-Dog?"

"Yeah..."

"Ahh—he's so cute."

"Crazy dog, good dog, likes to chase birds, just sits and watches them fly," James explains. "Anyway, I lost sight of where Joey-Dog was, and I was looking around and along the fence line on the other side of the canal. This big black crow or raven swoops down, real straight and just crashes into the ground. And all of a sudden it just starts jabbing away, gray and white fur flyin'."

Tyndall looks up perplexed. "You sure it wasn't a hawk?"

"No, all black, huge beak, real fluffy shaggy looking. Anyway…" James pauses and he shudders inside, thinking of the fierceness of the beak jabbing, red flesh, small chunks gobbled down with its head lifted and thrown back. "Aah, it just ripped this small rabbit to pieces."

He recalls that the raven picked just the best parts; it quickly ate what it could with an ever-descending mob of magpies ready to usurp his meal. It ripped the chest cavity open, gulping down the lungs and the heart. The still beating heart slid down the big black bird's esophagus in rhythmic pulsating beats.

"Did you try to save it?"

"No, it was so fast, quick. I bet within sixty seconds there were several magpies on the fence and in the shrubs just squawking away. They made the raven rip and peck faster and harder. By the time I knew it was a baby bunny there were another dozen magpies swooping down. It was insane."

Tyndall quickly adds, "Ravens don't usually actively hunt and kill like hawks—but they will be opportunistic and they do that occasionally. I've watched them walk in groups behind a tractor cutting hay and capture the mice exposed by the cleared grass. Just walking in one slow marauder line behind the tractor."

"Then it just flew away, leaving what was left for the dozen-plus magpies. They flew down, lifted the limp carcass, and flew away—all chasing and squawking."

The soft gray light of dusk descended; the red osiers, the blue-yellow willows, the furrowed bark of the cottonwoods all blended into a soft uniform flatness. It was all so calm and quiet, strangely peaceful, after such sudden terror and death. James found himself standing there. *Did it really happen? The ground was soft and muddy and his shoes were wet. It was so still. What just happened? It was so brief, gruesome in its finality. Where's the dog?* A haunting morose feeling weighed him down. Why did he watch, not look away, detached, mesmerized, a lone witness—a floating man.

35

INCARNATE

The smooth young hand of the scribe, the *Tlacuilo*, draws and paints with the eyes of his master over his shoulder. The room is large, rectangular with white plaster walls. Large expansive open windows and doors look out over the verdant canopy of the surrounding tropical forest. On top of the large pyramid of stone, is the thatched roof structure with a commanding view of the Caribbean to the east and the snow-covered cylindrical volcanoes to the west; prominent and gleaming, like the folded rounded tops of the white wings of a giant angel. Misty white fog wraps like a shawl draped across the steep canyons. The misty clouds open and close around the vegetation, revealing and then concealing a leafy world.

The high priest paces back and forth on the stone floor. Clutched in his hand is a small obsidian mirror, a scrying mirror. The blackish volcanic glass is polished to a shining, reflective, convex surface. Near the door, in the morning light, he turns the object in his hand. It gleams pure black for a moment, then a bright silvery greenish color. The black angle shows a perfect reflection; the silver green reveals waves of light, directional, white and bright through and into the glass. It is his special speculum for divination. A tear rolls down his cheek, with the stinging salty taste upon the corner of his lip. In a low guttural voice the incantation of the vision revealed in his mind.

On one knee, atop the stone table, the scribe draws and paints the pictograph described by the high priest. The glyph is an image of the profiles of two animal heads, one is deer-like with big ears and round eyes facing to the left, while the other animal profile is harsh and angular, contorted with a folded face and the small eye of a big-eared bat. The deer faces three small, round, red dots ending with a long, curved line like a closing ocher parentheses mark. The bat faces three small, rounded, green dashes and the accompanying parentheses mark. The whole image is underlined by three dark blue boxy lines. Below that glyph is another square painting. This glyph is of a Z-shaped serpent with its mouth up, agape, devouring circles and dashes that grow progressively bigger near its mouth. Alternating blue dashes and red circles enter its gaping mouth. Three straight blue lines, same as the above glyph, underline the bigger serpent painting.

The *Tlacuilo* painter dips his brushes into the bowls, dashes and draws out practice images on a brown palm leaf. Then with an affirming grunt from the high priest, the scribe puts the final image on the folded vellum of the Codex. Smoke starts to drift out of the large room as the heat of the tropical day emerges from the humid jungle below. Gray ash whirls on the stone floor at the bare feet of the high priest and the accompanying artisans. Six green parrots with short, fast wing beats whip across the top of the forest canopy. They have long tails and hints of blue and some red flashing from their feathers in the bright light of late morning.

36

DITCH DAY

James sits in class waiting for the bell and looking out the side window. He looks at a girl from across the room. Eyes shine backlit sprays of water in the cool morning light. James stares mesmerized; a large raindrop hits a leaf and sprays out a mist of a million diamond stars. She blinks, he takes a breath, his mouth opens so deep it is almost a gasp. A ball flies across the room. The fleeting moment. The moment of such intense beauty. So vibrant, deep and mysterious. Not rare, but ephemeral, unperceived and unnoticed like an eye blinking. Such as it is, an infinite number of times a day, in the bleak backdrop of white linoleum tiles and rows of desks under the shallow, flat fluorescent lights.

After class James meets up with the guys outside Tyndall's room. They plop down at the big table in the sun. James says, "Hey Tynd, can we hide out here during the Community Meeting?"

"No guys, not today. You seniors are such slackers—no. Unless you got some big assignment or something."

The boys exit through the back door laughing and floating through the courtyard. Hector says, "Hey, remember ditching back when we were freshman?"

Ryan smiles, "Yeah, we made such a big deal of it then. Now we just walk out and drive away."

"Ah, the roof top—I miss it," James says as he smiles and looks at Sialia holding the backdoor to the school. "Yeah, remember how we'd meet up and escape?"

The scrawny little freshman boys: James, Ryan and Hector meet up in the large atrium of open space outside the cafeteria and The Commons. Hector is shoveling a sandwich into his mouth as he says to Ryan, "What's the 'turkey report'?"

Ryan eyeing the students filing into the commons for the assemble known as the Community Meeting says, "Man it's Wednesday—ya know." All three boys get wide-eyed—"Town!" They say in unison.

Every Wednesday the principal and assistant principal are both gone all day for meetings—somewhere. Also, every Wednesday there is a school-wide community meeting before lunch. That means Mrs. Guglielmo—Mrs. G.—the school secretary, is in charge. The boys know from past experience that she will be too busy doing other stuff to tally the attendance for the afternoon classes. They are free to go downtown, eat and goof off. The afternoon is theirs. Wet snow sits in the shade next to the building. It is humid and damp out.

The way to town is directly to the north. It is a straight shot down the stairway along the creek and about six blocks to the 7-Eleven store. The store has everything a boy might want to eat plus some. The north side of the school is also the faculty parking lot and the bus roundabout is in the northwest corner. Mrs. G has corralled Mr. Jay from his normal copy machine routine to help her patrol the north school area. She knows it's ditch day, and the route the kids will take. Jay is pissed off about not being able to get some copies made, a wrath he is most likely to take out on whoever he catches. As he stands in the shade, on the wet cold pavement, his vigilance increases.

Hector heads off impetuously to the north doors right past the front office with James in step. Ryan lunges and grabs James's shoulder. "No," he says emphatically. He gestures with his hand to the long hallway to the east.

Hector, slow to react, comes running up. "Hey man where you going?" he says.

"This way," Ryan says. He is pointing coyly next to his waist. "Be cool. I'll show you." They slink off down the hallway, past the trophy cases, to the glass doors at the end of the hall. Hector kicks the chain and lock of the auxiliary gym, which he has never been in during the three months he has been a student. The boys quicken their pace as they approach the double doors, windows illuminated with a bright glare. They laugh, each looks over their shoulder, and with a striking force Ryan blasts the breaker bar on the door and they squirt out the building.

Ryan knows the way, and James has gone this way once before. Hector follows, in bewilderment, jabbering, "Where the fuck are we going?" The corner of the gym and the main building is where the service trucks deliver the food for the cafeteria.

James says to Ryan, "You got any money I can have?" in a whining voice.

Ryan says, "Fuck you, you're such a mooch; I lent you five bucks last week."

"Where we going?" Hector whines. The boys stop by a wall of brick, bumping into each other abruptly.

Ryan points to a large church across the street. "We cross here, cut through the church basement door and pop out over there." He points to his left. "Then we're practically in town," Ryan announces with authority. They bolt across the street to the east.

They continue running until they get to the stairway leading to a basement door. It smells musty, and there are old leaves in the clogged drain. The snow is mostly melted from the snowstorm the night before. It is all wet and musty. James creeps back up the stairs, looks back and gives a thumbs-up gesture. Once in the church, the boys run down the narrow hallways, not knowing exactly where they are going, but knowing the general northerly direction they need to go in. Hector puts his hand on James's shoulder as they run. James swings his arm back to shrug Hector's hand off. He looks back with an annoyed glare.

The boys pop out another door, facing north, and laugh out loud. Exhilarated, they slow from a run to a couple of skips, and then start to walk. They know that they are in the clear now. Ryan walks proud, with a smirk on his face.

Mrs. G, overwhelmed, heads off down the hall to find Bob Brown, the gym teacher. Mr. Bob, as the kids call him, has a plan period this afternoon. He is nowhere to be found, so she asks Jay where he is. "He's subbing for Taylor—remember?"

"Oh yeah; I called that in. She's out for a training for the new math curriculum. But the sub never showed, so Brown is subbing," she says in one long breath.

Flustered, Mrs. G returns to the office to man the phones. She hasn't even tallied the absences, and she knows kids are ditching. She will never get time to call all the parents of all those kids who are gone. She comes up with an idea to call the School Resource Officer who has an office at the school. She calls Joan, the financial secretary. "Hey, can I talk to Brian, I've got some kids ditching," she says with exasperation in her voice. Joan explains he's teaching Mr. Hunter's Street Law class because Hunter is also at a curriculum training.

Jon Stufa is standing at the head of a long wooden table at the district office. Mr. Combe turns and says, "You're good to go, whenever you are ready."

Projected on the screen is a slide that says Curriculum Adoption. Combe sits down next to the superintendent. The educational consultant, Joel Haustoria, is sitting to his right. The superintendent says to Haustoria, "We haven't seen you since August. How are things looking?"

"I just met yesterday, in Denver, with Congressmen Jones and Smith."

"So, does that mean we are initiating the statewide release of this curriculum?"

"Hopefully. It looks good. First the new tests this year, and next year we release your schools' curriculum data with the test results."

"I see."

"Is the funding statewide?"

"It should be finalized with the senators and congressmen and Bradmoor Publishing soon."

Combe turns and says to Haustoria, "We got the data and slides you sent. I think you'll like the way Jon and I put it together."

"Excellent. The senators and congressmen are very keen on this—it being midterm elections next year and all."

The lights are turned off and the superintendent turns and says, "Okay everyone let's have a seat."

Stufa starts up, "Today we are going to be intentionally unpacking the new curriculum in an informed way…" He stands there looking down at his laptop which displays a colorful slide showing children smiling and engaged in a classroom. The image is projected on the screen behind him. Both his hands move in circular motions in the air and his voice rings with a soft tone and resounding confidence. On his laptop screen, facing him, is a rippling greenish-black image of a monstrous creature with two animal faces. The beast's two hands move around and its head vibrates in jerky motions. The creature is picking up small rabbit-like animals and dropping them into a cavernous opening in the ground where a serpent-like creature is devouring them. White mist floats and curves over sinuous green mountain ridges, like a thin sheer cloth loosely draped over a beautiful naked woman. His hands continue to move, his voice sings, as bright blue and pink images are projected behind him.

37

ROOF TOP

George Caleb Bingham's painting *Fur Traders Descending the Missouri* shows an idyllic scene of two individuals floating downstream with the bright billowing clouds symbolizing a warm harmonious relationship with the opening freedom of the West. The silhouette of a tethered cat-like black animal is an ominous and realistic element within the scene. It is romantic and inviting, reminiscent of Tom Sawyer and Huck Finn.

Ryan, James, and Hector make their way into town. The afternoon is sunny and warming up. Most of the snow from the night before has melted, except in the shade of buildings and trees. Soon winter will set in, but for now, in the ever-shortening days of late October, an in-between exists. In the morning the world is dark, cold, winter-like and frozen; then it gives way to crisp late fall sun in the afternoon.

At the corner 7-Eleven store, the boys purchase all the junk food they can. They stuff it into two packs with thick string chords for arm straps. The strings cinch down at the top and close tight. The packs hang low on Ryan and Hector's backs. From there they wander down sidewalks past storefronts to the main alley. Down the alley they cut to the right and to the back of the hardware store. Here the store has a steel dumpster with a metal lid. With a quick gliding lunge, James leaps up the four and a half feet to the top of the lid, then lunges upright and takes a big step and without losing momentum grabs a two-inch pipe on the side of the brick wall. With one big pull, he hoists himself up to the low roof of the shed-like extension from the back of the hardware store. Ryan follows slowly and methodically the same route. Hector, more muscular and stockier, is far less graceful, thumping up to both knees to the top of the dumpster, and then hesitating at the pipe going up to the low roof. Ryan says, "Fuck, dude, keep it quiet, man."

From the first story roof there is a ladder up the next brick wall to the second story rooftop. The boys plop down, facing south, against the back of the façade wall of the storefront. Together they sit on the dry black asphalt rooftop in the warm Colorado sun.

Here on their rooftop perch they extract sixteen-ounce bottles of soda. Hector drinks a large energy drink. Food, drinks and cell phones are scattered about as the boys sit eating, drinking and texting. In about twenty minutes they pull out vaporizers and smoke and laugh away. Billowing clouds of steam dissipate into the cool air. The wall of the façade, about four feet tall, feels so warm on their backs. The metal ignitor glows for a fraction of the second, heats the liquid and delivers the flavored nicotine. The steam dissipates. The boys laugh.

38

THREE-THIRTY-ONE

After lounging around on the rooftop, the boys decide to get some more nicotine cartridges before heading to soccer practice. Being underage, it's always an ordeal and it takes quite a bit of arguing and strategizing. They approach the 7-Eleven from the pedestrian bridge. They stop at the back corner by the dumpster and scope out the situation.

"Okay, man, here's the ten bucks. Now go up and ask someone," Ryan says.

Hector looks back over his shoulder across a bridge. "How about that person?"

"No, too old." James says.

"Well then, who?"

"Can't your cousin just sell it to us?"

"No, no, there's cameras in the store and he can lose his job."

Ryan, pointing, says, "That dude pumping gas."

"Okay, I got this," James says as he grabs the ten-dollar bill from Ryan's hand.

"Be cool, Mali, be cool."

"Yeah, right." James walks up, explains what he wants to the guy and hands him the ten-dollar bill. He stands there at the gas pumps by the hood of the guy's car. The guy exits the building, hands James two nicotine cartridges for the vaporizers, opens the car door, plops in the seat and starts the car. "Hey man, what about the change?" The man smiles and drives away.

"But, what the fuck. Really!"

Back at the dumpsters, James is pissed off, and explains to the guys how they got two cartridges that cost seven dollars for ten dollars.

"Man, why didn't you get the change?"

"But, he just smiled and drove away."

"Let's get back to school for soccer practice."

"No, I want to go talk to my cousin, Jesus."

Jesus stands there at the counter, in his red and blue 7-Eleven work shirt. Hector and the boys go into the 7-Eleven and explain to Jesus what just happened. Jesus smiles and says, "Well, boys—3:31."

"What?"

"You see, it's now after school—you know 3:31—when the real lessons occur." Hector and Ryan laugh at James.

James says one last emphatic, "Fuck! The motherfucker took our money."

"Yeah, 3:31, man."

"Ah, fuck you guys."

At that time Ryan sees the girls walking and says, "Oh yeah, I been wantin' to talk to Helen."

Ryan skips on over across the parking lot. "Hey, Helen, you comin' to the game tomorrow?"

"Hey, Ryan, ah maybe." After that, Ryan is all smiles and floating high, jabbering away.

Then a car with senior guys pulls up. "Hey ladies you want a ride back up to school?" The girls jump in, leaving Ryan just standing there on the sidewalk. Inside the 7-Eleven, James turns to Hector and Jesus and says, "3:31." They all laugh in unison.

Laughing, they say, "Yeah—3:31."

39

WHAT'D YOU CALL
MY MOMMA?

It is the first full week of school. Students are still realigning their schedules, mostly in an attempt at being in the same class as their friends. This is a learned strategy, which works well at small high schools like Elysium Hills.

On the commute in, Tyndall gazes over at the horses in a pasture. In a small coral a horse shuffles its unshod feet in the bare dirt. Around the horse, red dust hangs backlit in the morning light. A man walks along a small irrigation canal. He is wearing blue jeans with hip waders and a tan shirt and has a shovel on his shoulder. A magpie flies across the road and proceeds across the pasture; its wings rhythmically blink black and white as it flies across the pasture. It alights on the coral fence next to the horse.

The bird looks over the back of the neck of the horse and sees stiff hairs lining the edge of the horse's ear and its wet round eye has prominent red-brown eyelashes. It also sees wicked sharp seeds and the barbed awns of dry cheat grass sticking out from the horse's lips with a bit of dried blood. Together they look across the fence at other horses in the expansive green pasture with water spilling over from the small irrigation ditch.

Tyndall, after all these years, has a strategy of keeping a couple of seats empty in the front of the class. If anyone causes trouble or comes in late, they get the "best" seat up front. But first period class has thirty-three students; all twenty-nine desks are occupied plus the back table and the three side tables. All great plans, yeah right.

Here on day one of class, all great plans are out the window. He knows that he has to be on top of this group. Fortunately, he is awake, and the students are not—yet.

A skinny young boy comes into class and says to Tyndall, "Yo, Fool, where's my seat?"

Tyndall responds, pointing to the seating chart on the screen in the front of the class.' "What's your name?"

"William."

"It's here, and don't call me 'Fool.'"

William plops down in his desk in the back row, and says, "So, Fool, do we get books or anything?"

"Yes, once we get up and started in a couple of days."

When class starts and everyone is seated Tyndall starts up, and William asks a question with a derogatory tone: "Yo, Fool…"

By day three, Tyndall has already moved William to a front desk for calling him a fool—as if it was a title. This morning at the start of class, William is absent. Tyndall thinks to himself, good, maybe he has moved to another class and teacher. Fifteen minutes into class, William floats in with a pass from the front office. Tyndall, annoyed, grabs the pass and with a dry erase marker draws a smiley face on it, and says, "Put this on your fridge at home." And then he says, "You lose nine minutes of your ten-minute break."

William, with a scowl on his face, says, "But. It says excused."

"Doesn't matter, you lose your break. Don't be late." Tyndall quickly barks.

Then he proceeds with the lesson; on the screen is an image of a figure from the book and he is outlining on the board the defining characteristics of life. He turns and looks at William and says, "You need to write this down." William sits there in the front seat in the center of the class, with his legs stretched out straight. He has no pencil or paper. He just scowls and obstinately stares at Tyndall.

"Now, William, get this written down." He just sits there, stares forward, not even a gesture. Tyndall, in midsentence taps his desk. He continues, now pointing to the slide on the screen next to the board, of an image of a cell, saying, "All life is comprised of the small units, called cells." Turning and facing the large class, annoyed now, that William still hasn't gotten paper and pencil out. William remains defiant, feet out, arms folded, staring straight ahead with deep set dark brown eyes with heavy eyelids. His thin face with prominent cheekbones and a square chin made more noticeable with his scowl. Tyndall, upon turning, takes a deep breath while dropping his head down and looking at the white linoleum floor. "Come on William—Yo momma could get a pencil out faster than you."

Immediately William lunges out of his desk, flying forward. His desk slides back and slams into the other desk, causing a text book to crash to the ground. William in one motion chest-butts Tyndall and screams in his face, "What'd you call my momma?"

Tyndall stands tall and motionless, William is bouncing up and down in front of him. "Now William, chill out man. No one is saying."

"What'd you fucking say!?" William screams back.

Tyndall asserts himself now and in the direct powerful voice, "Be cool man, it's just a joke. Hey, watch it, now—we're not going there. Sit down."

With a cross look, William says, "But you said…" Then he starts pumping his fist at his side.

"Fucking take it easy!"

"No, you said…"

The class is mesmerized; there is a deep moaning ultrasonic sound resonating through the floor of the room. A deep feeling, felt in the bones and not the head. The tension hums—an inaudible tone. The girls in the front desks are recoiled back, knees up and arms pulled in and up by their ears. In the back of the classroom, James and Ryan are sitting and Ryan loudly says, "Five bucks William kicks his ass."

James quickly says, "No, Tyndall will fuck him up."

"Ten bucks."

"You're on, man." Money is slammed on the desktop.

Tyndall pointing says, "Sit! It ain't going there today."

A silence falls; all eyes are looking at Tyndall and William squaring off in front of the class. William, tall and skinny, fists clenched, fidgeting. Tyndall stands hard, left shoulder to William, head up and pulled back, feet apart, his eyes looking hard at William's eyes, not flinching. He takes a breath in when

William does, and breathes out in rhythm and looks straight into his brown eyes—a lighter brown now, with a slight star pattern. He breathes in at the same time as William and then exhales. Tyndall gestures with his left hand out and away, hand open, and smiles with Williams exhale. Williams's shoulders drop. William reaches back and puts his right hand on the desk and with a flop, falls into the chair blinking and breathing hard.

In the back of the class Ryan says, "Man, no fight."

Tyndall takes another quick breath then says to the boys in back of the class "Hey! Keep quiet." James, with the back of his hand, whacks his friend on the shoulder.

Tyndall turns toward the board, he smiles to himself and under his breath says, "Fuck!" He inhales deeply, eyes closed, his back to the students, a slight smirk on his face. He thinks, *Fuck Lord mercy, day five of the school year and day three of class.* He jots down the corresponding page numbers from the book on the board. Standing at the board, he turns and says in a weak voice, "Now let's read this."

At lunch James and Ryan walk into Tyndall's room. Tyndall looks up from his desk while chewing his lunch, and says, "So you guys are laying down bets. What the fuck!" Tyndall exclaims emphatically, with his hand on top of his head, gesturing outward.

"Well, we were just betting," James says sheepishly.

"Hey, old dog always wins. You want to step outside into my office and I'll demonstrate?" Tyndall says, gesturing with his finger out the open door in back of his desk.

"No, we're good."

Tyndall says, "What the fuck is wrong with that kid?"

James says, "I don't know. He doesn't dress out in gym class either. Just does everything in jeans."

Ryan exclaims, "Oh, he's from L.A., gots an ankle bracelet on."

"How do you know?"

"I saw it the first day of class, when we sat on the bleachers," Ryan says defensively.

Tyndall looks up, swallowing a bite of his sandwich and taking a sip of tea, and says, "Oh, so that's it—a court order."

Ryan says, "A what?"

"The judge orders the kid to go to school or go to jail. So that's it," Tyndall says, looking up at the ceiling and rubbing his head with his hand. Tyndall thinks, *No information from the school or the principals. Class of 33 and he has to go through this dance. Blind. Not informed. Here he has his career threatened by a troubled kid, all the while, put in a situation like…175 days of school left to go.*

40

READING OF THE CODEX
(TESTING SEQUENCE)

Three days into their journey, Anci and Cualli stop to rest along a stream. The terrain is steep with lush tropical vegetation and steep foreboding canyons. After a swim and lying on a large warm rock, Cualli gets dressed and looks hard at the pack with the Codex. The skinny faces of the coati, with round eyes, made of blue colored stone beads, look back at him. He thinks, All that has happened in the past two months; the unraveling of his world. Actually, an unprecedented wave that would cover all. The membranous wings spread; light shines through the thin gray skin. Blood vessels, bone, and sinew are visible. The wings spread and envelop all. Cualli blinks slowly and long, and when his eyes are closed he still sees the horror. With a shudder, he opens his eyes.

He opens the pack, unhitching the antler buttons underneath the leather thong. The Codex, really just a large square book, feels heavy in his hands. At that moment Anci, the warrior, sees him and screams, "No, no you cannot." Running up to the rock, she lunges for the book; Cualli turns and flanks her with his muscular back. Her knife and belt are still on the rock at the stream side. Larger and stronger than her, Cualli keeps shifting and pivoting, holding the Codex out. Trained for battle, she deftly grabs his free wrist, counters his pivot and sticks her leg out and slams Cualli to the ground. He hits the ground with a grunt.

"No, we can't," Anci says.

"He never said..."

"We can't."

Cualli continues, "But why?"

"Not for your eyes."

"Who said, who?"

Anci straddles Cualli, submissive on his back, arms above his head, book in hand. She loosens her grip, he hands her the book. Cualli pleads, "Show me."

"No."

Cualli continues, "come on show me, what does it mean? They never said, we couldn't…. Think about it."

"No, not for your eyes. You do not know how to read it."

"So, show me."

The warrior explains, "No. You are not trained."

Cualli pleads, "I see, I see a dark blanket—when I close my eyes. What is it?"

Anci stands up, Cualli smiles. She walks over to a large boulder in the sun. In the lush canyon where the river comes down they can hear a beautiful and strange bird song. A long, high note, then a descending set of whistles, varied tones of great virtuosity, ending in the loose trill. It is the most haunting, beautiful, ethereal sound. She puts on her belt and knife, still scowling at Cualli.

"What bird is that? Is it a God? I have never heard it before," Cualli says.

Anci says, "That is a bird that is never seen; only heard. They say it is small and gray in color, yet its voice…a voice to stun all with its warbling beauty. Do not look for it, you cannot see it. It must be warm today, it sings out of season."

"The world burns behind us, we head to a far-off place. Show me, it is a sign," Cualli says.

"It's always in the mists on the sides of the mountain or by a waterfall that they sing. Where you cannot go." Cualli turns to run upstream, to find the bird. "Cualli, no." She lightly grabs his arm, slides her hand down and takes his hand. "That bird cannot be seen. The world burns in my dreams too; something has come, come from out of the cave. It does not go back; a veil of softness disguises it."

"I see it too." Cualli smiles. "It is winter, yet it is so warm today. Show me."

On the warm rock, streamside, Anci unfolds the Codex. She remembers her first teacher explaining the symbols and meanings. Water rhythmically sings as the winter day warms with the sun. She continues and explains, "The first pages—here, are about the time. The time it was written, the time and the cycles of events. Here these circles and dots on the outside indicate the days." There are thirteen small rectangles on the outside edge of the page; some with four red circles and others with nine green circles. They look like modern dominoes.

"It shows a year as we know it, from the spring planting to spring planting. But here, it shows nine phases of the moon, for the gestation of a baby in the womb. Strange it is out of sequence, the nine months start in autumn, here," she says pointing. "Here. The nine months of time are broken into four minor gods, and one major god appearing here at the spring equinox. The gods take measures of something. I have never known time sequences outlined as such. Nor have I known these gods, gods sent to measure. This one, with the deer-face and the bat-face on the same head, is the Two-handed One. The serpent, in the cave below, is the Overlord—hidden. A dictate of time, out of season. So curious. Four measures taken in nine months, plus one major measure. The major measure has its roots entangled in all the days. But the roots go up, up from the snake-like Overlord. But these beginning pages are the time, the time sequence, not the story."

Her face is contorted and strained while reading the beginning pages. Though formally trained to read, the glyphs are odd—especially the time sequences. So many references to the one major measure. There were so many glyphs of rabbits, indicating children. The meaning of time sequences, age of the rabbits and fate; the fate of the measures to come.

They take a break to spear prawn-like shrimp in the stream. Together they wade, plunging long pointed six-foot sticks with split trident-like ends into the water. The shrimp are skewered on sticks and cooked over a streamside fire. Then they continue to read the Codex. That afternoon the pair skip to the heart of the story. She points to the central page with one figure. "Here,

here is the story, the story and the players. This is the Overlord, here in the cave, and the roots. Same time symbols. See here, this is the Two-Handed One. He has two animal faces, but its arms and hands are human. The hand folded on top of the scepter means a value, something that is measured.

The next page has two rectangular glyphs on it, one with the Overlord and one with the Two-Handed One. The Overlord holds the Two-Handed One forward while remaining hidden in the Earth where the water flows under.

Anci continues, "The Two-Handed One oversees the children in the real world. His hands are always in motion; his body rocks back and forth with many jerky gestures. One side of his face is toward the sun and shines as a buck in velvet; the warm soft face of a deer, with long ears and glistening soft brown fur. He has round pleasing eyes that are inviting and wet.

"But here, the other side does not face the light. It is connected to the cave. It is the face of a bat, contorted with many folded membranous skin flaps and big ears with many strange inner folds. The bat's eyes are small and round. His face turns often in jerky motions. Look, one hand is in the cave, the Underworld, connected to the Overlord, here. The other hand is in the real world, and holds a rabbit, a child. The next glyph shows the sign for the sound of flowing water; this is his voice. And that sign is of a bat with its wings spread out, to cover what is hidden."

41

HIDDEN PREDATOR

Lunch is a special time. A time to find your friends, laugh and be free. After the initial fury and fray at the release from class, each person settles into a place. Every day "the crew," as they call themselves, tumbles haphazardly into Mr. Jay's room. The room is near the end of the hall, hot by late morning with large southeast facing windows. Unlike some teachers, he keeps his shades open. There is a small, inefficient microwave on the back counter. Mr. Jay sits at his tall front desk on a high chair, eats and grades papers or reads the newspaper. It is also his time.

Why or how the kids appear to eat, and mostly goof off, is unknown. Jay does not invite them here, or share food, or even advertise it. It is just a space which is safe sunny and warm with big tables. The crew precipitates out, unpacks lunch bags and drops down lunch trays. Their heads fly back as they laugh generously, potato chips dropping to the floor. A soccer ball bounces off James's foot; a constellation of dust flies outward expanding and swirling, backlit. Hector is transfixed by the beauty. He says nothing; the room is absolutely still for a moment—just the tumble of existence. James jives Hector about some girl, while Louie steals a chip. Hector suddenly, in a spastic gesture, falls out of his chair and the room erupts in boisterous laughter. Jay hardly looks up from his crumb covered newspaper. It is like the singing of birds in the morning—it is just there.

Sialia, Sandy, and Helen head out the front doors of school. "How much time do we have?" Helen says.

"About fifteen minutes," Sandy responds.

"I love this time of the year. Look! The dandelions are blooming over there," Sialia adds.

As the girls exit the building, educational consultant Joel Haustaria is entering. He is wearing a neat pale-yellow oxford dress shirt untucked and faded black jeans. He is in his early thirties, six feet tall, with thick brown hair loosely combed back. He smiles at the girls as they pass in the door entrance. The girls laugh and smile back. Sialia says, "Oh Helen, he's checking you out. That happens wherever we go. It's probably your new haircut."

Helen has a new hair style. Just in the last week she cut her hair short, dyed it back to its natural dark color with added highlights. She is an attractive young lady with a long neck and elegant features like a ballerina.

For the teachers who are new to the district, even ones that have taught for decades, this afternoon has been set aside for the monthly new teacher induction training. Every new high school teacher in the district has been pulled from their respective classrooms for an afternoon of training. Dr. Stufa and Joel Haustoria stand and greet the teachers as they file into the library. The teachers proceed inward as if doing penance with smiles on their faces. Stufa hands each incoming teacher a different colored sticky note with a number on it. Music is playing from a speaker, there are colored marker pens and colored paper sitting on the various tables. Stufa starts talking. "Today we will intentionally break into groups and share best practices with one another. Now when the music stops rotate groups…"

Melt the lead, and by mere contrivance, forge it into gold.

JR often eats outside in the front of the school. He tucks himself into a side bench along one of the footpaths, next to the community garden. He can see the east entrance doors and hear the bell from there. He chooses to remove himself from the commotion and noise. The garden is not well kept, but the flowers push their way up through the leaves and grass. It is about ten square feet, circular with round rocks around the perimeter. There is a large pear tree blooming in the center. The time when JR sits and eats is perhaps the only peaceful and quiet time in his day.

Along the side of the bench, the first flowers of spring are growing. In the lawn the dandelions are popping up. The three girls are collecting dandelions and bending the stems back through a hole torn in the stem to weave a headband-like crown of gold. "Here's what you do—tear a hole in the stem and loop this other one through here and just keep going," Sialia says.

"Like this?" Sandy asks.

"Yeah—you got it."

Sialia is the first to finish and crowns herself with the golden wreath of flowers. It stands out against her jet-black hair. Then she helps Helen finish her crown. She says, "I crown thee Princess Helen, slayer of all the boys with her beauty." As she lays the crown upon her friend's head, she silently smiles while looking at JR eating alone on the bench.

Next to the bench in the garden are some wallflowers blooming. Each plant has several erect stems with a tight bunch of yellow flowers at the top. As JR looks down to his right at the round flowers cluster, he sees something odd. He has to move over, stare down and look hard. Then something appears, then he loses sight of it, then it appears. In the flower cluster, on one flower, is a large yellow spider with long legs stretched out. It does not move.

The crab spider is an ambush predator. The beast that JR is observing has a large round abdomen, about the size of one of the round flower petals. Its four pairs of legs circle around its body and appear very crab-like. The spider does not weave a web. Instead it sits motionless in a flower waiting for its prey—an unsuspecting bee or fly. The color of this individual is almost exactly the same pale yellow as the wallflower petals. Only when it moves, crab-like sideways, does JR see it. He pulls out his phone and photographs it. It moves again as he lowers the phone.

The small sweat bee has a bright metallic green abdomen and a hairy light brown thorax; she flies around in search of food. She will gather pollen and nectar as food for her brood of young. She nests in a solitary hole in the bare ground. She lands in the flower, circles around the pollen laden anthers, grabs one or two anthers, rolls on her back and furiously pumps her hairy legs to strip the pollen off. She then circles around to the next anthers and does the same. Stopping, she cleans off her body and wings with her forelegs in a front to the back motion. The bee is packing the pollen onto special structures of hairs on her back legs, called pollen baskets. This is how the bee carries the pollen back to her nest. There, in her solitary tube-like hole in the soil she will deposit a loaf of pollen and nectar and one egg. The bee will seal the cell with a thin plaster of mud. Then off she goes again to tirelessly collect more pollen and nectar to provision a new cell-like chamber with another egg.

She flies off from the nest hole in search of more food for her young. She searches by using olfactory and visual cues. The wallflower is more than just yellow, it has nectar guides, often invisible to the human eye. The nectar guides are lines and patterns on the petals that are almost arrow-like and point to the flowers' nectarines. These features can be difficult to see, because bees can also see colors in additional wavelengths, such as ultraviolet. The insect can perceive what we humans cannot comprehend. Perhaps van Gogh had such vision, a perception of reality entirely unique. So penetrating.

The crab spider appears to JR, by his unique perception, the same yellow as the flowers. To the unsuspecting bee, it also appears as the same. These electromagnetic waves of energy bouncing back off the yellow petals and yellow spider, at a specific speed, are perceived by neurons in the bee's tiny ganglion of a brain. The crab spider is advertising the same generous reward of vitality and life as the flower. It is an insidious predator, sitting motionless, poised, legs spread out, waiting to quickly grasp its unsuspecting prey.

JR witnesses the green bee being grabbed by the spider. His head pulls back, and he reaches for his phone to take another picture. He thinks, *Mr. Tyndall will think this is cool. Whoa, so uncool to the bee. It didn't even know it was there. Brutal man, all so hidden.*

42

EMPTY MAGENTA BOX

Tyndall walks up to the front of the classroom. He leans to his right on the tall demonstration table at the front of the classroom. It is second period, a big class with thirty-four students. The group is remarkably functional, albeit high-energy. The boys in the front of the class are tossing a tape ball into a large plastic bowl.

"Gimme it," Jason shouts.

"Here," Rodrigo says. Then he says, "No, here," holding a roll of masking tape in his hand. He is feeding out long strips of tape to Jason, who then wraps it around the makeshift ball. Rodrigo wears a t-shirt with the pink, gold and blue face of Marilyn Monroe on a dull-gold background, a cheap replica of one of Andy Warhol's silkscreens.

Tyndall sighs, puts his mug of tea down, and silently holds out his hand. Jason reluctantly puts the ball in his hand. Tyndall then turns to his right and holds out his other hand to Rodrigo. "Don't hesitate Rigo, or you're eating lunch with me."

The roll of tape is placed on the front demonstration table, next to a deer skull, a fake wooden snake, and a couple of conch shells. The rest of the class shuffles in and gets seated. A couple of silent gestures by Tyndall and everyone is seated. Tyndall walks up and down the aisles, explaining the day's project. "Today we will review cell parts and organelles, watch about a five-minute video that takes us flying through the cell, then take a quick quiz and after that we'll start our cell posters." As he walks up and down the aisles he taps on a cell phone sitting on top of a desk. The kid quickly grabs it and puts it in her notebook. "No—in your pack," he says, pointing. Other kids put their phones into their pockets or packs. Some of the girls stick the phones down their shirts into their bras. These girls have learned that this is an awkward, even outright taunting gesture, to a male teacher. Tyndall shakes his head, looking down the girl's cleavage, turns, sips his tea, and continues a day's instructions. Then he says, "All right go. Remember your kindergarten skills now, children."

Tyndall tears off large three- by four-foot pieces of yellow poster paper from a large roll on the countertop by the window. The frogs sit silently on the bottom of the tank. Watching. Gazing upward and forward, never blinking. Four kids are absent and the students scatter. Tyndall thinks, *Yeah, four students are absent, this is just so, so very manageable.* He says to one group of girls, "No. You cannot work in a group of three, groups of two, or on your own next to a friend."

The girl who asked turns, giving a quick tisk sound.

"Hey don't do that to me."

"But…"

"Not today." Tyndall then turns to Jarret and says, "Don't take the whole box of color markers—like some chimpanzee hoarding."

"Can we work in the hall?" the young lady says in a pleasant almost flirting way, smiling at Tyndall.

"Yeah, but all of you have your books open, no phones, or you lose your privileges." Tyndall thinks to himself: He's not even supposed to cover this chapter. But it's so foundational, for the subsequent material. It is covered in seventh grade science. But he knows from years of experience that the kids don't actually remember the material. More importantly, about half the students never had seventh-grade science. For some, now in tenth grade, it is their first science class ever. They were yanked out of science classes by the administration in seventh grade to take more language classes. There are no state science tests in seventh grade. But there are state reading and writing tests. The principals there at the middle school know that those test scores are reflected in their pay and job security. So they schedule those kids deficient in language skills out of science and other subjects. But in Tyndall's mind, it is a good unit. Lots of opportunity for students to be successful. Besides, some of the best lab days are spent looking at real cells under the microscope.

Toward the last minutes of class, things start to break down. Tyndall strategically places himself in a location in the center of the room. Kids are sprawled out on the floor, drawing, coloring, and describing the cell parts. "Hey Janie, talk and color at the same time. Turn the page—there," he says, pointing to the book.

Then he floats back out to the hall and continues. He sits on the floor and stretches his hamstring, grabbing his right foot with his right hand, all the while talking to Raul and James about soccer.

"Why you stretch, Tynd?" Raul says.

"You guys make me tired, and my feet hurt from standing all day. That's why I wear running shoes."

Raul says with a big smirk on his face, "Sucks getting old."

Tyndall is quick to jibe back, "Sucks being a teenager." James smiles as he colors the cell red against the bright yellow paper.

Alisha, the girl who stuffed her cell phone in her shirt, is working at the large lab table in the room. There are about twenty-five minutes left in class. At that time Alisha's mom sticks her head in the door, waving to Tyndall, who is sitting in a chair in the middle of the room amongst three groups of students. He is laughing at some joke that Sandy has made.

"Oh, I just have to give this to Alisha."

"Ah, okay, sure," Tyndall says pointing to his right behind the chair. He thinks, *Parents, any adult for that matter, are not supposed to be roaming the hallways. Who's manning the front office?*

Alisha's mom bursts in, all bubbly and exuberant, and says hi to some kids. Then she says, "Oh here honey, it came today—express." She extracts a textbook sized box that is bright white with orange and bright magenta designs bursting out around a picture of a sleek Apple iPhone. The girls erupt into a minor frenzy with screams and hair being flung back. The couple of dozen students working in the room all start jabbering away.

Tyndall is clearly irked at the disruption. He's thinking, *Those fucking devices, trying to work here, keep it together.* He knows that Alisha's mom is a white "power parent." He says to the girls, "All right let's get back to work.

Now Alisha, put it in your pack until lunch in half an hour."

"Tynd, there's only twenty minutes left."

Another student says, "In your pack."

Scowling, Alisha obliges.

Tyndall walks out into the hallway with Alisha's mom, as she jabbers away about the volleyball game the previous night. Tyndall smiles, and walks down the hall saying, "Have a nice day. Come by any time, no worries." As he turns and walks back into his room he thinks, *Really this isn't grade school, perhaps bring cookies next time.*

When he returns, Alisha has torn the bright box open and is extracting the phone. The commotion is evident with boys hurdling desks. Tyndall says, "Put it away, play with it at lunch.

A boy from behind says, "But, Tynd, it's an iPhone 3B."

Another student says, "How'd you get it?"

Alisha bursts into an explanation about how they ordered it at midnight two nights before, and had it shipped express.

"If you're not going to put it away, I'll take it. And you can get it after school," Tyndall says.

Alisha bursts out with an audible sigh, then immediately looks down at the phone and starts pushing buttons.

Sandy and James are standing next to each other. Sandy has a shoebox of markers in her hand. James is dropping a handful of markers into the box with a limp hand. He is looking up and thinking about soccer. It is that moment, like on the ball field, where you see the play unfold. But there is a moment of hesitation, almost disbelief, at the way the play is in favor of the opponent. James sees the soccer ball bounce, then skip left, as he lunges hard to his right. The ball squirts straight down the sideline. Surprised, with angst on his face. Mud and grass fly. Grunts come from his opponent. He slips on the muddy ground, strains hard on his legs, and with hands splayed, spins around. As he pivots and runs his muscular arms fly upward, veins bulging in his forearm and biceps. Breathing in, he clenches his angular jaw.

Tyndall, takes the phone and drops it in his desk drawer. Alisha is scowling, with a tear falling down her cheek. "All right, let's clean up. Stack the posters here, we'll finish them next class."

He strolls assertively to the hall door and barks at the students in the hall to clean up. He resolutely goes to the front of the class and sits on the tall table, staring out at the commotion. "James, get that stuff, there," he says, pointing to a pile of open books and markers on the floor. He continues to babble about cell organelles and how the students need to focus on the functions, not worry about what color to draw it in. The class sits mostly silent in their seats. They know Tyndall is pissed off. It is awkward, strange to sit in a room crowded with teenagers and have it be silent. Besides, this is usually a fun class, not like this. A heavy pall descends. A frog silently swims to the surface, takes several breaths, then swims back under the submerged terra-cotta flowerpot at the bottom of the aquarium. Tyndall keeps the students seated and waits to release them. No one moves or says anything. Students stare at Tyndall, then back at the clock on the wall. Then he waves his arms emphatically out, and with a quick statement says, "Be gone."

On the soccer field a flurry of commotion breaks out in front of the goal. James catches up and blast the ball out into the crowd. His teammate in the goal pats James on the back, saying, "Nice."

Coach barks out, "Remember—squeeze the sideline."

"Yeah. Got it," James says, nodding his head up and down.

Alisha at first tries the cute girl's flirtatious approach. "Oh Tynd. Come on."

"I told you to put it away."

"But Tynd. Oh," as she cries looking up at Tyndall.

"You can get it after school. It's not up for discussion." Tyndall walks out into the hall and starts to walk away. Students are filing into his room to use a microwave to heat up their lunches. After Tyndall leaves the room Alisha walks up to Tyndall's desk and retrieves her new phone. The incessant use of these devices exasperates Tyndall. It's maddening how monstrous these teenagers are about these things. How dehumanizing.

43

CERULEAN BLUE TO ORANGE

At lunch, Sialia borrows JR's long skateboard. She, Sandy and Helen try to ride it at the same time. Sandy is seated on the back with Helen and Sialia standing on the skateboard as they glide down the sidewalk in front of school. The girls are laughing so hard that no one is in control as they careen down the walkway with people jumping out of the way. They crash dramatically, all splaying out on the grass. Helen laughs with her head down and eyes closed without making a sound. Sialia throws her head back roaring a boisterous cackle, while Sandy rolls around on the ground with her mouth wide open and screeching a high pitch laugh.

The girls come tumbling into the art room, their arms all entangled and still giggling so hard that they can barely stand up. It is a brilliant sunny day and the room glows in the afternoon sun. From the layered atmosphere of the sun, energy is emitted. Gas flows outward from the corona at super high speeds. From the surface of the sun a violent eruption of particles and radiation are emitted. These charged ions fly outward from the sun. Solar wind bathes each planet in a flood of particles. The charged particles are deflected by the Earth's magnetic field, the magnetosphere. It is a counter-wave of energy, making life possible on this tiny blue speck in space.

Light shines through the big glass windows of the art room at the corner of the building. A shiny blue fly buzzes frantically against one of the windows. Sialia sits at a high table on a round stool with a face painted on it. There on the tabletop is a shoe box full of small colored pieces of glass used for making stained glass windows. She is tumbling a blue piece of glass about one inch long in her right hand. She holds it up to the window so that it is backlit. The blue glass is wavy looking inside and a bit opaque. She steps over to the direct light shining bright through the window onto the countertop. There, in the warm light shining on her hand and the blue glass, she sees her hand's shadow and the light refracting through the glass. She twists her hand and slides a white piece of paper under it on the countertop. The light hits the far side of the blue glass, and on the near side, shines through as orange light. A wavy bright triangle of orange. Sialia blinks and twists her hand in a half circle motion. Perplexed, she turns and holds it up to the fluorescent light in the ceiling. Nothing; it is just bright blue glass.

On the other side of the room JR is painting. Ms. Rayleigh is gesturing and pointing at something next to JR. He is painting a blue damselfly on a green blade of grass. "I saw them along the canal last week while walking home," he says in a slow drawl. "Tynd gave me a net and helped me pin them. But the blue color's not the same. He points to the two dainty insects pinned in a small four- by six-inch tray with white foam on the bottom. He looks over his shoulder at Rayleigh, clearly frustrated. "That's not the blue they were yesterday, they've faded," he says directly to her.

"No. I've seen them, they're bright, almost iridescent blue. Not brown blue," Rayleigh says, with a puzzled look on her face.

"How do I do this—make that bright blue?" JR asks, pointing wildly with the paint brush at his painting.

Rayleigh responds, "Here you need to mix a better blue. I've got some other blue here, in my paints." With gliding steps, she floats across the room, and noisily fumbles through a plastic red fishing box with tubes of paint. "Here I'll show you. This one," she says, fumbling, and dropping the tube. "No, not that one. Where is it? Oh, it's around here somewhere. Come on. Cerulean blue, chromium." There is a #P 36 on the side of the tube. "Now mix this with titanium white. But just here add the smallest amount of cadmium yellow primrose." The tube has the same number system that identifies the color as #A 35. It is nearly squeezed empty and stained all bright yellow on the sides.

"Now mix these, just a little bit of blue," she says.

"How's that? It's too dark."

Gesturing with both arms, Rayleigh says, "Okay, here, little more white right here like this. That's it. Right about there—now paint it on in segments, like what you see on the insect; there, in segments, count them," as she points to the tray with the delicate insects. Then she says, "Now let that dry a minute and I'll show you a trick".

Sialia, listening in asks, "What is cadmium, and why is it in the name?"

"Oh, that's the element, a metal, which holds the color and makes a pigment," Rayleigh sings out, while giving a scowl to two students out of their seats on the other side of the room.

"Are there metals in all pigments?" Sialia asks.

"Not all, but many. For example, titanium is in pure white. Titanium is a super strong metal, like they use in artificial hips and things like fighter jets," Rayleigh says, still looking across the room.

JR asks, "Why are there different numbers on each paint?"

With the singsong voice, Rayleigh says, "Oh, that's because we need to define a specific color. My yellow is not the same as your yellow in your eyes and your brain. So, they figured we needed a number to quantify it so as not to be biased."

"Bias—that's what Tynd talks about when we're doing experiments," Sialia says.

"Here, now let me show you that trick." Rayleigh says, gesturing with both arms. As she paints, she says, "First put some tiny flecks—give me the brush—of yellow on top of the blue. And a few pure white specks, like this." She waves one dexterous hand and gestures with her other hand, all while bending her torso in a sideways motion. Then she steps back boldly.

JR cries out, "But there is no yellow in these bugs!"

"Oh—you'll see. Wait for it," Rayleigh says. "Now put a few strokes of complementary color along the edge of the abdomen. Make it slightly more orange, now here, swish here." She paints the slightest yellow-orange brushstroke along the thin blue abdomen of the insect.

"Whoa," both JR and Sialia say together in one breath.

"It's all bright and pops out now," Sialia said.

"You try now JR," Rayleigh says as she hands the brush to JR.

JR says, "Opposite in back, but just a little—got it."

44

AINT GOT NO SIX

After school, Dr. Stufa approaches Tyndall in the hallway. "So, Mr. Tyndall, Mrs. Albertson called me saying something about a phone and her daughter."

"Well sir…," Tyndall starts to say.

Stufa interrupts him. "We've set up a meeting today at 4:30."

"But Jon, the girl was clearly disruptive, and disrespectful…"

Holding his hand up, Stufa turns to talk to a student in the hallway about a homecoming poster, then continues, "Well—we have a process here to go through." He says this with a circular motion of his right hand, like the wax on/wax off from the *Karate Kid* movie.

"Mr. Tyndall, can we get our poster?" Sandy says, tapping his shoulder.

"Oh, okay. Let's go find it," Tyndall says, turning as Stufa signs some clipboard held by Coach Brown. Brown looks at Tyndall, seeing the frustration on his face.

The meeting in Stufa's office starts at 4:45 because Alisha's mom is late. She eventually enters the room talking on her phone. Stufa starts up, "Now Mrs. Albertson informs me you took her daughter's new iPhone." Dr. Stufa's Harvard degree, in a cheap gold frame, hangs on the wall behind Mrs. Albertson. She is looking down at her phone. The brazen logo of the university is displayed as three open books on a crimson coat of arms. The VI on one open book and the RI in another are set evenly apart, like two unblinking eyes overlooking the meeting.

"Yes, I had informed Alisha…" Then Stufa's phone rings in his pocket. It is an annoying singsong ring tone of a popular Beatles song. Midsentence, Tyndall sits there as Stufa bumbles around with his phone. He is holding it out at arm's length, then bringing the device closer and tapping the screen as he tries to silence the phone. Tyndall is beside himself at the interruption, the off-key bastardization of a great song, bleeping out in some high-pitched key. He thinks, *It's a meeting, what the fuck—be professional.*

Tyndall starts up again. This time Alisha bursts in, wearing her volleyball workout gear: tiny black, overly tight spandex shorts with a short skintight pink sports bra as a top. "Oh, mom can I have twenty dollars for pizza tonight? Hi Mr. Tyndall," she says with a smile on her face.

"Hi," Tyndall says, blinking a long, slow blink.

Stufa then just skips over to Mrs. Albertson, who says, "Well all I did was drop off lunch, and Alisha's new phone." Alisha departs, snatching the twenty-dollar bill from her mom's hand. Mom's red manicured fingernails let it go, as the thin gold bracelet, with red rubies, hangs limp on her wrist.

Stufa continues, "Well, Mrs. Albertson, we have a series of steps and protocols for this—it's all outlined here." He hands her a sheet of paper with numbers and letters. "See here at step 2B."

Alisha's mom has her phone in her hand and is reading a text from her daughter. Then she looks down at the paper and says, "Oh here. Okay."

"Once this step is reached, then we come to this next step—3A. From there…," Dr. Stufa continues with his hand waving in a circular motion.

At that moment Mr. Combe, the assistant principal, enters the room with an open laptop in his hand. Everyone is introduced; Combe starts hammering away on the laptop. He interjects, "See here, I'm filling out the form…"

"I was just going over that."

Everything is repeated: Stufa's phone rings, a student walks in, Mrs. Albertson sends a text, the protocol steps are repeated—and one hour and fifteen minutes later Tyndall is back in his room looking at colored markers in a small pile on the floor, in the corner of the room. Outside there is a loud hissing sound. The grounds crew is blowing out the sprinklers for the winter. It is late fall now and the shadow from the western ridge descends on the building.

Tyndall looks long and hard at the discarded bright white box with colorful patterns on it strewn on the counter by the roll of yellow poster paper. The oversized box sits where Alisha left it. The box is ten times the size of the phone. It is folded in upon itself to provide a chamber to hold the phone in its plastic sleeve. Most of the box is empty space. Other smaller chambers are folded within, origami-like, to hold the charger and various other accessories, each in their own plastic sleeves. So much empty space. Empty. Bright. An ergonomically designed device held solidly within so much space. Empty. He thinks about what happened and what was said at the meeting.

Mrs. Albertson said, "They weren't doing much. Mr. Tyndall was just sitting there in the middle the room talking to the kids. There was stuff everywhere, and kids out of their seats. So, I just thought…"

Mr. Combe's phone vibrated on the desk…

Stufa's phone rang again…

The secretary waved through the window, holding a piece of paper in her hand. She entered and said, "Here, on the last line, sign here."

Stufa babbled on, pointing and waving. "Then on the last line we reach step 4E…and there you have it.…Here we have a process.…Well, Mr. Tyndall, we have a process, a set of steps…"

Zach Tyndall remembers blinking slowly, shoving a wooden number two pencil into his shirt pocket and walking away. Combe remained seated, thumping away on his keyboard.

James is running through a hard rain; the soccer field is mud and puddles. He is kicked in the leg, by his opponent. He rolls over on his back grasping his shin, pain and agony on his face. A driving rain is falling sideways. Players from both teams rumble on by, mud, grass, and cleats around his face. The rain is falling. Nothing stops. James rolls back up to his feet, limping, grasping his right shin. The referee runs by, saying to James, "Play on, son."

45

THE RETREAT

In the east wing of the Smithsonian Art Museum hangs the painting *Among the Sierra Nevada California* by Albert Bierstadt. Sialia is not there to see it, but is stuck in English class. Exams are almost finished and in a couple of days summer vacation will start. She peruses the internet and views the painting and reads the following label about the artist and the painting.

Gallery Label

Albert Bierstadt's beautiful crafted painting played to a hot market in the 1860s for spectacular views of the nation's frontiers. Bierstadt was an immigrant and hardworking entrepreneur who had grown rich pairing his skill as a painter with a talent for self-promotion. He unveiled his canvases as theatrical events, selling tickets and planting news stories—strategies that one critic described as the "vast machinery of advertisement and puffery." A Bierstadt canvas was elaborately framed, installed in the darkened room, and hidden behind luxurious drapes. At the appointed time, the work was revealed to thunderous applause.

The painting was made in London and toured through Europe to St. Petersburg, fueling Europeans' interest in emigration. Buoyed by glowing reviews,

Bierstadt then offered the painting to American audiences who could take pride in the American artist's skill and in the natural splendors of the young nation.

—Exhibition Label, Smithsonian American Art Museum 2006

That same spring morning, a hundred-plus miles away, Dr. Jonathan Stufa is driving to a meeting at Arapaho Community College. The navigation screen in his car glows a black shadow of a two-faced monster with hands moving in erratic gestures. His car glides across the black asphalt of the near-empty parking lot and parks. It is early morning and the sprinklers are rhythmically spraying water over the lawn. To the west, the morning light illuminates the prominent red sandstone of the hogback overlooking Denver. He slams the car door and places his coffee cup on the hood of the car and extracts his shoulder bag from the back seat. The screen on the dash continues to flicker, like an old-time movie, a projection of molten gold flowing out into clay forms to make ingots. A man in armor stacks the glimmering gold ingots as high as his chest.

At EHHS on the last days of the schoolyear, Tyndall and the gang hang out in his room for lunch. It's the usual frantic end to it all, putting things away, trying to get the last projects and tests graded. But in many ways, it's just a normal early afternoon, sitting in the sunny room having coffee and food and talking away.

"So Sialia, now that the year is nearly done, what are you going to do this summer?" Tyndall says.

"Oh, sleep and babysit my little sister while my mom works."

Sialia sits at Tyndall's desk, twisting and turning in his swivel desk chair. Sandy sits essentially in her lap, as they share the chair. "And you Sandy?" Tyndall says.

"Sleep for sure, then go out to Oregon and see my cousins," Sandy says as she fumbles around with the rocks and bones sitting on Tyndall's desk. She grasps the black, palm-sized chunk of broken obsidian in her hand. Wavy green-white streaks illuminate a flickering image of armored horsemen riding down a long causeway with water all around it; green feathers float in the air and red blood drips from his long spear. The images glow bright then give way to a reflecting deep black, like the shiny waxed hood of a fancy car. The rock feels cold in her hand.

Sialia looks over at the frogs in the aquarium. "Are you going to take care of the frogs over the summer? Do you come in and feed them?"

"No, no—they go home with a kid for the summer. Froggy summer camp, you might say."

"So, who?"

"James is taking them."

"Mali? Mali will kill them."

"Well then, if they die, he won't graduate high school."

"You'll fail him—accordingly!" the girls say in unison, having heard Tyndall say this a bizillion times this past school year. The girls spin in the chair and rock back and forth. Sialia picks up a shiny piece of bismuth metal, which gleams with finger-like projections of purple and blue between two layers of dull gray metal. She places it down on top of the black obsidian. Waves of undulating black emanate from the rock like a shadow at night, and the bismuth sits like a colorful drake, floating.

Stufa ambles down the hallway to the conference room. The college has a photography exhibition of student work lining the hallway. Before he enters the conference room he looks at one of the photos. It is of a black water pond with lily pads and a wooden dock with a silver boat. A lone ragged dog stands on the end of the pier, head down, and looks into the indigo black water.

In the conference room Stufa meets with other principals and superintendents from four other school districts and ten other high schools. He knows many of the people and visits with them while placing donuts on a paper plate and refilling his coffee cup. Joel Haustoria is up front setting up the presentation with several publishing company salespersons and executives. Most everyone gets seated as Stufa sits down with the superintendent.

"Hello, I'm Joel Haustoria. Welcome to the Spring Forward Curriculum adoption meeting. As you know, we are finishing the initial two-year pre-adoption cycle, and all of your districts and schools have the opportunity to be on board for the initial phase. We have set up this meeting with Invino Group, another educational consulting firm. So, starting this fall all grades at your high schools will start up with our curriculum. As you know, with the new state tests this past year, most schools are anticipating student scores to drop. But now, with the Spring Forward Curriculum aligned to the new standards, you will create seeds of higher level thinking and achievement. This curriculum is a complete package that comes with staff training, online resources, and the books and materials needed. We now know how children learn. Data shows that with this new curriculum greater levels of achievement can be obtained for all students."

The following morning Stufa is picked up at the hotel by Haustoria. Stufa hoists his golf clubs into the trunk of Haustoria's black BMW sedan. "You'll love this place. Have you ever played at Arrowhead?" Haustoria says.

"No, I've heard so much about it. You see so many pictures—it's stunning, with all the red rock formations and the vista."

"We'll meet for a couple of hours in the clubhouse meeting room."

"So, who all will be there?"

"Just a subset from yesterday and some sales representatives from Bradmoor Publishing, and a couple of congressmen and senators, as well as some higher-ups from DC and New York."

"So, each of our schools will proceed with our assigned plans and agendas."

"Yeah, as we outlined yesterday," Haustoria says.

"The stakes are high."

"Ah, but the rewards for student achievement, not to mention your career, are great. This is an incredible opportunity for you, Jon."

"And in the afternoon?"

"I've set our tee-time with some senators from Missouri and Tennessee plus a couple of representatives from my company who were school principals for the previous testing and curricula round we did several years ago in their states. These senators were instrumental in bringing this curriculum to their respective states."

"So, you outlined yesterday this is a six-year cycle."

"Yes—and then we change the tests again, and the following year rotate in another set of new curricula. The beta-tests you do with the various schedules at your respective high schools will determine a great deal. Your work is very valuable to us."—*de novo curricle ad infinitum.*

As they drive up to the clubhouse, Stufa says, "So, in terms of the big picture, what really is the business plan?"

Haustoria responds, "Oh, I once spoke to some old timers at Bradmoor. They say the business plan is in a locked vault."

"This sounds like urban legend stuff."

"No, the guys really did see it."

Stufa adds, "I guess it outlines the testing and curriculum sequences?"

Haustoria continues, "Yeah, in essence it really is about the timing of the release of these materials. Do it too early or too late and the profit margin is lost."

"How do they know when?"

"In the old days they did some basic analysis of the testing data and made a best guess. But nowadays we control the ins and outs by making both the tests and the curricula."

Stufa continues, "So, what about the grants some schools receive to completely pay for the curriculum?"

"Those schools are chosen by their demographics as a measure of top potential scores."

Stufa then says, "Oh, you reward those teachers and schools by taking a measure of those scores. Basically, a litmus test for max achievement from a teacher trying really hard, in a stable school with a good population."

"Yeah, and when those students achieve at a certain level—then rotate the tests and curriculum."

"You advertise 'For everyone,' but then, in reality, base your analysis from that top tier," Stufa says.

"Exactly."

"Have you seen the plan?"

"No. Supposedly there is only one copy of it."

"Really, that is hard to believe. Surely it is in the hands of many?"

"No, it is all compartmentalized—you know I do training, L.A. does distribution, New York in-house publishing, and we outsource the analysis. And, as you know, each school is basically its own island." Haustoria parks the car and they head into the clubhouse for the meeting.

Outside on the warm face of a red sandstone fin, a canyon wren calls out a long descending trill; a white golf ball bounces with a dull sound on the carpet-like grass green. Standing there in the meeting room of the golf club Stufa is looking at a large sales map of the entire state of Colorado. The publishing company executive points to the map and says to Stufa, "This can all be yours."

The heavy purple drapes, with golden trim and embossed with dancing patterns, are pulled away. Dogmatic and rich in fantasy, the magnificent painting is unveiled. A universe fueled by expanding acceleration, similar to the way pushing on a balloon changes the air within and the outer shape. With fateful acceptance, manifest in a destiny revealed in a western landscape of grandeur unrealized. It is all there—held in the glistening eye of the stag overlooking the does and fawns in a clarity of light under cathedral peaks. Luminous colors, in warm sunlight, echoing a prophetic voice bestowed in the outreaching arms of sunbeams projected on a tranquil lake. Vividly detailed brush strokes held in absolute balance and symmetry in the atmospheric light. The deep background gives the illusion of a vast temple in a valley held in the hand of an imagined landscape. A magnificent contrived dreamscape shining free and verdant in the promised land.

46

THE READING OF THE CODEX
(CURRICULUM SEQUENCE)

Cualli and Anci take one last swim as the sun drops over the steep mountains to the west. The long, warm light of late afternoon gives way to
the cool shadows of the evening. The melodious whistling song of the bird in
the canyon echoes with the fading light. It is mesmerizing, and Cualli stops
in his tracks to gaze up at the steep canyon walls and the darkening green forest. They gather up more firewood, and stoke the fire lit earlier. He says, "Read
me more of the story."

Anci says, "No, it is not for your eyes."

"But we are bound with this task, and besides we know the power in the
horror that approaches." Cualli turns and looks back down the slope, east toward the ocean. "What about the time sequences?"

Anci, the warrior, reaches for the Codex and unfolds the pages. Cualli,
looking over her shoulder, points and says, "Here is the Overlord that gobbles
up the world." It is a glyph of the z-shaped serpent with its mouth agape, followed by colored circles. "And these signs?" he says, pointing to the symbols
surrounding the four sides on the edges of the page. "What are these around
the Beast?"

She says, "It's another time sequence, part of the calendar in the beginning pages. But these years, they are completely different, very different."

"Different time, what?"

"You know, the full year, rainy season of storms from the ocean to dry and then back again—the planting of maize and twelve full moons."

"Ah, yes."

"But the time is variable, six years depending on when the Overlord has eaten its fill. See here, satiated, like *el tigre* with tapir meat. See the belly— full. But it is not meat, it is the tax of corn, gold, silver, obsidian—here, look, given by all the people. It is seventy-two full moons or six winter dry seasons, and the harvest of maize each year. Then here on the year when he no longer has enough food, he changes."

Cualli, with a confused look on his face says, "He changes, changes what?"

"He changes not the food but the landscape; then more corn flows into his mouth."

"I don't understand."

"It is strange. It shows that the corn is collected for the children, then it is diverted to the Overlord—see the glyph for the rabbits and the payment in maize-grain. Here are the collectors—you know, once a year, and they feed the Overlord. It is planned in secret, underground in the Cave for two seasons. Then on the third season it is brought above to the children who are then lost in the new land. They wander and cannot find their way. But after four or five years they get to know the new country and can get home. At that time the Overlord changes everything again. Changes the mountains and the rivers again—see the glyphs here. Then great stores of riches: the tribute grain feeds the Overlord full again. Here the Two-Handed Monster appears again. The deer-side of his face is with the rabbits and that hand takes the corn while the bat-side of his face is with the Overlord and that hand feeds the Overlord the grain in the cave. Then it cycles back again, changes the features in the land- scape, collects the grain, feeds the Overlord. Then the Beast becomes full again."

"Why six years?"

"It maximizes what the Overlord devours."

"The rabbits, here." Cualli says, pointing to the glyph. "They are chil- dren? Then it is their corn, and it all goes beneath—into the cave, below."

Anci turns the page. "Yes, the payment is diverted to the Overlord. But look! Look, its mouth gets bigger with each cycle."

"The more he eats, the more he is hungry. But why two calendars?"

"I am not sure. One is for the rabbits, the other is for the Overlord."

"And the Two-Handed Monster?"

"He is in both time sequences. And, he exists in both the real world and the underground world."

"I never knew they counted the days and the years."

"For the high priests of my class and all the gods, they count everything. Everything is summed up."

"Summed?"

"That is another lesson."

47

BLAZING LUNCH

James and Hector come bumbling into Tyndall's room about ten minutes before lunch starts. "Hey Tynd, have you seen my math notebook? I can't find it anywhere," James says.

Tyndall sitting at his desk looks up and says, "You'd think, now that you're seniors, you wouldn't be losin' things like this. I don't know; a million things get left in this room. I just throw everything on the back table there, by the microwave."

James and Hector start rifling through stacks of papers, spiral notebooks, and three-ring binders. "Man, you got stuff from every class here. There's even a bottle of glitter here, and it's all over," Hector says.

"Yeah, a real interdisciplinary pile of…" Tyndall stops himself short. "Hey—when you're done—Hey!—pile it back up in one stack," he says to the boys, pointing at a now bigger mess spread all over the table.

"Oh, yeah—yeah, yeah."

"Tynd, this microwave is so old, it's an antique. And what you got this thing plugged into?"

"Still works, ah, sort of. Yeah, that is a funky old extension cord that I found in the back storeroom."

"Got it." James says. Then the boys quickly stack and pile the papers haphazardly. Hector pulls on the plug and extension cord and lays it down on a stack of papers. James, having fetched his math spiral notebook, leaves behind his yellow spiral notebook. Written on the cover, in black sharpie, are the words "English Composition." It sits on the pile of papers with the green extension cord atop it and is half behind the microwave. The boys depart. Lunch starts and Sandy opens her chicken noodle soup and spills some on the yellow notebook. It has many paper packets haphazardly stuck in it. Two of the paper packets have a paperclip and staple stuck together. Sandy hits the microwave start button. The machine hums. The intercom announces a "Code Pink" in the teachers' lounge. Tyndall looks up from his desk and smiles. He exits the room as James and Hector come back in. Other kids are coming and going with their lunches.

In the yellow spiral notebook which is wet with salty soup, purple phosphorescent sparks fly inbetween the metal spiral and the interlocking staples. Also, the metallic purple glitter is slightly covering everything—the way glitter does. In the yellow notebook, one of the sheets of paper is an outline of the Hero's Journey with an example from *Star Wars* and a long list of the characters. The other paper packet is a set of questions reviewing the book *One Flew Over The Cuckoo's Nest.*

As Tyndall leaves the room, Hector picks up the conch shell sitting on the front high table. It has a carved hole in the spiraling point, making the shell a horn. He blows hard into it; a deep pitched wailing sound echoes out of the room and reverberates into a symphony playing the opera *Faust.* Tyndall ambles down the hallway to the teachers' lounge. Opera music infuses the hallway. He sees a young lady sitting on the floor by her open locker and crying. He stands next to her, leans back against the adjacent locker and then squats down next to the girl and listens intently. He stands up, cruises another twenty feet down the hallway, stops and joins a circle of boys dribbling a soccer ball and kicks the ball with them. The high soprano echoes full crescendo as the ball flies. The microwave hums rhythmically, purple phosphorescent sparks dance and shine. The chorus sings as Tyndall kicks the ball with his left foot and then he spins to his right and exits the circle. He proceeds and stops at an open locker and with an assertive tone reminds a boy: "That lab is due. Today!—No exceptions—got it—capiche?" The tenor gives way to bass-baritone as the orchestra takes off. Sandy sits at Tyndall's desk and twirls a green lollipop with a scorpion in it with her left hand as she sips soup from a spoon in her right hand. Above the teachers' lounge, in the drop ceiling, a mouse scurries along an internet network cable. Sialia sits at the big lab table and spins a bluish dragonfly on a pin; its multifaceted eyes sparkle with tiny bristles between them. The soprano sings an aria, as the frogs float silently. A Frisbee slams, with a bang, against the outside of the window. Zach Tyndall enters the teachers' lounge.

The orchestra continues to play with everyone singing in French. The Man in Black, who wears a cape, stands with his hands, in black leather gloves, and undoes the Nurse in White's bra. His hands slide forward and grasp both her round, plump breasts and squeeze and pull on her bright red nipples. She is extracting the bottom-half of his black helmet. He then proceeds to lunge his mouth with tongue out onto her nipple. His hand slides up her skirt and inner thigh, past her white garter with white nylons. Her head arches back. Her white tiara-like nurse's cap is slightly off kilter, as she drops the bottom half of the mask. Purple sparks continue to fly and emanate from the notebook; hot pizza is extracted out of the microwave. The Nurse in White has both feet on the table and her back against the wall; the back of black helmet is buried between her legs and his right hand is pressing in, probing. Her white nylons are wrapped around his head. He licks away as she gives a soft moan interjected with high exhaling squeals.

The teachers' lounge is full of staff, and Tyndall stops by the copy machine to talk to Mr. Jay. The Man in Black is behind The Nurse, she has her elbows and face on the small table with papers, spiral notebooks, and three-ringed binders strewn about. The table bangs rhythmically against the wall with a hollow thumping sound to the opera music. Purple glitter bounces on the table top. In the teachers' lounge Dr. Jonathan Stufa is blowing out the candles to his birthday cake. Dark chocolate cake, pink frosting, with scoops of dripping white vanilla ice cream are passed out by the secretary on floral paper plates with plastic spoons.

48

COMPETITIVE EXCLUSION
PRINCIPLE

Sialia walks into Tyndall's room. "Hey, have you seen Helen and Sandy?"

"No."

"Thanks, Tynd, see ya."

At that moment Helen is walking down the hall toward the science room. Several other girls stand by their lockers watching her as she walks by. One of the girls turns to the others; Helen retreats from the weight of being watched. The monotonous gaze, from the eyes of others, festers in the mind of those who are watched. Things that are wanted, gliding by trance-like, seduced by the song in the mist of want.

Helen and Sialia return to the science room and join Sandy at the big stone-top table. Sialia bounces up and skips on over to Tyndall sitting at his desk. "Here," she says.

"What is it?"

"It's a flip book I made for you." She hands him an oversized white sticky note pad with drawings on it. "Here, you just flip through the pages, like this."

Tyndall flips the edges of the pages with drawings of stick figures that come and go, even of characters flipping pages in their own book. It is elaborately drawn and presents an amusing little story. "Wow! That's so cool. Did you do all of this?"

"Yeah—it is but a day."

At the end of the day Zach Tyndall sits at his desk. His room is a mess with text books on the floor and microscopes and lab supplies scattered on the countertops. On his desktop is a mishmash of open books and papers. He is outlining a lesson plan in ecology for next week's Biology class. James and Hector are fishing around in the pond aquarium with a plastic eye dropper, trying to catch a water flea. A microscope is set up next to them. On the computer in front of Tyndall a nature video is playing.

Tyndall is clearly overthinking all this. He has given this lesson before, but this time there will be Joel Haustoria observing him and his classroom. He can remember it well: *Principal Stufa came up to him and explained how some experts were going to observe his classes.* "These people are really experienced in optimizing educational time and lessons." In the perfect reflection of the prism sitting on Tyndall's desk, Stufa casts an undulating green-black image. Grotesque hands move in the air in a circular motion; dry yellow and purple corn flows out of the hand into a serpent's open mouth. Tyndall tried to explain that he was right in the middle of a lesson and didn't want to be disrupted with this. But no, next Tuesday, he would have to get a sub, travel to another school and tour around with an "expert." Then on Wednesday, the Master Teachers and Haustoria would be in his classroom to observe a lesson. "Which class will they observe?" Tyndall said with hesitation in his voice.

"Well, we don't know. Sometime in the afternoon," Principal Stufa explained with authority.

"So, should I plan on them visiting during my afternoon Biology or my River Watch class? Tyndall quickly asked. Hoping it would be River Watch; at least he had a few shining students in that class. His after-lunch Biology class on the other hand is a bunch of spazzes. Oh, what a nightmare. Now he had to over-plan two different lessons in two different subjects to look all slick and fancy for these educational experts. Dr. Stufa did not answer him.

In a coffee shop, across town, sit four former teachers and Haustoria. The teachers are all Teachers on a Special Assignment, or TSA's, with the title of Master Teacher. They are working together, each with their sleek laptops open in front of them. The TSA's combined salaries are equivalent to those of six full-time classroom teachers. They are preparing for a symposium being given by Bradmoor Publishing.

Tyndall is leaning forward starring at his computer screen with open books all around him. James and Hector exit, then reenter through the back door from the courtyard, amble through the room and leave through the hall door. Tyndall waves goodbye, with a motion of his hand. He does not look up from his books. The nature film continues to play on the screen before him. As the boys exit the door into the hall, Tyndall watches the nature video and the birds in the frame. He hits the volume button. Maybe he could show just this segment in the ecology lesson. Behind the screen, the black obsidian rock flickers and shines. A large hairy hand is gently placed on the shoulder of a child, as a monstrous deer-like face smiles while looking down at the kid. The microscope sits on the countertop, with the light on, as small creatures scurry about in a drop of water, a drop of water that is slowly shrinking and drying up.

Tyndall is watching a segment of a nature video about birds that forage on the bark of tree trunks. The first bird shown is a white-breasted nuthatch; it hops down the dark reddish-brown bark of the ponderosa pine and twists from side to side, inserting its long sturdy bill in the sinuous crevices of the bark. The narrator is explaining how the nuthatch climbs the sides of trees using only its feet, unlike woodpeckers and creepers which use their tail as props. The film shows a quick flash of a woodpecker propped on its tail as it forages. The narrator then explains how the nuthatch feeds by flying up the trunk, and then hops its way down, foraging along the way. The segment shows the tiny bird flittering up about ten feet and then hopping down the trunk in a zigzagging motion.

Next the nature video shows the brown creeper. Creepers are small, speckled brown, arboreal birds that also forage on the bark of trees. However, their bills are very thin and downward curved, adapted to gleaning and probing into tiny bark crevices to extract insects and spiders. The video and the narrator show and explain how these little birds fly down to the base of the tree and then work their way up the trunk foraging. The next segment shows both birds, with their classic foraging behaviors, in one frame hopping past each other on the same tree trunk. The narrator, as the video shows the birds foraging, goes on to say that according to the competitive exclusion principle: two species cannot coexist on the same limited resource. The reasons a nuthatch foraged by climbing down trees is that it may be able to spot prey hidden from creepers and woodpeckers and other upward-facing feeders.

The small, yet mighty, black and white bird flicks a flake of red bark off with its sturdy beak, revealing what is under the tree bark.

49

SLATE-COLORED SOLITAIRE

In the early dawn Cualli lies on the ground covered in a fur cloak. Not quite awake yet, he hears the warbling trill of the bird in the canyon. He rises and stands up; a heavy thick mist of fog hangs on the landscape. Cualli pulls his wolf skin cloak up around him. Dew drops hang on the edge of his fur hood and he gazes into the soft glowing whiteness. Anci is stirring and awakening. He is enchanted by the beautiful bird song emanating from a floating dreamscape. He feels dizzy, as if he is falling; he holds his arms out slightly as if to balance. In the soft white vale, he can see his very desires: Anci swimming naked, his family and home village, eating corn bread handed to him from a hot rock next to a fire. The descending whistle draws his very soul to step into the blank fog. It all rolls by from the bottom to the top, flashing all that he might ever want. Anci stands up next to him, her black hair hanging down around the tan puma skin draped over her shoulders.

"Do not chase the floating desires emanating from what you cannot see, or even find. The song will consume you, like a fire inside of you."

"But it is aloft and in the white mists of what I want."

"But when you touch it, it will be flat and gray with no color, and fall silent on your ears."

"But it is oh-so-beautiful, I cannot look away; so bright and soft, it rings and flashes by me. I can see it in the cloud."

"Let it ring inside of you, with all its beauty and carry it with you. And know—know the song is in your heart. But do not chase it, for it will sing forever in the mist just out of reach." She grabs his hand and they listen together for one more song.

Cualli smiles, listens, breathes in and says, "Here on this path now, and always in my heart, I will carry that song."

The fog wraps and rolls around the fingers of the descending ridges covered with lush tropical forest. A howler monkey calls, and in the far distance the sun rises over the blue green sea to the east. There is a slight pink hue to the clouds facing the sun.

50

ONE WING

It is a Tuesday evening in October and Joel Haustoria is seated at the long granite-topped Churchill Bar at the Brown Palace in Denver. Sitting to his left are two executives from Bradmoor Publishing. He says, "Our reservation is at 7:30."

The exec from Los Angeles replies, "Should we wait for them or go ahead and be seated?"

The exec from New York looks down at a text and says, "They're held up in a subcommittee meeting on The Hill."

"Okay, let's wait here at the bar until they get here."

Haustoria looks in the mirror at a smoky green-black reflection of a bright red painting. In the wavy reflection, hanging on the east wall of the lobby is a copy of the painting *Still Life with Parrots* by Jan Davidsz de Heem. It is ablaze in sumptuous scarlet with exotic fruit and a lobster spilling over draped velvet. A large, beautiful macaw and a gray parrot are perched atop overlooking the splendor of the opulent spread.

The exec from New York says, "Oh, this is a very exciting moment for us here at Bradmoor."

"If the legislators approve the adoption, it will be a guarantee of most schools having to adopt the curricula," Haustoria adds.

While gesturing to Haustoria, the exec from L.A. says, "Yeah, and you'll have a guarantee of training for Bradmoor. Then we'll rotate the tests again."

The exec from New York says, "The new tests, this last year, will really drive up sales for the new curricula."

Haustoria asks, "So, when do you decide to rotate new tests in?"

"When our team has finished the analysis of the test scores, and the scores fit the business model," the exec from LA. says.

"Well, have you seen this business plan?" Haustoria asks.

"No, but they say it is in a thick, oddly-shaped book, locked in a vault," the exec from New York says.

Haustoria pulls his head back as if it was a joke and looks down at his phone as it blinks with an incoming text. He reads the text then puts the phone down on the bar just as the LA. exec's phone rings. Haustoria listens and watches the exec talk. On his phone's screen, there are black images of two hands moving in circles in a misty white smoke.

"That's from the senators, they're on their way. Let's go ahead and get seated," the exec says. Haustoria places his phone into his pocket; the screen continues to flash flickering images of corn flowing into a serpent's open mouth, and processions of slaves, bound with rope, passing by a cave.

The next morning at EHHS, James and Hector come bustling into Tyndall's room. Hector is carrying a cardboard box, as James is talking away. "Tynd, Tynd," James barks, "look what we found." Then both boys start to talk at once. James goes on, "Its wing is broken; found it last night."

"Slow down guys," Tyndall says as he looks up from the stack of tests he is grading.

The adjoining door to Mr. Jay's room swings open and Jay sticks his head in. "Good, they found you." He says. "We figured you'd know what to do."

Sialia and Sandy come in frantically from behind Jay and commotion erupts in the room. The boys put the box on one of the big black stone-top tables. Everyone gathers around. Tyndall, cup of tea in hand, pulls on the teabag and says, "What do we have here?"

Sialia, more assertive and articulate, over talks them all. "Hector here found this baby hawk last night in the park by his house," she says matter-of-factly.

All talking at once. Baby, Tyndall thinks to himself, *It's the wrong time of the year for that—it's October.* By now a small procession of kids and faculty have filed into the room.

"Well, let's take a look," Tyndall says.

"Go slow." Sialia commands.

Hector undoes the lid on the box as James, kneeling on the table, tells how Hector and his dad caught it. "Got only one wing, just a bloody stub on the other wing," James says.

"Threw my jacket over it, to catch it," Hector says.

Tyndall looks in the box; everyone else crowds around the table. The bottom of the box is covered with torn paper towels. James points and says, "We put those worms in their last night." Tyndall sees the dry dead worms in the corner of the box. There is also the bottom half of a yogurt container with spilled water. In the bottom of the box, blinking frequently, is a male American kestrel. It flaps its wings. The left-wing is a bluish color, tapered and pointed. The right wing is a stub, severed clean at the elbow of the bird. Dry blood stains and mats its outside feathers. There is red-brown dry blood on the paper towels on the bottom of the box. The bird blinks a strange white eyelid from the side, and then blinks down with a dark eyelid. The little bird calls out a rapid, shrill kli kli kli kli.

Everyone is talking. Tyndall puts his cup of tea down. "Quiet, shh, quiet, now. Sandy, turn off the lights, please," he says, gesturing backwards toward the door. James starts talking. Tyndall continues, "No, no, quiet. It's not a baby, it's a male kestrel—a little falcon." He's thinking, *He had seen this before. At Jarett Nature Center in Michigan. He worked there right after college. He saw the same injury, to the same kind of bird. Must be something about how these little guys feed that makes them vulnerable to this specific injury.*

"So—as I was saying, these little guys feed by diving in a stoop for prey on the ground. Usually mice or grasshoppers. They end up hitting telephone or electric wires while diving down to get prey. I've actually seen this twice before," he says, going on to explain the way these birds hunt, their prey, how they are vulnerable to high wires. "Their eyesight is exceptional, with great focus on a specific spot; so specific that they do not see the wire between them and the ground. They fly at such high speeds that the wing can be severed off, clean." Tyndall reaches into the box with his bare hand. The bird frantically hops and flaps, kli kli kli, screaming out. Then the bird flips onto its back, little talons lunging upward, screaming the whole time.

"There, little one, got some fight left in you. Come on, baby, here we go." He grabs a wad of paper towels with his other hand. This kestrel lunges out and grabs the paper towels; Tyndall then subtly, but accurately, swiftly slides his hand along the belly and clasps both legs between his finger and thumb. "There, there, Little One." He folds the bird's good wing against his torso, with his left hand. "Close the blinds, everyone be still and quiet," he orders. "Now Ryan, grab the first aid kit, over there. Dump it on the counter—there." he gestures with his left ear. "There. That dark small bottle, the brown one. "Now open it up. All right, there's an eyedropper in there—careful it will stain your clothes. Hand it to me, when I say." Tyndall stretches the stump of the severed wing, and plucks a feather hanging loose. "Grab those scissors." Then he clips two feathers off. "Now hand me the iodine dropper." He squirts red-brown liquid all over the wing stub and the feathers. "Hector, James, get one of those eyedroppers you guys use to catch pond critters. Now cut off the tip. Fill it full of water, the bulb and all. Perfect." Tyndall then pries the bird's beak open and fishes the small plastic eyedropper down the throat of the little hawk. It gags. "Now, now, easy, there you go Little One," he says, as he squeezes the water down its gullet. "Now you're hydrated. Good. Not much more we can do now." He places the bird back in the box. "I'll put him in the back room, where it's quiet, until after school. I'll call my friend who's a vet; she can then get it to the raptor rehab people."

Sialia looks on with a strained look on her face, lips held tight and a lone tear rolls down her cheek. "So Tynd, it can't fly? Right?"

"Tyndall looks over and says, "No, I'm afraid not. Sorry kid."

Sialia looks down at the bird in the box and says, "It's worse than a bird in a cage; it can't fly."

Sialia can picture how it all happened; the American kestrel kites its way upward on a constant breeze. It rises straight up, flapping its wings in quick short wing beats. Its head is cocked downward, the whole while looking straight down. The bird rises. The air from the wind foils over its wings; its blue tail feathers fan out, cocking back and forth, holding the bird steady. It rises, then it remains stationary like a kite. All the while the kestrel stares straight down at the grasshopper. The grasshopper is flying erratically, clicking its orange, yellow and black wings in a crazy, up-down flight. The grasshopper lands on the dirt trail, folds its wings, and ambles straight ahead.

At that moment, the moment the grasshopper lands, the kestrel folds its blue-gray tail feathers and folds back its sharp falcon wings and stoops almost straight down from two hundred feet off the ground. The grasshopper refolds its orange and yellow wings, and shuffles along the stony ground. With laser vision and clarity, the little falcon dives. At thirty feet off the ground, along the gravel path, run the electric wires. The bird is moving at fifty miles an hour, bearing down on its prey on the ground. Vision so clear, so precise, keen and intent—eyeing its target. All is perfect, clear, he adjusts for the wind. The tall dry grass shifts in the breeze. The bird never sees the wire, neither does the grasshopper. Its wing is severed clean in the air in an instant. The little falcon tumbles sideways onto the ground, mouth agape, blinking its extra eyelid frantically, flapping in a small circle, tumbling in the tall, dry, golden grass.

51

BIRD IN THE HALLWAY

There are ten minutes between classes. It starts with a trickle as a handful of kids are released early by a teacher. Some students slyly wait till the teacher is encumbered and in a quick assertive voice say, "Goodbye, see ya." The teacher answers and waves and there it is—they are released three minutes early. In some classes they are seat bound until the appointed time. Still, in other classes the kids are all out of their seats piled up by the door, pressing and bumping into each other, backpacks and bodies jostling into one another, chairs left pushed out and in the way. In another class the teacher continues to babble about whatever the fuck it is that teachers say.

When it's all said and done, the hallways are an overcrowded jumble of awkward excited bodies flowing, clotting, separating, and coalescing. It is a narrow space with the doors of lockers stuck out, boys feigning a fight here or jiving each other there. There is no directional flow; some head down on the left side, some on the right. Backpacks, students and locker doors impede the flow. Some stand and watch, others move and text at the same time. This moment, in a defined parcel of time in a limited space, dynamically ebbs and flows. It is the random flow of energetic youth, uncoupled, uncooperative and yet somehow proceeding six times a day.

JR stands at the door of Mr. Klinker's room, waiting to be released. The pack on JR's back is big and hangs low. His basketball shorts are too big for his skinny, pale legs; he glides left running his fingers along the closed lockers. Then, with a quick step to the right around an open locker and a girl, like a boxer he shifts his head right to avoid the girl swinging her pack. Then he accelerates in the center of the hall, steps back left then careens far right, steps over a pack on the ground next to a locker. He presses his hands together, and like a swimmer doing the breaststroke, squeezes between a group of large boys proceeding the opposite way down the hall. Then he squirts out, steps hard left into the classroom, inadvertently kicking the wood doorstop as the door swings shut behind him. Other students, impeded by the closed-door, pile up, clogging the hallway. The grand procession continues as kids swirl around the imposed eddy of students banging on the door with annoyed gestures.

He plops down at his desk in Tyndall's science room for Homeroom. He sits at his desk and looks at the teardrop doodle he left on the desk the class before. Another student had added to it by drawing, in blue ink, the same repeating pattern. He extracts a pencil and continues the pattern outward. Someone finally opens the door and kids come piling in. Everyone spreads out as far from other students as they can get.

Tyndall starts up, "Okay, you guys, let's unplug and get to work. I want to…" And he is interrupted by the Pledge of Allegiance. Most of the students stand and halfheartedly say the pledge. Sialia and a few others remain seated, and do not recite the pledge.

Ryan pipes up, "Hey isn't it the law that you have to say the pledge?"

Sialia is quick to respond, "No! You don't have to say it."

Tyndall follows, "Yeah, the school just has to announce it."

"Ain't that wrong, shouldn't they have to say it?" Ryan says pointing to the Latino students seated on the side desk rows.

"No, we don't!" Sialia said.

"Don't you like the freedoms here?"

"We're free to not say it—that's freedom."

"But…"

Tyndall is quick to intervene, before it gets ugly. "Sialia's right, no one has to say it—the school just has to by law. You should respect their silence as much as they should respect your saying it. Does that make sense?"

"I guess."

52

INSIDIOUS

Christina's World
A thousand and one blades of grass
Pale pigment tempera
To nurture an expanse of lawn
So far away, so distant
How did you get there?
The weight of *Terra incognita* unrealized
No bird in sight, just grass
Your dress, so light, and free
A body so heavy, encumbered
Alone in the expanse
Look back, indignant to the distance
Feel the push and pull

—G.B.

The chickadee is a small bird. It is light gray and buffy white with a little black helmet of feathers, and flits from branch to branch. Mighty in its movements, assertive, as it nimbly hangs upside down gleaning insects from under the maple leaves. The storm approaches and stirs the forest. The bird takes off into the melee of swaying branches. It floats left, then flies straight, swerving right and dropping its wings to its sides, plunging below the branch and then above another. The dynamic flow of wind, wings, leaves, and branches guides the mighty small creature.

It is lunchtime on one of those first warm spring days. Tyndall works through lunch preparing sub plans. The next day he has an all-day training with Joel Haustoria, the educational consultant for the Spring Forward Curriculum. He and five other teachers from the building will sit all day in meetings going over the newly adopted curriculum. He's clearly annoyed at the disruption to his teaching. He had planned this great lab to grow pond critters in two-liter bottles. He certainly didn't want to leave that up to a substitute teacher. Instead the kids will do book work, and worksheets. But he knows the students really will just stare at their computers and phone screens and do nothing all class.

James, Sialia and Sandy come walking in through the back door, Sialia has an insect net in her hand.

"Any luck?" Tyndall says, looking up from the tall table at the front of the classroom. He is standing on a square piece of firewood, elbows on the desk top, stretching his left then his right calf muscle. He's looking through the itinerary for the training he has the next day. His feet are killing him; he has what feels like shin splints. Now that the snow is melted, he is hiking more. This mixed with standing on the concrete floors all day is a good recipe for shin splints.

"No, it's too windy," Sandy says.

Sialia looks down at her pant leg and pulls it up to her knee. She starts making funny noises and is pointing to the back of her leg. "Ahhhh, wheee, ah Mali—get it, do something—Mali."

"What?" James says, looking up from his cell phone.

On the back of her calf is a dark brown tick ambling up her leg. "Mali, please," Sialia says, standing frozen, elbows curled up against her body. "Hurry!"

James walks up and flicks it off her leg with his finger. "I hate ticks."

Tyndall, looking over, says, "Catch it, don't lose it. I don't want it in my room." James looks around on the dirty white linoleum tiles; there are foil gum wrappers, orange-red chips, and the patterns of dirt-covered soda spills on the floor.

"Tynd, your floor is ah—really dirty."

"Yeah, I know, they only mop, half ass, once every two or three weeks. I've stopped sending email requests—doesn't get cleaned anyway."

"Found it."

"Get it, for a specimen. Don't smash it. You guys better do a thorough check—it is tick season."

Sialia, turning her head to look at the back of her legs with a distressed look on her face, says, "I was just straightening my socks; I didn't even feel it."

Tyndall walks up, grabs a sheet of paper, and says, "Here brush it up on the paper." The tick just keeps ambling on, its legs just keep moving rhythmically from the floor to the paper. Sandy and Sialia are rubbing their scalps and inspecting each other's clothing.

Sialia asks, "How can it climb like that undetected?"

Tyndall walks over to the back cabinet and starts rifling through it. Not looking up, he says, "Well think about it. Would it get a blood meal if it was detected by its host? Say, like a dog."

"No."

"Keep in mind, blood is a high-quality food source, and then it can produce a lot of eggs. So, suppose you have a tick after a blood meal that lays a thousand eggs. Then you got a thousand ticks crawling around. Now, if the tick is detected by say a dog that bites it and kills it—those genes are gone. Right?"

"Yeah, I guess."

"Keep going with this," Tyndall says as he extracts a small glass vial from the messy cabinet and a plastic bottle marked: ET-OH in pen on the side. "Well, what happens to the noisy tick? Say—nine hundred noisy ticks?"

Sialia says, "So if you got nine hundred noisy, not sneaky, not stealth-like ticks starving or killed, that leaves the stealth-like ones. So only the sneaky ones that crawl undetected on the back of your leg get a blood meal."

"Here Mali, come here with it," Tyndall continues. "That's right, only ticks that: (1) get on a host, (2) are sneaky and undetected..."

Sandy quickly adds, "Get to reproduce and lay eggs after a blood meal."

Sialia says, "So they get better and better at being undetected."

"Yeah, in essence those sneaky genes get selected for."

Tyndall drops the tick into the small vial, and over the sink pours ethyl alcohol into the container. The vaporous fluid flows over his hands as well; it is cool, almost cold, as it quickly evaporates. He also knows that this is sterilizing his hands after handling the tick. In the vial of clear liquid, the tick continues to clamber away in the same rhythmic motion. Tyndall hands the vial to James.

"How long until it dies?"

"Not long, a minute or two." Sialia takes a photo of it with her phone while James, smiling, is out of focus behind the photo.

Tyndall says, "That critter is the vector of many diseases."

Sialia turns and says, "So a successful parasite remains unnoticed."

"Yeah, all its adaptations are highly refined, from how it crawls, to where it pierces the skin—almost like it's not there."

"Nasty little thing," James says.

"Yeah, but oh so good at being a parasite," Sialia finishes.

Ryan pulls up a close-up video clip of a tick's mouthparts going into skin. "Ah! Oh, that's fucked up. Tynd you got to see this." Their heads fly back and their faces grimaces.

Tyndall looks over the shoulders of the kids. "Look at those barbs, what a wicked adaptation. Oh nasty!"

The tick, vector of hidden disease that will incite a cascade of illness, waits to drop onto its host. It sits and waits on the terminal end of a blade of grass. There it sits with its legs fanned out waving in the wind on the end of the branch, questing. Sun, rain, wind, it waits. It can wait for months without feeding. When a pant leg of a human walks by, it drops onto its host. The tick clamors up silently, unperceived. Its legs furiously pumping as it crawls. The parasite will crawl up the backside of its host. There at the base of the hairline, on the neck, it will pierce the skin and suck blood. Unperceived in the interstitial spaces between the hairs it will engorge itself on nutritious blood. It will stretch and grow to twenty times its original size. Anticoagulant proteins keep the wound flowing as corkscrew shaped bacteria float into the host's bloodstream. The tick's mouth parts are particularly adept at piercing the skin and sucking blood. They first burrow into the skin with two mouth parts called chelicerae. Once the chelicerae are in the skin, they fan outward, and pull back. At this point the tick thrusts a third mouth appendage, called a hypostome, deep into the skin of the host. The spear-like hypostome is barbed along the sides and has a large furrowed groove, like a straw, for sucking blood. The tick will feast on its host's blood—unperceived. The sallow feverish child will see her doctor. Antibiotics will be dispersed, and the infection killed. But the immune system will have been incited, and a cascade of arthritic inflammation will plague the child for years after.

53

THE DISQUIETING MUSES

Tyndall did not get his sub plans done so he comes in early and is scrambling to complete them. It is just another inane, senseless training that will take him away from his own classroom, part of a bigger package that came with the purchase of the new curriculum. The ubiquitous quip of the school admin saying, "We have a grant for this," rings in Tyndall's head. He thinks, *Yeah, it's all tax dollars not getting to the kids.* It is disconcerting to put too much effort into something he knows the sub and the kids won't take seriously.

Zoom in and follow the electron, the great interconnectedness, moving at the speed of light down a pipe, from a server farm to bandwidth from a box in the ceiling of Tyndall's science room across the space in the room to a device on the desktop. The day's instructions are given by the sub, the students deftly turn on and interface the device—their heads peer down and fall into the void. The green mottled frog sits motionless, as if made of plastic, on the bottom of the aquarium. The rhythmic sound of water, flowing out the filter, fills the room like a song from a fountain.

Sitting alone next to each other, stare and forget, blank, gazing at the strong bleak shadows, cast heavily from the setting sun, or is it rising? And does it matter? Two prominent figures; one standing, one seated, and another lesser classical statue looks on, all faceless, head-on, head off, geometric color and a true vanishing point along the bricks to the red square building, offset to the adjacent chimney stacks of the factory piercing a green and black sky, bleak and stark, mysterious, disturbing, faceless, not centered, unbalanced, disproportional, a gaze-less place to look and fall into. Substitute, email, newspaper, sub plans, assignment on the board, logon, online quiz, upload, students gaze transfixed by flashing images of diamonds revealed from glowing screens; sculpted, bright, sexual, flash, open, download, sensual and easy, photoluminescent, thumbs and fingers flicking and scrolling, bottom to top, top to bottom, accessible, the bird sings a siren's call from the mists, the jewelry box the great Sultan made of gold and gemstones, the very light goes through the ruby projecting red, through the sapphire, blue with the very want of, the whistle, the flash, the tap, the mists upon the tree fern, the green emerald with light clipping off it, as a shaft of light hits a bromeliad on a branch of the oriental magenta inflorescence of desire, sweet upon the tongue of the exposed breasts flashing on the fold of a rose petal unfurled in the touch of the screen, a series of modulated algorithms complete and uploaded and transmitted to the eager disdain of wanting, clean and smooth, youthful, lesson plan unveiled, automated, bright, we now know how kids learn, flashes on the presentation screen, as a timeshare is booked on a white sand beach with the sapphire glowing Caribbean gleaming on the hip of a white bikini bottom gliding on the gem of commerce, freeing up occidental time, then scroll to what has been tallied next to a house on the golf course with the new car, sleek, soft and leisurely, arching back exhaled, driving in cars, uploading thyself, the red lips open, posting an innuendo of a party that does not exist, while separated in rolling cars, looking at the mists of a song forwarded, the penetrating voice, operated and set up like holidays uploaded in the down and low of a tiger mom with manicured cellophane wrapping in a hollow chamber of light inside a chunk of obsidian and relayed to a Queen's ear, the different maxims of concentrated touch, illuminating what is mine, what is yours, tailored to fit, flash from the descending set of notes ringing in a colorful box of narrowly emitting bandwidths of true color, not for the other, but to share, a full gamut of sound penetrating the light with the flick of soft tissue rolling under a finger, breathing in the remarkable rendering of form and shape as a million plus flickering screens lean against the hard phallus of desire.

54

ENRICHED MARROW

The Sleeping Gypsy
In our dreams it is still
Do you see yourself?
Lying down bathed in the blue hour
Your friend the lion
Like a silent musical instrument
The lucid freedom of slumber
The peace of not knowing

—G.B.

Sialia sits in her favorite comfy chair by the window in Ms. Rayleigh's art room. Her thick black hair hangs in a braid down her back. The braid is wide and loose near her head and tightens and narrows descending down her back. It contrasts against her red shirt.

An art book sits in her lap and Sialia's left-hand twirls a small lock of hair before tucking it into her braid behind her left ear. Her long thin fingers stick out from her long sleeve shirt, as she loosely grasps the ends of her sleeves. Her mind wanders; she turns and stares out the window across the top of the low bookshelves. She reaches out and grabs a color wheel from the shelf. It is a circular piece of stiff, shiny cardboard. There is an axis in the center in which two dials spin with windows that illuminate different colors and shades of color. She slowly spins the wheel. Arrows, triangles, and lines bisect descending shades of various colors. The wheel slides off the book into the crevice between the seat cushion and the arm of the chair.

She turns back to the art book. Colors, shapes and designs appear on each page. She flips the pages haphazardly and carefree. Her diaphragm rises and falls with each breath. The waves of energy continue, neurons fire, emotions emerge. It is more than a collection of neurophysiology and all the parts altogether interacting. She feels each piece of art. Not like in her muscles, but in her soul. Thoughts come and go, fleeting, remembered then forgotten. Her hand moves, she smells something, she lets out a scarcely audible sigh, invisible yet real.

Ms. Rayleigh comes into the room and looks over at the corner where Sialia sits next to the window. Outside the window, sheets of gray rain fall on the distant field. "Sialia, you'll melt into that chair," Ms. Rayleigh says. "Come on, you'll miss third period. Let's get a move on."

"Oh yeah. thanks Ms. Rayleigh," Sialia says in a whisper. She stands up and drops the book, in a haphazard manner, on the seat of the comfy chair. It bounces as it hits the seat pillow. The color wheel falls to the side, leaning between the book and the armrest at a delicate angle. Sialia looks down, blinks and turns abruptly for the door. She exits the room with an emphatic wave back to Ms. Rayleigh and tumbles into the hallway, bouncing off of other students as lockers slam around her. She is at once engulfed in a clamor of sound and movement. Her friend Sandy, coming up from behind her, grabs her hand and smiles. The very moment transcends the images in the art book; goes beyond the gilded and bright blue panels of the altar in the adorned church. They giggle in unison as Sialia throws her head back and smiles. Hand in hand, shoulder touching shoulder, the two girls float down the hallway. Happiness emerges.

The girls pass Stufa and Combe walking down the hall toward the office. Sialia notices them as they glide ominously along.

In the back of the office, in a hushed tone, Combe explains to Stufa, "Jay and Tyndall approached me about where the money for the new curriculum is coming from. They were particularly upset about their class sizes. Tyndall even mentioned Haustoria, specifically."

Stufa responds, "Oh, let me handle that. I'll address that in the faculty training this afternoon."

In the library Stufa prances around, all adamant with his gestures and tone, as he sets up the chairs in the customary half circle. At the beginning of the meeting he stands up front and puts on his reading glasses and looks down at his laptop screen. The lenses of his glasses have a violet, opaque reflection flickering with the jittery motions of his head. He says, "Bradmoor has been so generous with getting us all started with Spring Forward. I know you all think you are just teaching to the tests. All of you are such professionals, and in your classroom you each do what is best for the kids. I have so much confidence in you and what you are doing."

The staff sat silent, looked on and listened to the alchemy unfolding.

The gleaming sheeny light dances in his glasses as he removes them and puts them in his shirt pocket. On the other side of the school, in Tyndall's room, the chunk of obsidian flashes images of two hands moving. One hand is green and painted with yellow spots and the other is red with the same spots. The green hand moves in the light; while the other moves beneath in a cavernous opening in the ground. The black rock flickers with a luminous brilliance, like the Pacific just after the sun has passed, and the very moment before the stars appear. Occupation, rule, events, destiny, competing for empire, imposed by global corporations, the data scribbled on the balance sheet, company revenues, extorted out of taxes gained in a classic colonial economy, like opium and textiles moved for the weight of sterling silver holding the imperative of profit.

That evening, after the meeting, Stufa drives home, ever the entrepreneurial minded manager, the lure of financial gain; the twisted instruments of fingers welded with infinite optimism, manipulation, and trinkets for trade and gain for the Empire. So slick in melodious presentation, quick-practiced script flows effortlessly as the other hand moves pieces with insidious charm, with a most common touch. A sordid force, sway in his glance, a whiff of conviction, babbling menace, the infinite loop of protocol, glittering a soundless allure held in the balance of loss and gain. Phrases ring like some greed-driven East India Company trader: commerce, belief, and presentation, all in hands moving in incessant circles, like a snake eating its own tail.

Green at one angle, streaking white, uniform, then changing to smoke-black, all moving upon the cold coals burned through and out, to a pure black held in the hand and turned in the light. Beneath, a stealthy smile, commingling with absurdity, shimmering at the corner of his pale thin lips muttering fortitudes and pleasantries to placate. All this resonating from a black rock, soundless, inert, but not benign. Covered up in white gesso to add texture, to avert the eye of the viewer. His one hand full of trade beads for a heap of gold.

55

THIS RULER

The Slave Ship
To swim with shackles
Surrender to the depths
Can the sky really be
Stained red with blood?
Precious cargo to the depths
Oh my soul to keep
A mighty gray green—stained red
Silence in the depths
A cruel injustice
Blazing yellow leadership,
So justified in the decision
Morbid silence in the depths
A metric number clasped on
The weight of impossibility
Forever pulled to the depths

—G.B.

Tyndall drops the box on the table with a thunk. He pulls the test booklets out and stacks them into two piles. One pile is for math test booklets, the other for reading and writing. He then extracts the ruler and protractor punch-out tools, all sealed in clear shrink-wrap plastic. He dumps the box of pre-sharpened number-2 pencils and a baggie of red erasers cut in half out onto the table. The secretary comes in with a cart; on it are water bottles and snack bars that she counts off as she puts them on the table. She then noisily bumps into several chairs and tables with the squeaking cart as she haphazardly exits.

Tyndall stands silently reading the names of the students from a list taped to the top of the box. In the corner of the box white letters advertise Bradmoor Publishing. "Okay here we go," he mutters out loud. Twenty sullen children stare back at him as he drops each test booklet on each of their desks. There is a number and a long barcode in the upper left-hand corner of each test booklet. He thinks how the kids look paler and thinner. The constant chatter subsides and they fall silent. An eerie pall falls upon the room. The water tumbles out of the aquarium filter with a constant trickling sound. The frogs float and stare out. Never blinking. Sialia plops her entire chest and head on the desktop and sighs a mournful groan as her hands fall limp over the edge.

Tyndall reads the directions for the math test. "Today you will be taking…There will be no disturbance…Use a #2 wooden pencil…When you see a STOP ICON…You must not…If at any time you…" The children snap out their punch-out protractor and ruler. The ruler is six inches long, red on one edge, and yellow on the metric edge.

Sialia thinks about sitting in her comfy chair in the art room. In her reverie, her arms are folded across her chest, book in lap. Sialia, leaning to her right, comes upon Gustav Dore engravings of *Dante's Inferno*, canto 32, and something in Italian. The room is so very still, the vent in the ceiling clanks away above her head.

Now as Sialia sits at her desk, her feet are contorted and twisted underneath it, digging into the floor. Her right shoe is in a foot-shaped crater in the wood floor. Her foot twists with her right heel moving outward as she places her right elbow on the desktop. The test booklet slides to the left, she stares down, fidgets and rotates her foot as she measures the triangle with her ruler. Sparks fly red orange across the floor. Clanging metallic sounds ring in her ears. She leans forward, pivoting the other foot backward in a lesser crater. Unbalanced, she shifts her weight as she turns the page. In the canto 32 engraving, a monstrous upper body emerges from the ice. He is leaning over a smaller body and head. He is eating the other person, gnawing at his face. She finishes exactly half the math questions, then she stops and leaves the rest blank. It turns out that all the questions she did answer were correct.

In Tyndall's mind, The Teacher stands tall and proud. *He holds out the paper ruler at arm's length and emphatically yells out, "This ruler cost the state taxpayers millions of dollars and this ruler is all you get for taking the tests; this ruler, this measure. This ruler cost pennies to make and distribute and was sold to the taxpayers for a dollar. There are roughly one million schoolchildren in this state—so how much did this test company make on this ruler? This measure?"*

The students recede as he speaks. He holds the yellow and red six-inch ruler at arm's length; tiny script in the corner of the ruler says Bradmoor Publishing. The ocean waves roll back at his feet. In front of him is the setting sun, burning fiery pink-orange. In back of him is the full moon rising, pale yellow against the purple-blue horizon. The ocean recedes and with it the children in their desks, looking up with sallow complexions and sunken eyes, #2 pencils held listlessly in their hands. He speaks louder; the way you do when you're trying to over talk another speaker. Frustration and anxiety crackle in his voice. Like a prophet he bellows, *"This ruler!"*

The mass of the lunar satellite orbiting the Earth conspires with the mass of the Sun so very far away. The pull of gravity, the spinning of the planet, the shape of the continental shelf all beneath, above and around him. Pull. Pull invisibly. Pull. Bulge the water, drop the glacier, and wreck the ship upon the reef. Forces so far away, unseen, ripple through Our World. Underneath his feet, in the wet sand of the receding wave, a sand crab scurries on the sand surface, then buries itself. Bubbles follow it, the dimple in the sand can be seen, and then vanishes to a flat monotone of tan. Tyndall blinks and breathes in.

After three tests and an entire morning, the students are released from their testing rooms. They run across a burned and charred black landscape with skeletons of trees standing erect. The children run, in the loose charred soil, slipping as black dust flies from their feet. Feet scrape the charcoal with a squeaking, crushing sound. Burnt branches slash back violently, whacking against their shirts as they run through the foreboding landscape. Their shirts are stained with black swashes. An acrid, dry smell burns their throats. All fades to an artisan engraving a copper plate. Black ink drips from a roller, and the press rolls out the engraved image. With a swishing noise each print slides out and is lifted onto a drying rack by the artisan. The team works away. A leopard leaps out of a childlike jungle to devour a shadow of a man.

56

STARLINGS DESCEND
IN THE LIGHT

The school year has now proceeded past the inviting and exuberant start. With early October's cold mornings, the first sputtering anomalies of the broken heating system are coming into play. The rambunctious time of Homecoming and all of that has passed. A resplendent reality has set in. Upon rising from bed, Tyndall walks over to the open bedroom window. In the pale light of dawn, he stares out at the eastern sky. A waning crescent moon hangs as a bowl-shaped sliver, with Venus shining bright just below it. Another smaller, less bright planet is aligned just above the moon. He does not know what planet it is. Cold air flows through the open bedroom window, making him shiver. Purple, blue, and black; silver white piercing through the parchment of memory and space. By the time Tyndall has started his day, the reflected light off the celestial spheres has been consumed by the aurora. The planets and the moon are still there, just not revealed in the brilliance of the day.

At lunch, Sialia and James walk together down the hall, smiling at each other. From the side a small freshman boy runs up. "Mali, Mali, look what I have," he says, with a big smile on his face. In his hand is a string of firecrackers. "Yeah, dude I'm gonna throw these into the girls bathroom—watch," he says, fidgeting and bouncing in front of them.

James smiles, Sialia frowns. The younger kid starts to run off. James looks over at Sialia, who touches his arm and says, "Mali."

James is quick to call the kid back, "Hey, kid." The freshman stops and bounces back to them. "Don't do that. It'll be nothing but trouble," James says.

"But, Mali? You did all this, ya know what I'm sayin'?"

The kid starts talking and James holds up his hand and says, "No, ya gotta see it. Like how it is for others."

In the freshman boy's mind, he sees the lit firecrackers, hears the loud bang, and how his friends laugh and think he's cool. James looks hard at him and says, "No, no, not that way, the way other people feel it. Ya know, how it might hurt and shit."

The younger kid sees the girls exiting the bathroom, how upset they are with the ringing in their ears and the foul smell of smoke in their hair.

James says, "Think about it, ya know what I mean?"

During the last class of the day, Tyndall does his best to get the attention of the River Watch class. "All right you guys here's what we're gonna do this week. Today we'll head out to the bike path to collect some chokecherries. Then, next class on Thursday, we will make jam."

The day before he had scouted out the chokecherries growing on the bike path in front of school. There he found several loose thickets of chokecherry trees heavily laden with the small, round, dark purple cherries. Today, the afternoon is picture-perfect, deep blue sky and the surrounding landscape a patchwork of brilliant yellow, orange, and red with the changing autumn leaves. It is absolutely dazzling in the bright afternoon light. Tyndall and twenty-four students are heading down the bike path in front of the school.

"Guys, move over when a bike comes by," Tyndall barks out at the kids running around in front of him. As two bicyclists pass, a dozen kids jump out to the side. All in unison they raise their hands over their heads and give a whoaaaa chant, as if the bike riders were a football team. It's all good fun, and the two lady riders laugh at the kids' playful antics. A Frisbee flies over the fence into the hay meadow. Hector, running and without breaking stride, leaps up with his left foot onto the top wire strand and clears the fence. The disc flies back; James grabbing it over the heads of Sialia, Sandy and Helen. As they approach the chokecherries, Tyndall shuffles his feet and comes to an abrupt stop as the kids behind him bump into him.

"What's up Tynd?"

"They're gone."

"What's gone?"

"The chokecherries they…" And with a long pause. "They were here yesterday. There were thousands of them."

"Thousands of what?"

"Chokecherries."

"Huh? Hey guys, gather up here. So, it looks like the chokecherries got eaten since I was here yesterday."

"Was it a bear?"

"No. I don't think so. They usually break branches and trunks, and don't quite pick it so clean," Tyndall says with authority.

"Sure, sure you know where you're going?" James says jiving Tyndall. James, pointing a little further down the path says, "How about those guys?" he points to three mottled, striped and spotted black birds at the top of a clump of chokecherry trees.

"Ah, yes there we go. Okay guys one lesson gone. Hold still just for a minute—this is a good bit of bird ecology. At least we can learn you something today," Tyndall says.

"Yeah, learn us good Tynd," James quips.

"Yeah, okay—it looks like all the chokecherries got eaten by starlings—those black birds over there," Tyndall says, pointing to the birds on top of the chokecherry trees growing about fifteen feet tall in a clump next to the path. "Those birds are weeds, a nonnative invasive species that has taken over."

"So, they're flying weeds?" James adds with a funny smile on his face.

Tyndall continues, "This is kind of a crazy story. So back in the late 1800s some guy in New York City thought that America—the New World was incomplete—because it was missing the birds mentioned by Shakespeare. So, he went to England, captured some starlings—those guys, and brought them back to New York. And he let them go—well they died, so the next year he went back to Europe…"

"You're making this up, Tynd."

"Oh no, oh Horatio, there are more things…or something…in Heaven and Earth than are dreamt of in your—ahhh something."

"What?"

"He's quoting Shakespeare," Sialia says.

"Well...not exactly a quote but something close to that. For art thou— or something. Yeah, this dude, I can't remember his name, really did this. America was incomplete without the songs of the birds mentioned by Shakespeare. Poor America. Well as I've said before, oh humanity—leave it up to humanity to screw things up, and here's a great ecological screw-up. Long story short, on the second try, these birds took hold. They have since expanded across all of North America. They form huge flocks that descend and eat all the food. They are extremely aggressive; they take the nest cavities of other birds."

Sialia adds, "And they screwed up River Watch making chokecherry jam this year."

"Indeed. All great plans...and whatever would Horatio say back to Hamlet? Well guys, all right, let's walk further down, see what we can find. If not, I'll go out tonight and get some by my house."

As the group of kids and Tyndall approach, the last starling flies off. But before it flies, it rapidly grabs the last couple of cherries and ravenously gulps them down into its already-full gullet.

As the kids walk down the bike path, Sialia asks Tyndall, "Do you think we'll find more chokecherries?"

"For that is the question," Tyndall replies.

Long after sunrise, the light of dawn hung with an extended softness under a low ceiling of leaden clouds. The sun broke through a sliver of open sky and the light shot through a linear space between the Earth and the gray clouds. Sandwiched in between, the long shot of light illuminated and raced westward with the turning planet. As the light hit the golden cottonwoods, several hundred starlings alighted into the air. The birds swooped left then careened right in a rippling murmuration and descended on a patch of chokecherry trees on the bench-like hill of Elysium. In a rapacious frenzy of beaks and wings the flock consumed all that was there. Each bird actively gulped down a chokecherry and quickly grabbed another. Within minutes thousands of chokecherries were consumed. The Earth rotated on its axis; and the sunlight was extinguished by the clouds. A soft even light, a voided flatness, enveloped the entire landscape. The birds flew off.

57

THE HUNT

It is lunch on one of those first cold days in November. Tyndall sits at his desk as kids parade into the classroom to microwave their lunches. It is the usual commotion-filled start to lunch, before everyone falls into some niche to eat and chill out for a well-defined timeslot in the middle of the day. James, Ryan, and Hector come bustling in through the back outside door which is held ajar with a flat brick.

Hector, looking down at his phone, says, "Fucking no shit, I'll send you the link."

Tyndall swivels in his chair and with a fierce look says, "Hey."

"Oh, oh sorry, Mr. Tyndall, but…"

"I don't want to know, just watch what you say."

"Sorry."

James, while digging into his backpack, asks, "So Tynd, is it true that if we catch a muskrat and bring it in, we get an A in River Watch class?"

"Yeah, but it's got to be a live muskrat."

Ryan is quick to say, "We'll just order one on the Internet."

"Go ahead, can't get a live one," Tyndall says, taking another bite of the salad and placing his feet on the desk.

"So, we catch one and we get an A for the year?" James asks.

"No, not quite, you catch one, and one of you gets an A for the semester—got it?"

"Can we both get B's?" Hector quickly asks.

"No."

"What about we bring you a dead muskrat?"

"Then you both get F's."

"We'll get graded accordingly," the three boys say in unison.

"What if it's alive, then it dies?"

"I'll fail you accordingly, for both semesters." Tyndall continues, "Live, not dead, any fool can kill a muskrat. Alive."

"Where do we find a muskrat?"

James is quick to enlighten Hector: "Remember the reading, by the woman writer?"

Tyndall pipes up, "Annie Dillard; *Pilgrim—Pilgrim at Tinker Creek.*"

James continues where Tyndall leaves off. "Yeah, the woman sneaks up on muskrats, muskrats are like God, everywhere, but you can't see them unless you look and don't look at the same time."

Smiling, Tyndall says, "Well, pretty much so, like that."

Tyndall sits and picks through his salad and watches the boys jibe each other about catching a muskrat. James pulls up a photo on his phone and passes it around. All the while Tyndall watches and wonders why some kids can think about a reading or painting and actually see the metaphor, while others just can't breach the gap.

James, with a funny smile, points to the phone in Hector's hand, and says, "See if you can find one in a white robe, sandals and a beard?"

"What?"

"Or with a crown of thorns"

James throwing his head back laughing, looks down at his phone and says, "Yeah that's gotta be here."

"What?"

"What the fuck are you talking about?"

"The muskrat is Jesus."

"What?"

"Never mind."

"How do we catch it?"

In a direct manner, Tyndall looks hard at the boys and says, "I'm not going to help you, that would be too easy."

Hector walks over to the wall next to Tyndall's desk and grabs the net leaning on the wall and says, "Can we use your net?"

Tyndall snaps back quickly, "That's for butterflies and insects."

Tyndall gets up from his desk and walks through the side door of the adjoining classroom of Mr. Jay. He enters the storeroom and grabs three dip nets– sturdy aquatic nets with a D-shaped net and a four and a half foot handle. Just as he's coming back through Mr. Jay's room the boys burst in, jabbering away. "You'll need some waders too, he says." He points to a cabinet in the corner of the room. Jay looks up from eating his burrito, chewing and reading the newspaper.

With a wry smile on his face, Tyndall says, "They're going out to catch muskrats."

With food in his mouth, "Oh yeah," Jay says in a drawl.

"Okay, where do we go?"

"Still water, slow moving, not the river—but a pond, like downtown where the taco place used to be."

Hector adds, "Yeah, yeah I've seen them there."

"No, you haven't, you're full of shit."

Tyndall, gesturing with his hand, says, "Okay guys, get out of here, good luck. Here's three nets and three pairs of waders—now be gone."

Tyndall looks at Jay, and says, "I think the world was safer when soccer was in season and they didn't have so much energy."

Jay looks up from his paper. "Yeah, it'll never be safe."

Tyndall smiles, "Yeah, what can go wrong?"

Jay, smiling, turns to Tyndall and says, "Good thing it's warm out."

Tyndall continues to wave the boys away, saying. "Lord have mercy, happy hunting. Grab a bucket in my room on your way out—now go. What could possibly go wrong? Good thing it's warm out." The two men turn and look out the windows as the three boys bounce through the courtyard, arms full of gear, as leaves blow on the ground and some snowflakes start to fall.

The boys drive downtown where there is a small pond to the side of the river. The pond has an inlet on the one side with a large roundish concrete pipe. On the far side, water flows over a spillway to a slow, wide canal that dumps into the river about a hundred yards down from the pond. They joke around while pulling the hip waders over their jeans. Hector has a stocking cap pulled over his ears and a down vest on. James and Ryan have hoodies on with the hoods pulled up. Each has a net in one hand, and Hector carries the big orange five-gallon bucket in his other hand. He slowly bangs the bucket with the handle of the net, making a rhythmic hollow clunking sound. The hunt. The hunt is a primal endeavor as old as time. As they near the pond the boys are remarkably quiet. They have funny smiles on their faces, looking over at each other as they cruise the nearshore of the small pond.

"Look!" Hector says, pointing with his net.

"No way! Fuck." Right at a broad flat sweep of cattails growing at the intake is a brown, cat-sized, round beast slowly swimming up the narrow muddy channel. James gives hand signals for Hector to go over the top of the intake pipe and circle around and down. The other two boys charge into the mud flats with the cattails where the large pipe comes out. The muskrat dives and swims into the pipe. A set of rebar barriers are laid up against the pipe opening where it exits from the berm-like hillside. James and Ryan are stuck in the mud in the cattails, laughing and cursing. Hector rounds the berm and slides down the bank into the willows at the edge of the pipe outlet.

After some struggle, the boys meet on the flat concrete pad where the pipe disappears under the berm. James pulls a wader off one foot; his right foot sock and pant leg are all wet and slick with stinky black mud. As he dumps the water out of the wader boot, the boys look at each other. Shallow six-inch-deep water flows on the wide concrete slab. The pipe is oblong, about eight feet wide and about six feet tall. The barrier of rebar is broken on one side. The water is dark and blackish in color; it flows about three feet wide and about a foot deep inside the pipe. There is a hollow echoing sound to the flowing water, with a strange silver sliver discernible from where the boys stand looking in.

"Did it go in here?"

"Yeah."

"I don't know."

"No, I saw it, dove in here."

"We're going to fucking die."

"Fuck, it's cold."

James pushes at the rebar which is not attached at the bottom, and says, "Come on." The rebar swings like a pendulum to the side because it is still attached at the top. The boys enter; the pipe echoes in a strange way, their boots make a swishing sound. Each has a smile on his face and they emanate strange, funny laughter. Ryan swishes the net in the dark water. The boys fumble around with their cell phones to turn on the flashlights. The water is now a yellow-tan in the broad white light of their cell phone lights; the air is heavy and almost foggy in the darkness.

"Now what the fuck, where is it?"

"Just keep the nets ready."

"Ready for what?"

"The fucking rat." Hector tucks his phone into the fold of his ski cap, so it is like a headlamp. James sticks his in his shirt pocket, light sticking out the top. A fog comes from their breath as they speak in hushed whispers. Hector grabs James by the back of his hoodie; James swings his arm back to make him let go. The water gets deeper as the pipe becomes more rectangular in shape. At the junctions of the pipe sections, red orange tangles of roots protrude through, hanging and clinging to the sides of the concrete. Strange whitish fingers of film dance in the slow current of yellow-tan water.

Images seem to appear as the light bounces off the water, reflecting dancing waves of light on the pipe ceiling and side walls. In the foggy dream-like atmosphere; Paleolithic cave art paintings, like those in the caves of Lascaux and Chauvet in France, blink on and off as if illuminated by an old-time movie projector. The overlapping heads of lions, with no manes, seem to be animated and look on at the boys. A group of rhinos, again with overlapping huge blocky bodies, does not blink, as one rhino faces the opposite direction. Horses, deer stags, and bull-like aurochs of red, yellow and black undulate in the light of the flashlights. The boys continue down the long tunnel as if on some shamanistic ritual.

"I don't know about this..."

"Shut up man, the fucking rat is in here."

Ryan, pointing with his net, in a screeching whisper says, "There." A dark brown shadow darts under their feet. They jab their nets frantically into the shallow water.

James slips and falls back, grabbing his phone light and thrusting it up above the water. Many curse words echo in the dark chamber. James pushes himself up and swishes the net in a mad anger through the water. The muskrat flaps up against the curved vertical wall of the concrete. James runs and lunges forward, scooping the large rodent into the net. He yells, "Get the bucket." With a loud thud, the animal is in the bucket thrashing around, the sound of its tail and toenails on the hard plastic.

The boys emerge from the pipe laughing. James is all wet, teeth chattering, jeans wet. One wader is full of water as he extracts it off his foot, he yells, "Keep the net over the bucket."

"Dude, you got it."

"We fucking got it. Tynd is going to freak." Laughing. "Dude, you're going to get hypothermia—come on, man."

As they approach the car, the girls drive up; Sandy, Helen and Sialia, all smiles and texting away. They park the car. Sialia sees James shivering in his wet hoodie and jeans says, "Oh Mali, you're a mess. Here—take my jacket."

James yanks his wet hoodie and shirt off with his trembling hands. He extracts his soccer jersey from a pile in the back of his car. Sandy gives him her orange ski cap which is folded perfectly to show the label in the front. He then puts on Sialia's ski jacket over the soccer jersey. It is smaller than his jersey and the jersey sleeves stick out in a comical way. Hector, reaching into the trunk, pulls out a pair of soccer sweat pants and says, "Here, man, put these on." The girls, looking on, start giggling as Sandy lifts her phone to take a photo of James stripping down his pants around the side of the car. Sialia swiftly raises her hand, deflecting her friend's arm to prevent the photo.

Sialia gazes at the taut muscles on the side of James' thigh and calf. An image of a bronze life-sized statue, *contrapposto*, seems to come to life, as he bends his leg to pull his sweat pants on.

James looking down, shivering and pointing says, "Thanks you guys— look."

In the orange bucket under the net is a brown, furry, wet muskrat. Sandy exclaims, "It's so pretty, but a hideous tail."

"Juxtaposition," they say in unison, laughing. Each emanating the word they memorized for an AP-English exam.

James clenching his chattering teeth, smiles. A victory smile, successful in the hunt.

Hector says, "Come on, let's go to 7-Eleven. My cousin Jesus works there, we can get some hot mocha and warm up."

"Tynd is going to freak out."

Sandy, smiling, says, "Look at its big whiskers, so cute."

Helen exclaims, "But that tail. Keep it away from me!"

Sialia, in a cooing soft voice, says, "But it's so cute."

The boys drive with the net over the bucket and the handle sticking out the window of the car. After a quick stop to show Jesus and get hot drinks, the boys return triumphant from the hunt. Sialia is in her car, and Hector is driving James' car as they all pull up to the back parking lot. Photos of a large, wet, brown rodent in a circular orange bucket are quickly posted and shared, and are circulated around the school instantly.

58

THREE-LEGGED DOG

Cualli and Anci walk down a narrow trail in a cloud forest on the high ridge. The ground is an interlocking weave of roots covered with green moss. All around them are stunted trees and stout tree ferns covered with epiphytes and moss all dripping wet. From here they will descend onto the high interior plateau. In the afternoon they stop at some large sloping boulders overlooking the immense valley with the volcanoes looming to the southwest. At this spot they dry out their cloaks and rest. Here they read one last story from the Codex.

"Here, I am familiar with this story," Anci says.

Looking over her shoulder, Cualli says, "Is that…that what I think it is?"

"Yes, probably. This is the three-legged dog. See, here, how it is eating its own leg," she says, pointing to the glyph of the dog gnawing on a bloody stump of a front leg.

"But why?"

"You will see. Now here is the year cycle, and the five days in between, you know, set for fate and destiny with no festivals."

"Ah, that is elsewhere in the book."

"Yes, but see. The following year it is eating a different leg—and that front leg from before has grown back."

"But then it is still hobbled—right?"

"Yes. And the cycle continues the next year."

Anci the warrior, and Cualli approach the last segment of their journey to deliver the Codex. The tops of the volcanos gleam silver-white, while steam rises from one. Tensions are high with the people they meet and pass on the road. A line of warriors passes in spotted jaguar costumes; others are waving feathers of the Eagles Sect, all marching at a slight jog. Anci, pointing to the people in jaguar outfits, says, "That is the sect of warriors that I was training with." A procession of thirty men goes by; each carries a long stick with big flakes of black obsidian glued into grooves on two sides, making a club-like sword.

"Where do we go from here?"

"There is a flat plaza with no prominent temples or pyramids over there," she says, pointing to the west. "That is where the three nation tribes meet to do battle and the sacrifices occur after the battles. It is a place used by different empires: the Aztec Mexicana from the northwest, the Tarascan from the west, and Our People from the Rising Sun on the water. I do not know how we will be received, so use caution. Remember you are wearing the clothes of a noble, made out of cotton, so they will approach you as if you are a noble. Take your sandals off as we enter the plaza, carry them in your left hand, and look down when approaching."

They enter the plaza, which is actually several platform-like open areas of dark gray limestone paving stones. A warrior approaches them holding a serpent headed spear thrower in his right hand and a feathered shield with three long darts in his other hand. He has a feathered crest on his head stretching from ear to ear. His ears and nose are pierced with turquoise, and gold tassels hang from his cotton loincloth. He wears sandals and has a serious, stern look on his face.

"Remember, look down, let me do the talking," Anci says, as she removes her sandals and walks up to the warrior with her right hand on the handle of her obsidian knife. They are led to the prominent overlook and are joined by several priests. The Codex is extracted from its pack and placed on an altar. The coati eyes look on; the blue and green feathers on the pack dance in the wind. On the large stone altar sits the obsidian mirror. Anci looks into it and sees a horse charging down a stone road bearing a Spaniard wielding a steel sword. A wooden shield, covered in bright blue feathers, shatters; the feathers explode out into the air. There is much deliberation. The priests and Anci and

Cualli meet and discuss the Spaniards, their weapons, and how they appeared from the floating cities. Cualli explains his observations of gunpowder and how he witnessed a true lust for gold and women. For three days they meet with various priests at the plaza. They are treated well and discuss what they had seen. It is decided: the Codex will be hidden in the caverns below the plaza.

Upon leaving the high terrace of the plaza, Cualli recognizes and points to a series of white limestone reliefs of dogs eating their own legs. Each carving is about six feet tall and superimposed over the next relief to give the impression of different legs being eaten while the dog hobbles around. It plays out like movie images as they descend the stairs to the lowest plaza and on down. Smooth, rounded white-stone reliefs surrounded by gray pavement stones, flickering in the bright light.

With little ceremony, the Codex enclosed in the coati pack was hidden in the caverns below the plaza, a place where today stands the Puebla Cathedral, where the huge dog reliefs were chipped away at and re-carved into icons of Catholic saints and domineering archangels. And the shadows dance in the bright Mexican light giving an impression of movement. The fluorescent beating wings of an archangel, carved with Spanish-steel chisels, created from the gnawing teeth of a dog eating its own leg. And the gray paving stones of the plaza were reused to build the church.

59

MUSKRAT HEAVEN

After lunch, Tyndall's class is taking a test; as usual he has gathered up all the phones in a large black plastic flower pot. The container sits on the side counter and flashes light out the top, and hums and buzzes at various pitches as the devices incessantly go off.

It's about an hour into class as Tyndall is collecting tests. James cracks the back door of Tyndall's room with a smile on his face and his matted, wet hair sticking out from under Sandy's orange ski cap. He has purple sweatpants on and three jackets of different sizes oddly layered with the sleeves sticking out in a funny way. Tyndall lets out a short laugh under his breath and starts to shake his head. James turns and runs back to the car where everyone is standing.

As they walk up to the back door through the courtyard, Hectors says to James, "Mali, you're getting an A for this semester. You probably already have one, but now you won't have to do anything. Wow, I met with the counselor yesterday and they warned me that I might not even have enough credits to graduate."

James looks down at the wet chocolate brown muskrat in the bucket softly swaying as he carries it. Then he swings the bucket over to Hector, "Here."

"But…"

"Fuck you. Take it, it's okay."

"Mali, no, it don't do me any good anyways."

James smiles as he pulls the back door open and shoves his friend in the room and says, "You should've seen Hector catch that rodent."

"But Mali, you—"

James quickly whacks his friend in the arm. The girls are smiling and looking on. Sialia smiles and looks hard, like a frozen cave painting, at James.

Hector, holding the bucket, "Do I get an A—really?"

Tyndall, shaking his head side to side, as if to say no, and slightly laughing in disbelief says, "Yeah. I never thought…Yeah, you get an A—but you still have to come to class, understand?"

Hector, with a funny smile, says, "That's my first A ever!"

Mr. Jay comes in, smiling while his whole class trails behind. Commotion sets in, cameras are snapping, photos are quickly posted. The kids are attracted to the little brown muskrat. Jay turns to Tyndall and says, "A two-pound rodent in the school; what can go wrong?"

Tyndall turns and looks up, and in a slow drawn out breath, mutters, "Oooh yeah."

After loud and rambunctious stories of the capture and the hunt, Tyndall calls James over to him. "James Malachite," he says, as he gestures for him to come over to the back door. James walks over and Tyndall grabs James' jacket, pulls him in close, and says, "Mr. Malachite, here's what you're going to do. It's a wild animal, so go let it go, where you caught it. Got it? Now the critter has had a hard day, so let it go now." James just looks Tyndall straight in the eye and nods.

As the group walks back to the car through the back courtyard, the back hall door flies open and another group of kids wants to see the muskrat. James and the boys step into the back hallway to show off their catch. What could go wrong?

Tyndall returns back in his room, and things settle down. He is busy explaining the natural history of muskrats, and how it all worked in River Watch class. Then a student burst through the hallway door, "Tynd, Tynd, you got to come quick!" Tyndall stands there, does a very long blink, closes his eyes, breathes in deep, and heads out the door.

The muskrat had jumped out of the bucket in the hallway and all hell broke loose. It ran straight down the hall through the legs of kids as teachers closed doors and screams and yelling broke out. The boys had bounded after it, leaping and diving as they tried to catch it. Phones were instantly out, capturing images of the critter striding and dodging over books, in between legs, and then across the perpendicular hallway and straight into the library.

Now the boys bound after it along with a growing group of people trying to video the whole thing as it runs. Shit is flying in every direction as the insane dash to catch it from behind proceeds. Students dive and run out of its way in front of it. Whole book shelves tumble down, laptops and phones fly from hands. There are bloodcurdling screams and students jump on tables and then tumble over and out of the way.

Tyndall doesn't need to ask where to go. He can tell by the noise and commotion where the action is. When he comes into the library, some kids are on the ground laughing so hard they can't stand up, while others are curled in little balls sitting on top of tables holding their knees to their chest and crying. It is like a tornado hit, with people frantically running and screaming at the rodent. Tyndall grabs a kid, points and says, "Back door—open it! Forget the alarm," and shoves the kid, yelling, "Go!" The kid pushes the door open and a fire alarm-like rhythmic squawking beep screams into the commotion. The muskrat bounds on down book piles, people and books flying in its wake. The critter runs out the open back door, galloping down the hill. It is remarkably fast for a semi-aquatic rodent.

Tyndall just stands there and takes in the scene, some kids are crying and others laughing. The library is a total pandemonium of books, magazines, laptops, kids standing on tables, kids hiding under tables. The back-door alarm is screaming. The rodent is still running, on past the parking lot, then the bike path and then down to the dry irrigation ditch lined by overhanging willows.

Tyndall looks around sees the three boys and calls to them. The librarian, Mrs. Hall, is yelling frantically at Tyndall, but he's not paying attention to her. Her screaming is actually more distressing than the whole incident. Tyndall gestures to the boys to step into the conference room in the back corner of the library. Tyndall looks back at the kid he had commanded earlier; he is still standing there holding the screaming door open, as if he were a statue. Pointing to the back door, Tyndall calmly gestures and says, "Just close it."

They step into the conference room and Tyndall closes the door behind them. "Fuck, Lord mercy, we're going to get in trouble now," are the first words out of his mouth.

The boys all start talking at once, "Tynd, Johnny reached, and Jorge dropped his phone in the bucket and…"

"Shut up and listen. Don't say anything, we only got a minute. Just don't blame anyone; just get in trouble. Take it on the chin. Don't lie; whatever you do, don't lie. Get in trouble—got it? Get in trouble—capiche?"

"Capiche," the three boys say in unison.

"And start cleaning up this mess, just clean up—and get whoever you can to help you, or the fucking librarian will kill us all."

Hector says, "This is a hard day."

Tyndall quickly says, "Yeah, but not as hard as it was for the rodent." They all smile. Just then Principal Stufa walks in.

The muskrat continues down the dry ditch, through the fields, then through the culvert under the highway. It can hear the river water flowing. It proceeds down the long tunnel of willows all bent over the canal, now devoid of water for the winter, with only a little snow and ice mixed with the willow leaves. Just as it approaches the last stretch to the river, a coyote jumps out from the tall bare bankside vegetation. Snaps it up in its jaws and in one swift shake, kills the muskrat. The death shake is an astonishing action; so fast and cruel in its gripping finality. It hangs limp in the coyote's jaw. She trots off in a smooth bouncing gate, chocolate brown muskrat hanging in her mouth, as dusk gives way to night. A little way up the canal she drops the dead muskrat for her now grown pups to eat. Tails wag and tongues lick her face, welcoming a good meal before the onset of winter.

60

EL SALVADOR V

There in the side parking lot of the palapa bar, evening falls and with it a stillness in the surrounding jungle as the frogs just begin to sing. Just a slight way down the road, Juan is finishing changing the flat tire. A man jumps out of the blue pickup truck with one kilogram of cocaine in plastic wrapping, hanging heavy in a thin plastic grocery bag. The bag sways pendulously back and forth as the man walks up to the pickup truck and places it on the hood. The bag vibrates rhythmically on the hood of the running truck. He pulls out his knife and slices a slit in the center of the plastic. He pulls and presses a crack in the layers of plastic wrapping. He sticks his knife blade into the white powder and lifts the blade of glistening white cocaine to his tongue. The cool taste numbs his mouth and with a rush he breathes in.

At that moment the first gun shots are fired; with his eyes wide open and pupils dilated, the man is shot and drops the one kilogram of cocaine in the torn wrapping. His partner jumps out of the truck firing a gun back at the other truck. Crouching behind the open door he reaches over the shot man and grabs the cocaine in the plastic grocery bag. It spills a white trail as he backs up and dives into the open door of his truck. About half of the white powder gets spilled on the ground. After some pursuit down the winding road the truck crashes and flips. His pursuer, in the other truck, reaches in and grabs the now half kilogram in the grocery bag. The white powders spills in a heap at his feet. It is at that time another car drives up and he is shot. Two men jump out and grab the spilled coke and drive away with what now weighs about two hundred and fifty grams. In a blitz of action one of the two kills the other later that night and makes off with a hundred and twenty-five grams of coke. So, it continues through the night. And in the end, two men stand face to face, eyes wet and glazed; each with a handful of cocaine in one hand and a gun in the other. Within a second, they both lie dead on the muddy ground. Half blows away in the wind, half washes away with the morning rain. Cut in half, in a trail of violence and tears.

Down the road from the bar, little Juanito is inadvertently shot dead next to the truck his father is repairing. Miguel Angel's father stands crying over the body of his son. Green and purple mangos lie scattered on the ground next to the truck. The tire iron drops out of his hand to the ground with a sharp resounding clang and echoes into the surrounding jungle.

61

THE TURNIP FACTORY

The ravens assemble on the west-facing cliff on this warm, sunny and windy spring afternoon. The gypsum outcrop has eroded into a cliff that forms a natural amphitheater. Here the ravens gather to fly on the rising heat of the exposed rock, which is all bent, curved, and sinuous evaporate strata. Along with the cliff's particular aspect, and the heat rising up from the sun-baked rock, the wind makes the amphitheater a perfect playground. The big black birds converge on this special spot in the landscape. The strong wind allows them to glide motionless above the ridgeline. They fold their wings and plummet, twist, and whirl and tumble in freefall, wings spread, and launch them back up into the air. After gliding steadily on the foil of air, they again fold their wings back and plummet upside down, tumbling effortlessly under another raven hovering. From the branch of a pinyon pine, a bird sits and watches, clasping the branch and spreading its wings but not letting go. It bounces and is lifted upward, springing on the branch. The raven lets go with the gust of wind—free. The bird, with outstretched wings, is lifted straight up, free flying, legs hanging down. Then waits—pulls the legs up, tucks the wings slightly back and stoops forward, tumbling in the bright air, careening backwards and to the side, going with the freedom of the wind.

The boys ride in the bed of the pickup truck which pulls up to the field for practice. They launch themselves into the air, lacrosse sticks in one hand and sports drinks in the other. Spring sports have begun and it's the second day of lacrosse practice. The snow has just melted and the ballfield is muddy.

A chinook wind is blowing at a steady 40 mph out of the southwest.

"Hey Malachite, you and Ryan show the freshman boys how to collect the balls over in crazy McCload's field over the fence."

"Yeah, coach."

Ryan and James look at each other, then start jogging for the fence in the back of the lacrosse goal. On the way they each grab a smaller freshman boy by the back of their hoodie.

"Don't let Farmer McCload catch you; so, explain it to the newbies," the coach barks out at James and Ryan.

There are about twice as many players out early in the season. There are so many annoying little freshmen that can't throw or catch, so there are balls all over the place. The air feels warm and humid, smells sweet, and the wind is incessant. The more experienced boys place athletic tape over the ear holes on their lacrosse helmets to block the howling noise made by the strong wind.

James and Ryan and the two younger boys arrive at the barbed wire fence line in back of the ballfields. Here there is an expansive set of hay meadows lined by small irrigation ditches. "Okay guys, ya jump the fence here. Then collect up the balls and chuck them to the corner of the playing field, else you'll take out somebody's nuts. Go fast; if the farmer guy comes on his ATV, just head back, he'll have a shit-ka-fit with coach. Don't get into it with him, just head back—let coach take care of it—else we'll all be running."

As one of the younger boys attempts to climb the fence, he says, "What's up about this hay field and our lacrosse balls?"

"Something about school land in his family's land. Some weird happening," James says.

Just then the little guy falls with his foot caught in the top rung of the barb wire fence. Ryan and James stand there and laugh, drop their sticks, and walk back to the fence and help extract him.

Ryan says, "Never climb a fence before? Ya okay, kid?"

"Yeah."

The little guy is all embarrassed and is trying to smile and laugh it off. James grabs the freshman's lacrosse stick and hands it to him, saying, "Come on spread out and get the balls, fast." The lower leg of the boy's gray sweatpants is torn, and his leg is bleeding a little.

James, with his big oversized lacrosse glove, hits Ryan on the shoulder and says, "Come on, I've always wanted to check this out," as he gestures to the collapsed wood rafters of a half-buried structure in the hay meadow. Ryan looks around, back at the ballfield and all the busy running and throwing. He smiles looking through the facemask of his lacrosse helmet, then turns to the younger boys and says, "Yeah, spread out, don't miss any."

James and Ryan run off to the old potato root cellar structure at the far end of the hay meadow. They approach from the northeast corner of the structure. It is about the size and shape of a small single-car garage; its far end is sunk into a shallow hill and has round skull sized black basalt rocks as part of its foundation. It has a door facing toward the lacrosse field. The door is held by only the top hinge and is open exposing the sunken room inside. The roof is made of rough log beams covered with a foot-thick sod of soil and grass. The roof is partially collapsed farther in the room, illuminating the interior in a dull light. Rock steps, grown over with long winter-dead grass, lead down to the door and the interior of the root cellar.

"I've always wanted to check this out," James says, dropping his lacrosse stick and taking off his helmet and gloves.

Ryan and James step in. Round dark rocks with soil between them line the interior walls. The cellar is about seven feet deep from the dirt floor to the wooden beam roof. The far collapsed end is completely underground and at the door end it is about four feet underground. Jutting out from the soil and rock walls are long, thin, creeping vine-like roots with stems. There is a pile of rusty, old metal saw blades and the axle of a tractor in one corner. There is also a stack of car tires falling over against the wall by the collapsed corner of the roof.

"Mali, what is all this?" Ryan asks.

"It's a potato cellar, from when they grew potatoes here a hundred years ago. Yeah, it's like an underground frigerator. Tynd talked about it once."

"Whatever."

It is cool, damp and very quiet inside. Through the opening in the roof, James can see the white wisps of clouds against the bright blue sky; it is a very dreamlike perspective. His mind feels like it is floating weightless as he gazes at the sky. But the dark interior feels like a big flat rock has been placed on his chest—a shudder of cold hits him like a wave. There is a musky smell, like onions or maybe carrots. Ryan pulls on the white, lanky vines jutting out from the inside wall.

James says, "Huh, growing with no light, how weird."

"Yeah, they look like they're fake, plastic," Ryan says. Looking back around he says, "Come on, coach's gonna get to asking."

"Yeah, let's get those little guys and head back," James says.

From the rock steps, James takes one last look into the cellar. In the near corner is a pack rat midden piled high from the floor to the ceiling. It is one tall chimney of rat excrement mixed with pinecones, small round rocks, sticks and an occasional feather or bone. For decades a procession of pack rats has collected and piled the stuff of their world into one cylindrical layered pile of debris. Each layered level is material deposited from successive generations of pack rats. The stratigraphy of each layer is a testament to a particular window of time. Toward the bottom of the pile is a round, fist-sized, half chewed up, petrified turnip. James blinks hard, looking at it briefly from the side before he steps back into the brightness and wind of the spring day. Grabbing his lacrosse gear, he starts jogging back to the ballfield.

On the outer rock wall of the potato cellar there is matrimony vine growing. Here along the warm, south-facing stone it forms loose clumps of trailing, weak woody vines about three feet in height. The frosty gray-green stems hang over with a few shriveled orange-red berries. On the inside wall, though, the roots grow out and the vines shoot out into the interior blackness of the space. The vines growing in the pit-like chamber are long and a creamy white, and trail on for five to ten feet, with white little nodes where leaves are supposed to grow. They grow and clamber, whirl, ever reaching, striving to find light, growing out into the damp dark void.

The McCload family homesteaded on this parcel of land back in the 1890s. Late in the 1920s the three sons split up the land into separate ranches and farms. The family called the bench-like hill above the valley Elysium Hills. The name has something to do with some old story their father, from Scotland, told them. Something about the way the morning light illuminated the bench. The old man fancied himself an old-time bard from the Highlands. He would wax on about "the sheeny light on those fields. There on the hill bathed in the ethereal purple light with the morning dew wisped away." Then he would stop talking, there in the big kitchen, and just gaze out the window as if he could really see the light upon those fields. His silence would break as he continued in Scottish Gaelic from the old country. But his steely gray eyes continued to stare transfixed. The name Elysium Hills is just a place name; it is not a town or a township or even denoted officially on any map—it is just a name—just a place.

The middle brother, sometime during the Great Depression, got some cockamamie scheme in his head to grow turnips instead of potatoes. He had it all planned out. Grow the turnips and feed the cows the top leafy part in the summer. Then harvest the big roots and feed the cows the roots in the winter. He came home one day talking about some Russian scientist in the new Soviet Union who came up with the whole idea. This guy, Lysenko, was a genius; he had a revolutionary technique of wetting and cooling the seeds called vernalization. It was supposed to increase yields by four times. But in the end, the whole scheme went south: The turnips made the milk taste odd, and they didn't store as well as potatoes. The families argued and fought. There was a good market for potatoes, they had all the equipment for potatoes, people eat potatoes—it had all been working. "Turnips? What, why—turnips? Fucking turnips!" the oldest brother would yell in the big kitchen, spilling the coffee in the mug in his hand.

The vector of the turnip enterprise was set in motion with its own peculiar time, space, and angle. The turnip farm was foreclosed and confiscated by the banks with a small parcel sold to the state of Colorado. This state parcel is now the school property. The oldest brother's ranch is essentially the housing subdivision at the bottom of the hill. The third ranch survived and evolved into the operation it is today with grass/alfalfa-hay and cattle. But when it built the new school, the state acquired some acreage from the surviving ranch through eminent domain. This acreage is now the ballfields in back of the school. And now on that sunny bench above the valley, glowing in the light of dawn, shines the campus of Elysium Hills High School. And there in a hayfield in back of the school is a potato cellar, with a pack rat midden, with a turnip in a layer from 1930. It is a testament, a history, preserved in the cool, damp, dark chamber. And for nearly a century the vines have grown into an empty space, reaching out for a light that is never there.

There in the darkness below Elysium; there, in what lies beneath.

62

DEUS EX MACHINA

At the end of the school day, the staff assembles for the weekly meeting at the library. And so the meeting begins. Dr. Stufa, Joel Haustoria, and the superintendent are busy setting up the tables and chairs in the library. Each table has several different colored sticky notepads, multiple colored scented markers, plus three giant sheets of presentation poster paper. Music is playing and the secretary is rolling in the cart with coffee, donuts, and oranges and bananas to the corner near the doors. One side of the room has forty-three chairs aligned right next to each other, in a giant semi-circle. The chairs are facing a large flat screen TV in the ceiling corner. Stufa has strategically put out forty-three chairs for the forty-eight teachers and staff. This is his managerial technique, so that anyone coming in late has to disruptively fetch a chair and shove it into the half circle, thus calling attention to their tardiness. Stufa finishes things up by closing the blinds to the windows; wouldn't want anyone daydreaming at the vista of mountains in the bright Colorado sunlight. One of the blinds is broken and hangs stuck at an odd diagonal.

Stufa starts off, "Now everyone, let's have a seat over here and get started. You'll notice that the music has stopped playing; that's the signal to get to our spots or later at different stations set up at the tables over there."

Haustoria and Mr. Combe are wrestling with the computer and the projection on the screen as Stufa continues with his arms moving in a circular motion. Coach Brown comes in. He was on the phone with another athletic director about the upcoming games this week. He stops and stands outside the circle and listens. Stufa interjects, "Now Coach Brown get a chair, join the circle. We are all one big team on this crew."

Haustoria steps up and says, "Now we're passing out the results from last spring's state tests. Each packet is color-coded on different colored sheets. Now, do we have the projector yet?" as he looks back over his shoulder at Combe frantically pecking at buttons on his laptop while looking up and then back down at his computer. Finally, the image comes up on the screen. It is of a black and white spreadsheet with various columns and rows highlighted in different colors.

"Which one are we on?" a teacher barks out.

"This should be your yellow paper, this year's sophomores."

"But on our sheets the rows are just gray, and it's colored on the screen." Also, the spreadsheet on the flat screen is projected so small that only about half the people in the circle of chairs can make out the numbers.

Now Stufa, Haustoria and the superintendent are all standing next to each other explaining in unison how…

"Now that we know how students learn…," the superintendent says.

"And with these test results and the new curriculum aligned to the new standards…," Haustoria says.

The superintendent then adds, "With the grant we have obtained and the training, you all will be successful in intentionally achieving higher levels of thinking for the students…"

Stufa continues, pointing to the numbers on the screen that no one can read…

At that moment sunlight comes streaming in through the catawampus shade. Stufa, Haustoria, and the superintendent turn to the side and start wheeling in a huge steel and wooden crane with large wooden wheels up to the front of the half circle. Haustoria is heaving his entire weight on a massive crank handle as the cable and hook are maneuvered by Stufa and the superintendent. The crane with cable crashes through the drop ceiling and a rainbow and sunshine appear as they lower a gleaming white unicorn into the center of the circle. The teachers are all pointing to the colored sheets, looking up at the screen and frantically writing on their colored paper packets. Some have both hands in the air; others are clapping in unison, there are tears, and laughter. The unicorn is lowered to the ground, rears up and gallops around the tables with the multicolored sticky notes flying in the air behind it. It gallops around the circle, abruptly stops and takes a dump on the outskirts of the circle. Stufa walks over and starts the music. The steaming pile of shit is covered and infused with pink glitter. It sits there as a prominent pile that all enthusiastically look at and admire. Everyone is gleefully turning to each other, pointing and smiling in overexuberant gestures, as if pantomiming on stage with the orchestra playing some singsongy Gershwin musical tune.

Someone exclaims, "Ah! This is all so magnificent. This is the best of all possible worlds."

"We need to incorporate this into the Rubric."

"The Formative Assessments culminate in higher level thinking."

Another teacher points and adds, "Oh look at all this—now the children will be engaged. All is for the best."

"Oh, can you smell that?"

"Ah yes, it's familiar—kind of pleasant, what is it?"

"Oh, I know that. What is that?"

"Oh, oh I know—lavender."

"Yes, lavender—oh my."

63

HARRIER HUNTING

Knight, Death and the Devil
Steadfast
True
Faithful by his side
The impending wheel of time
Ever pursued by the silent menace
Pressed upon from the side
The weight from above
Stand tall and ride on

—G.B.

It is Thursday, the last day of school for the week. The next day is teacher training, so the kids have a long weekend. The wind blows hard and steady as Sialia and Sandy jog around the soccer field. Sandy says, "I wish I remembered my tights."

"Yeah, it's like this every spring. It's warm out, but with this wind it's cold—really, you know." Looking over at the track, Sialia waves to Helen, who is walking on the track interspersed with exaggerated high steps. She dances a wave back to them, her dark hair blowing madly around her face. She is preparing herself for interval sprints.

In the near hayfield, a pair of harrier hawks are hunting in the strong spring wind. The smaller gray male swoops down on a mallard duck sitting on her nest along the irrigation canal.

At soccer practice, Sialia stands in line behind two other girls parallel to another line of girls for a passing drill. "Now full speed here," the soccer coach yells out. His voice is buffeted by the wind and most of the girls have the hoods of their sweatshirts pulled up. Breathing heavily, Sialia looks into the wind at the expanse of hay meadows; she sees the pair of hawks flying low, swooping back and forth in the strong wind. She and Sandy rotate up. Sialia drops the ball, dribbles it with her feet, and kicks it hard in front of Sandy, who lunges forward and gets the ball. She kicks the ball back, and Sialia responds with another quick kick back to Sandy.

The second hawk, a brown female, rhythmically turns right and drops down on the duck, just as the gray individual veers off. The mottled female duck lies low with her wings spread over the eggs in the nest.

Sandy jumps up to manage the high bouncing ball. Sialia thinks about her morning and can hear her little sister crying, and her mom responding.

The track coach barks out, "Now keep track of your own run-time and rest-time." Helen sprinting, lets up. Winded, she walks around the corner of the track, all the while looking down at her wristwatch. She knows that the next sprint will be against the wind. Her left ear stings from the incessant wind, and her hair whips across her face.

The two hawks swoop downwind, then turn, lift up, careen back upward, turn and come back with the wind behind them. They lunge upon the nest with the hen lying low in the nest.

Sialia's mom responds, "Now eat your cereal, you've got a bus to catch."

The ball is dribbled.

The track coach yells, "Go—full speed!" Helen stops, leans in, looks at her watch and sprints head down into the wind. Her hair is blown back, bouncing on the back of her neck.

The hawks split, the brown individual flushes the duck out of the nest while the gray hawk swoops up and turns.

Sialia can hear her sister crying, having a tantrum in Spanish. Mom stands there with a carton of milk in one hand and the cereal box in the other hand.

Sialia veers off to the sideline to retrieve an errant pass and kicks hard to get it back in play.

Boom! and in a flurry of feathers the gray hawk slams into the duck. The next moment the hawk is standing, clutching the duck in its talons while the duck's one wing flutters, then withers into a vibrating twitch. The wind blows steady and strong, as the brown hawk glides, just inches above the now greening hay grass, back to its mate.

Helen, looking down at her watch, turns the corner of the track, now with the wind at her back. With deep heaving breaths she gazes at her watch and readies herself for another sprint. Her hair furiously slaps around both sides of her face.

Sialia lunges to her left for the ball thinking about English class and the teacher saying, "I told you, stick to the rubric."

"But the paper's complete."

The teacher says, "Well, you get a partial grade.

"But, but it's in before the long weekend."

"I warned you to stick to what's outlined here," the teacher said, pointing to the rubric.

"It seems it's more about your grading rubric and not the writing."

"Matter's done. This will go on your quarter grade."

Sialia stood in the doorway, turned around and said, "So, what are you doing for the long weekend?"

"Well, I'll be grading these," the teacher said, gesturing with her open hand over the stack of papers.

"Have a nice weekend," Sialia said, then turned abruptly while exiting the room with a scowl on her face. Now, Sialia blasts the ball as far she can, way past Sandy, who looks over perplexed. She stops running and stands there holding her hands out, palms up.

"I got it," Sialia says, holding her hand up apologetically while running off to get the ball.

64

BUS RIDE REFLECTION

Jose Maria Velasco's painting, *The Valley of Mexico from the Santa Isabel Mountain Range,* was painted in 1875. The oil on canvas painting is on display at the Museo Nacional de Arte in Mexico City. It shows a vast open landscape with the two prominent volcanos far in the distance, and some people in the foreground, and everything in between shines in focus in the bright light. It is a world that is gone; now an expanse of urban sprawl on a massive scale, and some of the worst air quality in the Americas.

It's Thursday night, after soccer practice. Sialia asks her mom about using the car on Friday to go watch the boys' lacrosse game in the next town twenty-five miles away.

"What do you mean you don't have school tomorrow? You kids get so many days off. Just seems that teachers are in training all the time—you should be in school."

"Well, mamma, can I have the car?"

"No, you have to stay here and watch your little sister."

"But mamma, the game's not until four o'clock. She'll only be alone for an hour before you get home."

"I don't know. Let me think about it—can't you get a ride with Sandy?"

"No, no that won't work."

Earlier that evening, coming home from soccer practice with Sandy and Helen, they stopped at Starbucks for a fancy coffee drink. Sialia was the last to walk in after fumbling around in the parking lot with her phone—texting her mom. Sandy was standing, talking to Alisha and a couple of other mean girls at the long center communal table in the cafe. It was one of those inexplicable moments when somebody says something unwanted.

Alisha said, "What's with Sialia? She's always got her hair in some braid, like some Indian girl. How can you hang out with such a Mexican Beaner?"

Sandy stood there frozen, not knowing what to say. She turned around and Sialia was standing right in back of her, having heard the whole thing. Sialia didn't know what to say back. Upset she turned and said, "I think I'll walk home from here."

"Sialia, no! It's not what you think." Sandy sent off a quick text, but the message got fumbled up and misconstrued, just making matters worse.

Now it's Friday afternoon, and Sialia is supposed to stay with her sister, but she leaves at 3:40 to catch the bus up to the game. She keeps pulling out her phone and looking at it. Rereading the mis-sent text message from Sandy. She types a response back, does not send it, and then deletes it.

On the nearly empty bus, she sits in the third seat on the passenger side, and in the late afternoon sun stares out the window at the housing subdivisions, the traffic, and the mountains rolling by. There is a constant deep humming sound coming from the big tires on the asphalt. From where she sits, and the light at that time of day, she can see five different reflected images; plus, three actual images. She can see the side of the road and vegetation rolling by to her right; also, the oncoming traffic ahead, and the traffic and buildings speeding by in the opposite direction. In the near window, to her right, she sees a reflection of the traffic going by on her left. Across the aisle, to her left, she sees the reflection of the vegetation and houses to her right. There are also three mirrors with multiple reflected images swimming by, some of which are reflections of reflections.

But in her mind all the reflected images and the reality flowing by blend into one long twisted set of memories. She can see in the reflection herself and her family crossing the US-Mexico border at the river, there in the Chihuahua Desert. She remembers riding The Beast, the rumbling steel train with so many desperate souls. And waiting there in the bushes and tall reeds along the river. She can see the giant twelve-foot reeds, with the fluffy tops, swaying in the cold night wind. The reflection in the mirror shows her and her family hiding on the shoreline of the Rio Grande River, looking out at an asphalt wasteland. The very weight of hope, sitting there waiting for her uncle to drive up in his big blue pickup truck. The other window reflects the ocotillo and agave blooming, orange-red and cream white, there in the rocky desert. And in the mirror, above the driver, she can see the train and feel it rumble. In the side mirror to her right she sees her mom holding her infant sister, swaddled and wrapped in a big maroon shawl. On the far window, across the aisle, she sees a reflection of the bright lights of the border crossing miles down the river from where she hides in the streamside vegetation. In the near window reflection, she sees her feet stepping into the cold muddy river at night and disappearing into the chocolate colored water. Anger wells up inside, as she reminisces at the reflection of Sandy and her on the school playground at recess. She can see them together on the jungle gym, laughing. How can she know? The multiple reflections blink on and off playing vivid images of her memories. All the while, the rumbling hum of asphalt under her feet vibrates inside her bones.

At the game Sialia stares out across the field, as the boys, with lacrosse sticks in hand, run by. Sandy and Helen sit on the far side in the bleachers. Helen says, "Are you going to go talk to her? You know, fix it."

The girls stand and stare at each other across the field. Sandy holds her arms out to her side and mouths the words, "I'm sorry."

Sialia responds by holding her hands out to her side palms out and mouthing, "What the fuck?" Sialia's phone vibrates; she reads the text: "I'm sorry let me explain." She texts back: "I don't understand." Emotion wells up in her throat, tears flow, chest heaving with deep breaths as she tries to contain herself. Around the corner of the field, behind the far goal, along the fence they approach each other.

Sandy says, "Sialia come on, it's me, it didn't happen like you think."

"I don't understand."

"Let me explain. I was just standin' there, and that bitch just started saying nasty things, just when you walked in."

"But why? But how? But, but why didn't you say something?"

"But, you know. I just froze, didn't know what to say. You know what I'm saying?"

"But, how can you let her say that?"

"I didn't let her say that, she just said it. You know what a bitch she is—so nasty."

"But…"

"Come on girl, it's me. I'm sorry, I was slow to respond, I didn't know what to say—and then you are just standing there. I froze."

Sialia is wiping a tear off her cheek. Sandy reaches up and pushes a strand of hair back behind Sialia's ear. She steps forward and hugs her friend. "Come on, let's watch the rest of the game. You can get a ride home with me. James was asking about you; he's worried, too."

On the ride home Sandy and Helen sit in the front seat. James and Sialia sit in the back seat. James is all sweaty with his hood pulled up, hair all matted against his cheek, and grass stains on his forearm and elbow. His big lacrosse duffel bag is on the car floor; their feet sit awkwardly on top of his gear. Sialia silently sits there, with a tear rolling down her cheek. As she inhales, the last resurgence of fading emotion emerges, then tumbles down her soft cheek. James leans over and touches his shoulder to hers. He smells strong; a mix of grass, dirt and sweat. But it's not unpleasant; it actually smells like the wind on your face—something real and tangible. She grabs his hand, interlocks her fingers with his, and leans into him.

65

INTERFACE

Hey guys, let's stay unplugged and work together with this. I'll put the music on shuffle up here."

Helen, standing next to Tyndall, says, "Tynd, can you help me get a good stonefly?"

"Yeah, sure. Here." Tyndall grabs a pair of forceps and picks through the jar of insects preserved in alcohol. He plops down the large insect into a petri dish. "See here, it has two tails and these prominent wing pads. So, do you remember where the gills are on this critter?"

"No."

"Well, get your lecture packet out. That'll help you identify the structures."

Josue looks over Tyndall's shoulder at the bug in the dish. Helen says to him, "You want to draw this guy with me?"

"Yeah, sure. I've got the lecture packet here." They sit opposite one another at a lab table. "Mr. Tyndall, what's the front called?"

"Ventral, and the back is the dorsal side," he says, in an assertive voice so that everyone can hear him. "Make sure you guys label the structures on your drawings," he barks out. Sitting at his desk, he asks, "So Helen, where are you going to college?"

"Oh, CSU."

"Great, I think you'll like it there. And you Josue?"

"I don't know, probably Arapaho Community College. But I have to work."

Sialia joins in, "That's where I'm going. At least for the first two years." Sialia blinks and looks hard at Helen and Josue sitting together. She looks around the room at Ryan, Hector and James sitting together. She looks to her left at Sandy next to her at the same table. She smiles, then gets a serious look on her face as she peers around the room. The music screams out of the speakers at the front of the room. The frogs float silently adrift in the current from the filter. In the momentary lapse between songs with the ringing of the flowing water, Sialia sits straight up and loudly starts to talk. "You ever notice how we all still hang out with the same group of people. Hector, do you ever sit with Miguel Angel?"

"Ah, no."

"But aren't you on the same soccer team?"

"Well, yeah."

"And Sandy, we girls always sit on our own. It's the end here. High school is essentially over. It don't matter now. We're all going off to all these different places. Leaving. Come on you guys, we're all different, now we don't have to…" She pauses. "It don't matter that I'm from Mexico or wherever, we are all gonna leave this place. We are like—gone; but we're here. Maybe just now, here at the end we can be together; like in a new way. You know, it's real."

James stands and says, "Who's drawing a mayfly?"

"I am."

"Well then, can I draw it with you?"

"Yeah, I guess."

Sialia says one more thing, "We now know. Don't we? We know!"

The mayfly floats up to the bubbling surface of the rapid and rides the wave downstream. It tumbles down the riffles and eddies out in the corner of a foamy pool. Its skin splits and its wings emerge straight up and dry in the sunlit swirl of light and water. There, at the very interface.

Sialia exits out the back door into the sunny courtyard. As the sun warms her shoulders, she takes off her sweater. She unties her braid and runs her fingers through her hair. She lies on her back atop the picnic table with her sweater as a pillow. Her long black hair hangs down over the edge of the table. James lies down next to her on the lower bench and he closes his eyes in the warm sunshine. She lowers her hand and holds James' hand.

66

THE FATE OF THE CODEX

After delivering the Codex, Anci and Cualli remain together. They return home to find that the Spanish have destroyed their way of life. Their tribe, from the coastal region, had aligned themselves with the Spaniards. They pass processions of natives and conquistadors heading together over the mountain pass to the interior. The new alliance was traveling inland to fight the mighty Aztecs in the causeway city of Mexicana.

Anci and Cualli stand holding hands as they watch the armored Spaniards pass with native slaves pushing small canons up the winding mountain road. At the end they know, they know they cannot go back, forever changed—like after the atomic bomb. Imposed from the outside, strangely attracted to them—the other; with so much power, the allure of, to be seduced by. And to carry the weight of desire. They stand witness, knowing, knowing both worlds; the before and the after, they cannot go back, cannot be free, free from the cultural assault.

In the year 1647, the Franciscan monk Santiago de Santo Alvarez paces in front of the church doors of the Cathedral of Pueblo in the colonial town of Ciudad de Puebla, New Spain. The morning air is cool and crisp, and the snow line on the prominent volcanos on the western horizon gleams in the morning light. He stops by a lemon tree next to a wall in the big plaza with brick paving stones. Lapis lazuli rosary beads are rolling through his fingers as he looks down at the copper chain and the shiny blue brown beads. He is waiting to meet with the Bishop of Puebla, Juan de Palafox y Mendoza, about an important matter. Seven years before, the Bishop had assigned him the duties of overseeing the continued construction of the cathedral. Construction of this doctrina had started sixty-five years earlier on the top of a sacred Native American site. Tiny dark-skinned native women walk by slowly in their red and orange woven skirts with bundled blankets on top of their heads. They are heading to the market.

Bishop Palafox had also founded the Biblioteca Palafoxiana in 1646, the first public library in Mexico, and some say the New World. He was a renowned lover of books and was quoted as saying: "He who succeeds without books is in an inconsolable darkness, on a mountain without company, on a path without a crosier, in the darkness without a guide."

The monk is also holding a black velvet bag with a large heavy square object in it. In the bag is the Codex of The Two-Handed One. The Codex had been found in the crypts below the church. There, under a skeleton, overlooked by onyx and alabaster sculptures of saints and archangels, it was found. According to legend, the cathedral sits atop of a labyrinth of caves and an underground river.

There is a distinct metallic clanking sound as the latches on the central church doors are unlocked. Father Alvarez looks up, rosary beads in one hand, the heavy book in the velvet bag in the other. The large arched central doors swing open with a slow moaning sound. He slings the beaded chain and crucifix around his neck and approaches the door, and proceeds down through the great central hall to an office in the back. Here he meets with the bishop and extracts the Codex from the bag, places it on top of his large wooden desk, and steps back.

"Where did you find this?"

"In the catacombs below the south tower. We were excavating to reinforce the foundation for the new south bell tower. The cave walls are covered with metallic ground-up rock; it makes the tunnels, in torchlight, look like the stars shimmering at night."

The Bishop does the sign of a cross, and whispers a prayer under his breath, then says to Father Alvarez, "This is different, it is older, from before the conquest. Very few have survived." He picks up the Codex and walks it over to a window, places it on another table, and opens the book. "This is unusual, in that it is not just pagan rituals, but something different."

"Should it be destroyed?"

"There have been many changes since the conquest, and political changes are on the wind. The Jesuits are coming to power. I do not know if Our Order will prevail here in New Spain."

"So, what shall we do?"

"I will be sending an emissary to Rome in the spring with the trade winds. I will have him consult with the Pope then. Until then do not speak of this. Understood?"

"Yes, Your Excellence."

In 1648, Bishop Palafox sends an emissary to Pope Innocent X. They meet in the Vatican and the emissary presents him with the Codex. To this day the ancient book is in The Vatican Secrete Archives. There it sits in the darkness of a wooden cabinet, in a small room to the side of the Sistine Hall with its ornate frescos glowing brightly.

The ancient book was created to foretell a catastrophe. A story reflected in a translucent black stone polished to a mirror finish. Essentially, the ultimate business plan. Dualistic pictorial presentation of wealth tapped and redistributed. A road map to Cibola. Hidden away, after the unforeseen invasion, by both the native priests and the Catholics. Only one copy of the beautifully crafted text was ever made. The illustrious Count of Dagsburg, part of the noble House of Luxembourg, Montague senior par Bradmoor, received the copy directly from the Pope in 1709.

67

WOODED PATH

In the year 1400, Renaissance sculptor Lorenzo Ghiberti fled Florence, Italy, during an outbreak of the plague. On a hot day in August 1401 he returns. In that same year, he wins a commission to make the second set of bronze doors for the Baptistery of San Giovanni. He shuffles his feet on the messy stone floor of his studio. Sweat drips down his face and his muscular arms are covered with a thin layer of dust and grime. He is holding a hammer and an incising tool as he chases—that is, hammers out—the bronze casting of God bending over Adam as he extracts a rib to make Eve.

The very depth of the sculpted relief gives the illusion of dynamic movement. That, and the multiple story lines in each panel, present a revolutionary leap in sculpting technique. Movement, incised and hammered from an incandescent vision of blending sculpture and delicate relief. Embossed and covered in gold leaf; burnished with exquisite features of depth and movement. Ten panels from ten chapters in the Bible, an additional twenty-four figures and twenty-four heads surround the panels. For twenty-seven years he and his artisans labored.

Each episode unfolds on the east-facing doors, gleaming brilliant in the cool crisp Italian morning. The doors glow with a pantheon of light. Shining in the bright spring light, so bright that the viewer has to squint at the reflected light.

It is Friday afternoon, the backdoor is open, music is playing, and the inbox is overflowing. Tyndall sits with JR playing chess. Sialia is coloring and shading in an elaborate drawing of a stonefly nymph. Grasped in her one hand are a yellow, a brown and a light-green colored pencil. The motions of her other hand are free and light as the lines stretch across the page. Her bare feet play with James' bare feet under the table as he writes the final description of an insect. "So, Tynd, which one is this?" he asks.

"Oh, that's the green-drake mayfly."

JR adds, "Hey wasn't there a blue one?"

"Yeah, that would be the blue-winged olive mayfly."

Miguel Angel asks Ryan, "Hey, do you have a soccer ball?"

"No, let's ask Jay." They head off together into his adjacent room.

James says, "Hey, I'm gonna do a different cover for my book." He grabs a sharpie and some paper and starts a rough doodle-like drawing of a treasure map.

Sandy interjects, "Oh, give the monster one eye."

Josue adds, "No, no. Misspell school, like a little kid would."

Hector adds, "Mali, burn the edges of the paper, so it looks old, like a treasure map—hey Tynd, you got a lighter?"

Miguel Angel finishes dribbling the soccer ball and heads off to the art room to get some paints to make a Salvadoran flag for the top of his graduation cap. He comes in and starts doing a practice painting on paper.

Sialia says, "What are you doing, Miguel?"

"I'm going to paint the El Salvador flag on my cap."

"Cool, you should make it blend into an American flag."

"Oh, I don't know if I am skilled enough to do that painting."

"It's okay, I'll help you. I'll be right back, I'm going to get some red, white, and blue from Ms. Raleigh." Upon returning, Sialia sits with Miguel Angel and sketches out, with her color pencils, what she was thinking. Miguel Angel smiles as the prominent center white strip in the Salvadoran flag blends into the white and red stripes of the American flag, and the blue blends into the blue with white stars flying on the US flag. "This is a good idea, I think I'll do the same with the Mexico flag on my cap."

Helen asks, "Hey Tynd, are you coming to our graduation party?"

"Who all will be there?"

"Pretty much everyone here now—so you gotta come."

"I'll try."

"Yeah, everyone," she says.

On one side of James' drawing there is a small building with a steeple and underneath it has the word school misspelled as SKOOL, with the L backwards. A dotted line leads past a blob-like monster with one eye and two hands. The dotted line finally finishes at a desert island with one palm tree with an X underneath it. The outline edge of the paper is burned, giving it a brownish tinge.

The next day, Tyndall wakes early and heads out on the trail with his dog. Later that afternoon he will be attending graduation. He reflects on the upcoming ceremony and this particular group of kids. In his mind's eye he sees the gang; energetic, vibrant and beautiful, poised on the edge of unprecedented opportunity, so ready to leave and go on.

Tyndall heads down a wide path through the woods. It is an old logging or mine road from long ago. Tyndall saunters down the corridor under the newly leafing-out trees. He walks east into the morning sun. The new leaves are backlit, scarcely trembling in the growing warmth of the day. The forest floor is a carpet of green emerging from cracks in the dry leaves. Spring beauties of delicate pink and purple violets are a refreshing reprieve from the winter. The understory shrubs of maple and serviceberry have yet to flush out their leaves.

A woodpecker drums a fast, hollow rhythm on a distant tree. Chickadees, in several directions, blast out a high-pitched dee dee dee call. He can identify the birds by their distinct songs. But this morning he chooses not to. A large bumblebee flies along the ground with a deep buzzing sound. *Bombus*, he says in his head; what a cool scientific name he thinks—so fitting. He knows it's a queen this time of the year; she is flying low and conspicuously. She is searching for a mouse hole to make a nest in. The blooming spring beauties fuel her search with nectar. A new plant punches a hole through a dry leaf; a tenacious push for the first light and space to grow.

It is a floating experience to walk down the trail in the morning light. Within the moment there are a thousand dots of light; bright, backlit, and vibrant. A cacophony of singing birds echoes from the trees all around. The dog chases a chipmunk under a log. He returns and looks up at Tyndall for reassurance, before leaping off in a new direction.

In the distance, so bright, children run with white shirts and dresses. They dodge in and out of sight amongst the trees. They run, for that is how children move. An exquisite photo-like aura of movement and freedom surrounds them. The light intensifies; a blazing yellow and green, dappled in white. The children are like butterflies, floating for a moment, then fluttering off in some direction, up and down, in view and out. Two girls grab hands, look back, and continue. A boy crouches by a rotted log, looks over and touches something. Another grabs the new leaves on a low branch and pulls them through his hand as he floats by. A robin hops on the ground down the distant trail. There, the light is cooler and he can see more clearly.

> But the place, the moment,
> the bright soft light does exist.
> The warming day.
> The effortless movement.
> The first wind in the trees.

EPILOGUE

So, I can remember the inception of this story. There I sat in the art room with the school staff enduring another inane staff training on how to administer a standardized test. I was not listening, but was penning a reasoned and logical essay on how these tests are harmful. Looking around the room at the art posters and thumbing through an art book, it dawned on me that maybe I should pull on the heart strings with a story. A pilgrimage, like Dante, with sins of ambition (pride), greed, gluttony, hatred, want and desire. A real story, no gurus or magic, of transcendence by the kids past their own innate tribalism as a microcosm of the world.

I ended up wrapping so much of the story around Socrates's "know thyself," and Buddhism's "to see." Also, the important question: What is transcendence? To know, see, and transcend is all something on the inside with ever so subtle actions on the outside.

If we could see and know the personal journeys. If we could follow the tax money, the grant money, the tax shelters, the incentives, the business plan, the entrepreneurial schemes and see the effects on attendance, class size, discipline, honesty, and infrastructure. I ended up gravitating to writing about natural history, history and art to tell these stories. The kid's world, I'm afraid to say, is defined by inequality and xenophobia, which is also a reflection of our greater world. Within all this is the ever-pervasive loss of our own humanity through our interactions with the internet.

Huge sums of money are flowing to build a monolith. Like most monoliths, it is a collective cultural madness. The money is not getting to the kids. Follow the money. The highfalutin expensive curricula, the tests, and the consultants are cleptoparasites. They just hover, waiting to steal from the children. This is not a working relationship/partnership (as school principals and superintendents would say), it is just parasitism. The primary pathogenesis is no longer just a parasite on a host—the parasite has become the primary organism.

The perfect reflection and the bent light reveals a pamphlet with the emblem of Bradmoor Publishing; zoom-in to the opulent executive boardroom, a long red cherry table with many chairs around it, executives sipping coffee looking at sales projections and profit margins on neat slick graphs on the sparkling projection screen, printing presses noisily spitting out state tests that are then loaded into green and white boxes, slides projected of the calendar and rotational schemes for the tests and curricula that are constantly changed to maximize profits, senators and congresspersons meeting with publishing executives in posh new hip restaurants in downtown Los Angeles, New York, and Chicago, a superintendent and principal meeting with publishing executives and a senator, the slick integrated teacher training, requested by teachers themselves, the burning pyres of dead bodies with an armored conquistador standing leaning on his spear, state and federal tax forms, moving the stone monoliths of staggering size, the Aztec high priest gazing into an obsidian mirror, the press release about how poorly American students perform on the tests, those bad teachers, must do something, panic, the tide of the ocean pulling away the unanchored ship into a gray sea with patches of floating ice closing in, the last gleam of light from the winter sun, soon to be gone, the educational consultant, fresh from the Harvard Graduate School of Education, with entrepreneurial aspiration dances in front of the projection screen, as teachers look on, copper breast plate gleaming from the gold sheen brought out by the acid bath, a thick green oil underneath the white linoleum floor, as the frogs drift in the current from the overflowing filter in the aquarium, never blinking as they digest worms in their guts, piles of revenue move, distributed way upstream so that the river no longer reaches the sea, neutrinos pass and hit the detector made of ancient lead, plumbing the very makeup of the universe, see the monster with two hands and a serpent underneath devouring all. It really is just a business plan, a blessed business plan, with guaranteed profits built into mandates and laws.

Perhaps it is time for some oversight by educational ethicists. Like a medical ethicist, someone who is removed from politics, career, status, pay, and job security. A moral guide for all those that cannot act or speak out for fear of losing their jobs.

Education needs just three things: (1) a little honesty, (2) functioning infrastructure, (3) stability.

ACKNOWLEDGEMENTS

Many thanks to my friend Don Silver for working so hard on this project, and understanding how to tell a crazy story. To Kitty Riley for editing and tirelessly giving such great feedback. And to the incomparable Marjorie DeLuca for editing and book design and layout. Special thanks to Hannah Condon for the cover drawing.

Most of all, thanks to all the young people who I spent so much time with— you helped me learn the real lessons about our humanity.

M ark Duff spent eighteen years teaching science in a public high school. He also taught environmental education, and science at the college level. He spends most of his days sauntering through the woods while talking to dogs and photographing wildflowers. He lives in Colorado.